BILLION DOLLAR FANTASY

BILLION

THE HIGH-STAKES GAME BETWEEN

DOLLAR

FANDUEL & DRAFTKINGS

FANTASY

THAT UPENDED SPORTS IN AMERICA

ALBERT CHEN

Houghton Mifflin Harcourt
Boston   New York
2019

For information about permission to reproduce selections from this book, write to trade.permissions@hmhco.com or to Permissions, Houghton Mifflin Harcourt Publishing Company, 3 Park Avenue, 19th Floor, New York, New York 10016.

hmhbooks.com

Library of Congress Cataloging-in-Publication Data is available.
ISBN 978-0-544-91114-7

Book design by Chloe Foster

Printed in the United States of America
DOC 10 9 8 7 6 5 4 3 2 1

Insert: *p. 1 top* Photo used with permission, *middle* Photo used with permission, *bottom* Bryan Steffy / Getty Images for DraftStreet; *p. 2 top left* Courtesy Mark Nerenberg, *top right* Ken Richardson, *bottom* Photo used with permission; *p. 3 top* Photo used with permission, *bottom* CNBC; *p. 4 top* Photo used with permission, *bottom* Photo used with permission; *p. 5 top* Jane Barlow, *middle* David L. Ryan / The *Boston Globe* via Getty Images, *bottom* Photo used with permission; *p. 6 top* Richard Drew / AP / Shutterstock, *middle* Michael Dwyer / AP / Shutterstock, *bottom* Photo used with permission; *p. 7 top* Courtesy of the author, *middle* Robert Beck / Getty Images, *bottom left* Photo used with permission, *bottom right* Darren McCollester / Getty Images for DraftKings

p. 8 collage AP Photo / Mark Lennihan; John Ourand / SBJ Staff; KeithAllisonPhoto.com; Erik Jacobs / The *New York Times* / Redux; Erick W. Rasco / *Sports Illustrated* / Getty Images

To Andrea and Leo

CONTENTS

CAST OF CHARACTERS

DraftStreet
Brian Schwartz / *CEO*
Mark Nerenberg / *Chief Product Officer*

FanDuel
Nigel Eccles / *CEO*
Lesley Eccles / *Chief Marketing Officer*
Tom Griffiths / *Chief Product Officer*
Christian Genetski / *Chief Legal Officer*
Justine Sacco / *Communications Director*

DraftKings
Jason Robins / *CEO*
Matt Kalish / *Chief Revenue Officer*
Paul Liberman / *Chief Operating Officer*

The Industry
Cory Albertson / *Rayofhope*
Jeremy Kudon / *Partner, Orrick, Herrington & Sutcliffe*
Mike LaSalle / *Partner, Shamrock Capital*
Vic Salerno / *President, US Bookmaking*
Peter Schoenke / *Cofounder, RotoWire*

TIMELINE

October 1992: Professional and Amateur Sports Protection Act
   (PASPA), prohibiting betting outside Nevada, is signed into law

October 2006: Unlawful Internet Gambling Enforcement Act (UIGEA), legalizing fantasy sports, is enacted

Summer 2009: FanDuel launches

Spring 2012: DraftKings launches

July 2014: DraftKings acquires DraftStreet

July 2015: DraftKings and FanDuel announce funding rounds that total $575 million

Summer 2015: DraftKings and FanDuel are each valued at over $1 billion

September 2015: DraftKings and FanDuel become largest advertisers in America

October 2015: The FBI and the Department of Justice open probes into daily fantasy sports companies

Winter 2015–Spring 2016: DraftKings and FanDuel are shut down in half a dozen states

August 2016: New York State passes bill legalizing daily fantasy games

June 2017: The Federal Trade Commission blocks proposed merger between DraftKings and FanDuel

May 2018: US Supreme Court strikes down Professional and Amateur Sports Protection Act of 1992

PREFACE: VISIONS IN THE DESERT

W̲e will, soon enough, get to the unicorns and the sharks, the billion-dollar game of Prisoner's Dilemma and the carpet-bombing that unleashed the mayhem, the FBI investigations, the conspiracy theories, and the nerds and impostors who waged a battle that forever rearranged the landscape of sports in America. First, though, we must begin with the three prophets in the desert, the men who saw a war coming and sought to win it long before it started.

It was 1991, and the three men had a plan. They would travel across the country, coast to coast, pitching their idea to anyone willing to listen. Inside casinos and horse-racing tracks, they would install establishments where people could wager on the outcome of sporting events and in turn win, or lose, money. These outfits — sports books, they were called — would be linked through a computer line, a line connected to a hub in central Nevada, a hub the three of them owned and controlled. They only had a vague idea of what this network could be worth one day, but they knew that the line would give them an edge in a clash they were certain was about to erupt.

If anyone understood what was at stake, it was these three men from that neon-lit oasis in the desert, gambling's birthplace in America — Las Vegas. Art Manteris lorded over the sports book inside the opulent Las Vegas Hilton, then the largest hotel in the world, a modern-day Versailles that illuminated the entire Strip like a great lantern. Roxy Roxborough was the most influential oddsmaker in town — every morning in his office in a downtown strip mall he sat at his desk in a resplendent suit and set the opening line for the entire world, from Vegas to Monte Carlo to Macau. Vic Salerno ran Leroy's Horse & Sports Place, Vegas's largest independent sports book, a dark, smoke-filled, gin-stinking parlor where the town's biggest sharps and wiseguys gathered to place their bets and watch their fortunes rise and fall.

This concept of linked sports books had worked for them before, beautifully, on a smaller scale. With the help of a computer whiz kid from Pakistan, Vic built the first electronic system that took bets, which meant that he no longer had to lug home trash bags from Leroy's, cursing as the bags burst with pencil-scribbled tickets that he would sift through late into the night at his kitchen table, sorting the winning tickets from the losers. In 1989, when Art opened up a sports book down the road from the Hilton, at the Flamingo, he used Vic's computerized system to connect his operations. "It was so easy — easier than anyone imagined it would be," says Art. The result was the first linked sports book in America.

Years earlier, Art had arrived in Vegas, in this world, in a roundabout way. The son of Greek immigrants, he was twenty-one when he dropped out of community college, left home in Pittsburgh, and headed west to become an actor. On his way to LA, he made a stop in Nevada to make money for rent, working as a cashier for his uncle's business: the sports book in the Barbary Coast, a little shop with golden chandeliers and faux stained glass that sat on a prime corner of the Strip, the nexus of what was, in the early 1980s, a fledgling industry in America. Sports betting — then legal in Nevada and, on a much smaller scale, in Oregon, Montana, and Delaware — was always the odd, slightly uncouth child of the gambling family. Its stature began to grow after an obscure tax cut in 1974: when Congress slashed the sports betting tax rate from 10 percent to 2, it was worthwhile for someone like Vic Salerno to walk away from his career as a dentist and go into business as a full-time bookie. In 1983, just as Art arrived in Vegas, the tax was slashed again, from 2 percent to just 0.25 percent, and that peculiar profession became a potentially profitable one. The Nevada handle — the total amount placed in bets — had ballooned by 450 percent after the first tax cut and rose to $894 million after the second in 1983, and with all the money that was gushing into this world, Art's aspiration to become Hollywood's next leading man was put on hold.

Art had a handsome face and, even in his twenties, a dignified presence; he floated above the wiseguys and fleas around him, but without an air of condescension. Within a few years, by 1987, he was running the sports book at Caesars, at twenty-six years old the youngest director in town. A few years later, he was cutting the ribbon at the entrance of the glittery, $17 million, state-of-the-art SuperBook at the Hilton — a magical realm in which men sat in leather chairs sipping on Stolichnayas at 11 a.m., all of them gazing up at one of the fifty-three flashing, cinema-scale TV screens with live sporting events beamed in from around the world. The SuperBook was the first of its kind — a case study for every casino in town on how to create the ultimate man cave for any out-of-towner.

It was now the early 1990s, and Art was leading a new venture that was even more ambitious: if he, Vic, and Roxy could persuade casino and racetrack operators outside Nevada to let them provide the infrastructure and expertise to bring sports betting to their states, then they could be the ones leading the movement to take sports gambling nationwide. A tsunami, they believed, was coming. At the time, legislatures in more than a dozen states, salivating over the prospect of increased tax revenue, were considering proposals to legalize gambling on sports. The potential value of the network of connected lines that the three of them were trying to build was unknowable. Even to take a stab at a ballpark estimate, by extrapolating the numbers, was a pointless exercise in imagination: if the handle in the state of Nevada, where the population was less than one million, was nearly $1 billion, then the nationwide handle, with New York, Boston, Philly, and Los Angeles all in play . . . well, the numbers were mind-blowing. Vic put the figure for the potential nationwide handle at, conservatively, somewhere around $300 billion; other longtime Vegas bookies floated $1 trillion with a straight face. To anyone who thought that Vic's number was preposterous, to anyone who didn't seem to grasp how pervasive this activity was, Vic liked to note that he knew of a town of one thousand in rural Wisconsin that alone had *three* illegal bookies to service people's desire to bet the farm on the Packers.

In pockets across the country, plenty of casinos and racetracks, it turned out, wanted to listen to what the three men from the desert had to say — from the dingy Boardwalk in Atlantic City, New Jersey, to the regal Churchill Downs estate in Kentucky and the quaint Laurel Park racetrack in Maryland, where the owners were most eager to pounce. This could happen fast, Art thought, as the track in Laurel began erecting booths and hanging TV sets for an on-site sports book. But as word trickled out that a racetrack just outside the Beltway was sniffing around the possibility of expanding sports betting, opposition voices, many out of Maryland and Washington, DC, suddenly emerged — and loudest of all were other local racetrack owners, who thought that sports gambling would steer their customers away from betting on horses. "That it was Laurel that was most interested initially turned out to be the most harmful thing for our project," says Art. "It was right outside of Washington, and once there was some opposition, well, there was a lot of it."

In late 1991, those racetrack owners took meetings on Capitol Hill to discuss a piece of legislation that had been introduced in Congress: called the Professional and Amateur Sports Protection Act, it would effectively ban sports betting outside the state of Nevada. To hear the politicians tell it — foremost among them Bill Bradley, the New Jersey senator and former New York Knicks star who introduced the legislation — the law was about nothing less than saving the souls of our children. "Our youngsters will be learning to shave points before they're able to shave their beards!" howled one lawmaker. But as with any piece of legislation in Washington, there were other, hidden forces behind it — perhaps none more influential than the hard-lobbying campaign initiated by the multibillion-dollar horse-racing industry. Suddenly, here came the sports league officials to join the lobbyists and lawmakers in their antigambling rants, tripping over themselves to rail against this new threat to society, refusing to admit that their sport reaped any benefit, that there was any relationship at all between the popularity of their product and fans' eagerness to toss their favorite team into a three-team parlay to make their Sundays just a bit more dangerous. The National Football League's television-rights deals, coinciding with the rise of Nevada's sports gambling industry, had risen from a total of $400 million per year in 1982 to $900 million by 1990. Where did the NFL think its money was coming from? The games themselves weren't suddenly *that* good. With the NFL and others behind it, PASPA was passed on June 2, 1992, by an 88–5 vote, making sports gambling illegal outside of Nevada. "The way this came out of nowhere and became the law of the land — it was eye-opening, to say the least," says Art. His plan was crushed; the war Art saw as inevitable never began.

Roxy, who had relocated himself and his business to Atlantic City, expecting the Boardwalk to be the center of action outside the desert, closed up shop and returned home. Vic channeled his energy back into Leroy's, expanding it to multiple locations and eventually selling the franchise to UK bookmaking titan William Hill for $18 million. Art had been teaching a sports book management course at the University of Nevada at Las Vegas, grooming future bookmakers and casino directors for a bright, shiny world in which gambling was prevalent coast to coast, border to border, a world in which the kind of expertise that Art Manteris could provide was rare and vital. While the outside universe clung to an image of gambling as two shadowy characters from an Elmore Leonard novel surreptitiously exchanging cash on a street corner, Art represented order and integrity in the regulated, thriving industry in Vegas. It was Art who, in 1999, would lead the Nevada Gaming Control Board in uncovering one of the most notorious point-shaving scandals in the history of American sports; Art who would be the only bookmaker in town who possessed the indomitable will to refuse bets from the most ruthless shark in the industry, a high-stakes gambler named Billy Walters, and from the growing pool of cold-blooded, algorithm-equipped bettors making a killing off the sports books.

Art had once envisioned a national system not so much modeled on Nevada's as subsumed in it, with the state's regulatory infrastructure in place across the country and the state's bookmakers and casino directors acting as leaders for this billion-dollar industry. After PASPA, though, he didn't know what to tell those bright-eyed students about the future and their place in it. The course was canceled. With the signing of that bill, the idea of legalized gambling across America had become a fantasy. Art's worst fears were about to be realized: billions of dollars of liquidity were funneled underground, sustaining a thriving black-market industry that would ride the crest of the online gaming explosion of the late 1990s and 2000s and that existed in a legal and commercial phantom world, beyond the reach of regulation, authority, and the law. That bright, shiny world? Art had lost all hope that he would ever see it.

Then one night many years later, Art was returning home to Las Vegas. He was now in his fifties, softened around the edges since settling into a more serene life as the director of a chain of understated, elegant sports books for the locals, away from the rowdy out-of-towners, miles off the Strip. Art was walking out of his gate and through McCarran Airport, which was lined with rows of blinking slot machines, when he gazed up at one billboard-sized sign that seemed to shine brighter than any of the others in the terminal. He couldn't turn away.

A NEW FANTASY MILLIONAIRE EVERY WEEK — PLAY FREE
DAILY FANTASY SPORTS.

And then a strange word, in lime green and white script font, under a sparkling golden crown: DRAFTKINGS.

Art thought to himself, *What the hell is* that?

Somehow the world today still clings to the old sepia-rinsed image of sports gambling — of a man with a bag of cash walking up to a booth to place a bet in a cavernous, dimly lit room full of other men in bowler hats, or in a dark corner on the phone whispering a series of cities and dollar figures with life-or-death urgency. Those images are of a bygone time; the world it depicts is fading, replaced by a new world that is much more complex and one in which the money at stake is many magnitudes larger. This new world, fueled by a gushing spigot of venture capital, reflects the rapid and radical social and technological changes around us; in this world, gambling is becoming so widespread that one will be able to bet as often and for as much as one wishes, so long as there is a device nearby.

This book describes how this new world came to be through the story of a high-stakes game between two unlikely startups and the entrepreneurs who did battle: the individuals who were both uniquely suited to the moment and also completely unprepared for what it was about to do to them. Some would make a small fortune; others would be left shattered, or even destroyed.

As it turns out, the sign that Art Manteris laid eyes on that night at McCarran Airport was a weapon in the game between the startups. Art didn't know who was behind that sign; he only had a quickly growing stack of questions: What exactly were *daily* fantasy sports games? How were these games *not* gambling operations? Art was aware of every single sports betting outfit in his state, so what was this one that he'd never heard of? One that had never gone through the gauntlet of his state gaming board — how were these guys operating in plain sight, *in his own backyard?* And finally: How were the people behind the sign not getting a loud and angry knock at their door from the FBI, like any other illicit gambling operation in America? How was this *legal?*

Art was about to find out that the battle he saw as inevitable back in 1990 was now, unbeknownst to him, being waged by a group of accidental disrupters: a band of nerds from Boston and a group of Brits who weren't even sports fans. Soon there would be international scandal, FBI investigations, congressional hearings, and a historic Supreme Court ruling, in 2018, that would rearrange the landscape in ways that even the three men from the desert never foresaw.

How did the story of this war begin? Like the story of any startup, really. It began with a fantasy.

PROLOGUE: EDINBURGH, 2014

They were sitting around a conference room table, face to face, for the first time. On one side were the Brits: with their lilting accents, measured demeanors, and pale complexions, they could seem more like a group of academics than tech entrepreneurs. On the other side were the investors from America who had blustered into glum, gray-rinsed Edinburgh from the glitz of West Los Angeles: perfectly coiffed and, as the Brits later marveled to each other, tan — so improbably *tan*.

These visitors, partners from the private equity firm Shamrock Capital, looked around at the office space, which was a dreary contrast to the glimmering tech offices in the United States: dimly lit, cluttered, decorated with an incongruous mix of British propaganda posters (YOUR RESOLUTION WILL BRING US VICTORY) and a curiously curated collection of American sports paraphernalia. They were here because they believed that the Brits' creation, a startup company called FanDuel, was the key to unlocking the future of sports in America, though when they saw the cheap stickers of NFL team logos slapped on the walls next to outdated posters of players on former teams from forgotten eras, the visitors had second thoughts. It was 2014 — what was Brett Favre in a *Vikings* uniform doing here?

They may not have been authentic sports fans, but the Brits possessed the credentials that suggested they had the experience and intellect to lead a transformative company. Nigel, the boyish, cerebral CEO, was a former media executive and McKinsey man, and that morning, as he presented a picture of how they were going to win the exploding fantasy sports market in America, the Shamrock partners were reminded of why they had felt, when they first met with Nigel months earlier, that the CEO's analytical, efficient approach aligned perfectly with theirs.

The investors were also familiar with the two technologists who unveiled FanDuel's new product features. Tom, the chief product officer, was Cambridge-educated, a former PhD candidate, and Rob, the creative director, had already had a hand in cofounding three startups; their collective talent was reflected in the new app, which was as sleek as a Bentley.

The Shamrock partners, however, were not yet familiar with the fourth founder, the last to take the floor. The job of the chief marketing officer, Lesley, was to take the money they had raised and turn it into paying customers. Now, not only was FanDuel a company with tens of thousands of paying customers playing their online game, with millions of dollars of revenue flowing in weekly, but it was also, with a new infusion of capital from the new partners from Shamrock, a startup with over $70 million of investment money bubbling in their tank.

"This is a make-or-break year for us," Lesley declared to the room. "We're going to have to be very aggressive."

The screen behind her changed to a slide that described an evolving market. Because FanDuel rewarded winners with prize money, many were beginning to view the games they offered — a subset of fantasy sports called *daily* fantasy sports games — as a kind of Trojan horse brought into the sports gambling market, territory from which media companies and sports leagues had long been excluded. But now, with a new NFL season weeks away, not only was a media titan, ESPN, in play as an advertiser, but professional sports teams were also returning Lesley's calls, eager to strike deals.

"We can't hold back," Lesley said. There was another factor, she added, just as critical to consider: a startup that had entered the space only two years earlier but was willing to burn through astounding sums of cash to acquire customers. Their ads were appearing on TV and radio and billboards across the United States, everywhere from Boston, the company's home base, to Las Vegas, where it was catching the attention — and ire — of regulators and gambling operators.

These new rivals seemed hell-bent on taking over the fantasy sports world, even if it meant blowing up the entire industry in the process. They were called DraftKings, though some in the industry called the company by a different name: the suicide bombers.

Earlier that summer, there had been rumors swirling in the industry that FanDuel was closing in on a monster investment; the word was that Nigel had been able to secure $40 million. Soon after, around the time of Shamrock's visit to Edinburgh, DraftKings announced it had closed on a venture-capital-backed Series B round. That total: $41 million. The number was a warning shot.

The suicide bombers were coming.

"We're going to need a significant push to keep our lead," Lesley continued. The screen flickered to the next slide: the marketing plan for the upcoming NFL season, just weeks away in September. A year ago, in 2013, FanDuel had spent $10 million in advertising for the entire year. Now a figure representing their planned spend for the 2014 NFL season appeared: $43 million.

The FanDuel founders watched their visitors' jaws drop to the floor. On their faces was a look that said: *Are you out of your mind?*

"We agreed," boomed a voice from the table. It belonged to Shamrock partner Mike LaSalle, who just days earlier had been on a call with Nigel, discussing these very plans for the season. "We talked about this. Twenty million dollars," LaSalle said, looking at Nigel, even as he was beginning to realize that the final say belonged not to the CEO but to the woman standing at the front of the room.

Lesley was small and thin, with a mask that was impossible to read — long dark-brown hair with ringed curls framed a strong-boned, purse-lipped face that at rest conveyed a hardened skepticism about the world around her. That mask, and her way of cutting to an uncomfortable truth, made her a stark contrast to her genial cofounders. To make her case, she needed only to show the simple math. Radio, print, digital, partnerships with teams and leagues, TV . . . the numbers added up: $43 million.

"There are diminishing returns," LaSalle said. "You are pushing your limits."

"It has to be forty-three — not a penny less," Lesley said.

There was a stunned silence in the room, from both sides of the table. From his seat, the CEO shot Lesley a look: *Are we really doing this?*

Nigel should have known better — known that his CMO would not back down to the investors; known that she would not allow a rival company to take what was theirs; known that she would do everything to protect what she and her cofounders had spent the last six harrowing years building together. Nigel should have known better because he knew the CMO better than anyone else: Lesley was his wife.

Years later, when asked to describe the thinking behind the decisions that led to the war and how all the players in it allowed the stakes to reach such unimaginable heights, Nigel would say, "The thinking of everyone inside this world was, *Given what I can control, this is the best decision for us.* Everyone's making rational decisions. That may be the case. But the output? The output is insanity." In the summer of 2014, at FanDuel, the $43 million ad spend was a calculated bet — no one, not even the founders, could have anticipated that, within months, that bet would erupt into a $70 million carpet-bombing. Or that in just over a year FanDuel would become the largest advertiser in all of America.

"We're going to shut this down if it's not working," Mike LaSalle finally said to the room — to the Brits and to the other Americans, who were now in this together. "And then it will be on to plan B."

Nigel and Lesley nodded, then glanced at each other. They both knew. There was no plan B. There never was. They were, from the very start, all in.

PART I
THE WAR
2008-2015

Are your dreams big enough to cash a giant check? . . . **DID TURNING $6 INTO $60,000 GET THIS DUDE LAID? . . .** *This is the feeling of turning a game you love into a lifetime of cash* . . . **PICK YOUR SPORT. PICK YOUR PLAYERS. PICK UP YOUR CASH** . . . Football is already exciting. This is taking it to a whole other level . . . *I won $15,000 off a $5 entry* . . . **100% GUARANTEE MONEY BACK. NOTHING TO LOSE** . . . *There's nothing special about me. The difference is that I played, and they didn't* . . . *CLICK ON THE MICROPHONE. GET UP TO $200 FREE* . . . **TURN $20 INTO $1 MILLION! . . .** You can win a *SHIPLOAD* of money . . . **THE MONEY IS REAL! . . .** *The night I did win the money, it was one of the best feelings I've ever had in my life* . . . **IMMEDIATE CASH PAYOUTS. . . .** *More and more people are starting to find out that this is the way to play. . . .* It's like the best adrenaline rush ever . . . **BET SMALL, WIN BIG, IT'S THAT EASY** . . . *I've deposited a total of $35 and won over $2 million. . . .* **WELCOME TO THE BIG TIME.**

1

BETTING ON BRETT FAVRE WITH
BAR MITZVAH MONEY

(And Other Hidden Origin Stories)

2008–2013

This peculiar idea of his, which could have sunk to the bottom of the abyss of abandoned dreams, had a strange way of surfacing from time to time with the urgency of a vision that would change the world around him. Perhaps it wasn't a coincidence that it always happened to Mark when he was in a drunken haze. Usually, it was along the long oak bar where Mark had an eye on one of the TVs split into four screens flashing with the afternoon slate, as his head swirled inside the brain-assaulting bar noise and that second or maybe third drink was beginning to settle in the part of his brain that allowed him sometimes to resist the urge that was the essential thing about him. Some stranger at the bar had taken out his phone and showed him his lineup, and while "Let me tell you about my fantasy lineup . . ." was a line that should be uttered only by someone who wants a conversation to crash into a dead end or a brain to go numb, Mark never felt exactly the way others did, that listening to someone talk about his fantasy sports team was as interesting as listening to someone go on about his dog's sweater collection. Instead, when Mark listened to a person admiring what Mark in an instant could see was a frankly terrible selection of players, he felt that urge that was as difficult to fight as gravity: Mark wanted to teach this minnow a lesson and, while he was at it, make some money.

There were two types of people in the world: those who saw the world as a matrix of sharks and minnows, and those who didn't. Mark Nerenberg was the type who always walked through a room looking for an edge, whether it was a poker room in Vegas, a room full of suits in his day job as an options trader, or this sweaty sports bar in Minneapolis overflowing with fish. When Mark was growing up in the suburbs of the Twin Cities, his father, Lex, would return from poker night with his long-time crew, and Mark would listen and absorb his father's analysis of how the night had unfolded, each hand and tell methodically broken down and dissected by this internist by day and poker shark by night. By the time Mark was a rebellious eighth grader who'd been suspended from school more times than he could remember, he was mobilizing his buddies to join his own version of the old-school, season-long fantasy football games their dads played. His notebooks were overrun by stats from weekly games that he had meticulously compiled and charted and reset after each NFL Sunday, when his friends would put into the pool another $10, $20 each — a small chunk of bar mitzvah money for Mark's circle of friends who found a little thrill in having some stake in the performances of a god like Brett Favre, Marshall Faulk, or Randy Moss. Mark's wiring was completed in college during those hours spent hunched over a laptop on his frat-house couch, jazzing a second or third Red Bull and a cigarette and a line into PartyPoker live; he had turned hours of repetitive labor into more pocket money than a student in a sleepy college town knew what to do with, winning five figures in one night and somehow blowing it all during a one-week bender in Atlantic City.

Online poker was a beautiful moneymaker for him and other skilled poker players because of the vast ocean of minnows. When strangers showed him their terrible fantasy lineups, Mark couldn't help seeing another vast ocean to exploit, except for one problem: unlike in poker, there was no way for fantasy football players to take strangers on for instant money. And from that problem of Mark's emerged an idea.

One night in 2007, after too many rounds at the bar, Mark stumbled home, sat down with his laptop, and fired off a drunken email to one of his old University of Maryland buddies.

I want to create an online fantasy sports website where customers can:

- Deposit and withdraw funds
- Participate in live drafts and auctions with people they have never met all over the world
- Chat with other participants
- Know that their money and personal information is 100% secured

He added:

> If this site was up and running the way I envision it, there would be so much traffic it's ridiculous. $$$$

It was exhilarating to tell others about this idea that had been cooking in his head, but Mark didn't have the faintest clue where to begin making it more than an idea and a drunken email. Ultimately, there was one person whose opinion he valued most — his dad's. While he was certainly not going to ask his father for money, Mark knew that the odds of him actually doing something about this idea were slim without his dad's blessing. Lex could be hard on his son, but he also admired the kid's edge — his audacity, his refusal to accept convention. "Son, this is a good idea," he said to Mark in his deep and commanding voice, like a judge's. Lex meant it: the idea was inspired.

Though he also had another thought about Mark's game, one that he kept to himself.

No way in hell is it legal.

One of Mark's first memories was of a rumbling, rising elevator and opening doors that led to a room where a group of men assembled, dressed in attire that resembled clown outfits — an assortment of hats and T-shirts and jerseys slathered in a variety of radioactive colors. Mark sat in a corner and watched middle-aged men groan and sigh and belch and deliberate solemnly, as if over real estate transactions, as they convened around a table covered with scribbled legal pads and spreadsheets and glossy sports magazines and mulled the value of players they would draft onto their imaginary teams. This was little Mark's first glimpse into his father's secret society. All of its longtime members were men of roughly the same age, many of whom had grown up together, and some of whom returned home specifically for this occasion. Now, as middle-aged adults with young children, they assembled once a year to draft their teams in a fantasy football league that, by the time young Mark attended his first draft, had existed for decades.

When Mark was young, his father often told him that he invented fantasy football. Lex was kidding but not kidding. As a premed student at the University of Minnesota, Lex had the idea when some friends of his who were visiting from Canada told him about a game they played based on the statistics of hockey players during the NHL playoffs. Lex took that concept and created an NFL version of the game for his room-mates and friends. He had stacks of papers from 1978 to prove it to his son. There it was, documented on a gridded sheet on yellowing paper: in the first draft of the league, held in a kitchen in a Saint Paul apartment complex, Terry Bradshaw of the Pittsburgh Steelers went first; a kicker (*Can you believe it, son, a kicker?!?*) was taken next. A fantasy football league was born.

Lex knew that he didn't invent the game he played, but he also knew that any claim to be the origin story for fantasy sports was probably not so. For instance, he and countless others had heard the story of a group of fans coming up with the idea for a fantasy baseball league in the early 1980s in New York City; this was the neat yarn for the origin of fantasy games of all kinds, a tale that would be passed around and written about in books and celebrated in film. An idea hatched during a cross-country flight. Eleven founding members. A French restaurant in Manhattan.*

---

* Rotisserie baseball's founders, a who's who of the publishing world, met at a midtown New York City restaurant called La Rotisserie Francaise. Decades later, having seen what he'd created, the group's ringleader, the writer and editor Daniel Okrent,

The details were polished and smoothed over through the years, and while there was no reason to dispute any of the facts, the idea that the early 1980s was the dawn of fantasy sports games was simply hogwash, since Lex and his pals were playing a kind of fantasy game years earlier.

Beneath one origin story, there was always another origin story.

Lex assumed that games like the one he'd come up with were already being played in living rooms and dormitories and offices by like-minded sports geeks of his generation. Many years later he would be able to read about a league that had been started a decade before his, in a basement in Oakland, by the staff of an NFL team. The story went something like this: The Oakland Raiders professional football team was approaching the end of a sixteen-day East Coast road trip when one night, in a Manhattan hotel room in the winter of 1962, the general manager, a man named Wilfred Winkenbach, and a sportswriter for the *Oakland Tribune* came up with the blueprint and the rules as the night progressed and the cocktails flowed. The first documented fantasy draft was, fittingly, held in someone's basement — Winkenbach's basement — and from the start the goals and purpose of the fantasy games were clear: to make the real games more interesting to watch, with bragging rights and money at stake, and to "bring together some of Oakland's finest Saturday-morning gridiron forecasters," it read in the original rules, "to pit their respective brains (and cash) against each other."

The cash: it was essential to make things interesting. So began the first fantasy football league — on record at least. No one in Winkenbach's league got famous or rich off their idea for a fantasy sports game. No one in the original Rotisserie baseball league did either. In the late 1980s, Lex had the thought of trying to make some money because he and others were putting so much time into sifting through every box score to manage the stats and scoring of the teams in the league. Why not do it for others across the country, for profit?

---

would say: "I feel the way J. Robert Oppenheimer felt after having invented the atomic bomb: If I'd only known this plague that I've visited upon the world."

Lex called up the local newspaper and asked to put in an ad for a statistical service.

"No way — this is gambling!" was the response he got. Perhaps so — but a year later Lex opened up that newspaper and saw that it had decided to start running Vegas odds on professional games, even though sports betting was illegal virtually everywhere in America outside of Nevada.

For years, during breaks, in between seeing patients, Lex closed the door to his office, took out his yellow legal pad and the week's NFL box scores, and at his desk began compiling the scoring for the teams in his leagues. Nothing gave him more joy during his day. Each week he mailed the league standings to the members. Those standings arrived sooner with the advent of the fax machine, and in the late 1990s another technological game-changer appeared: the internet allowed Lex to email updates (and, of course, trash talk) and later also let players log on to online services that did the scoring for the leagues. By then, the popularity of fantasy games had spread so far and wide that they had the endorsement of the professional leagues, which at first had seemed to keep their distance from this thing that sure smelled like gambling. Now they were embracing the games as a mainstream component of the fan experience. And yet, despite all these changes, in just about every other way Lex's league through the decades remained basically the same as in those days when little Mark followed along to the draft meetings: the same scoring, the same rules, the same team names. Countless friends, coworkers, and neighbors passed through Lex's life over the years, but the nine other men in his fantasy football league — these blustery, obnoxious, vulgar, beautiful men — were constants.

Their game didn't change, but the world was changing, fast. Now those who fell in love with live snake drafts and five-hour auctions and the day-to-day micromanaging of a single team over many months, all for the reward of bragging rights and a few hundred bucks at the conclusion of an interminable season, were in their fifties and sixties, with adult children who lived in an instant gratification world of 140-character quips and six-second videos, a generation for whom the idea of playing one game over several months seemed as old-fashioned as Parcheesi. This generation was ready for a new kind of game, even if they didn't know it.

Two years — two miserable, soul-crushing years at his desk job as an options trader — had passed since Mark first sat down and riffed about his idea for a new game, and during those two years, while most people on the other end of his idea agreed with him that there was *something* there, no one had the faintest idea what to do next. All that time, though, another like-minded soul was waiting to hear an idea like Mark's. When Mark connected with Brian Schwartz for the first time, through a mutual friend, Brian was sitting at his desk in a drab cubicle in Manhattan; he was making good money just a few years out of the University of Wisconsin at a marketing job where he spent his days dreaming about doing something entirely different. One day, Mark reached out to Brian and explained his game.

> MARK: It's fantasy against total strangers for money.
> BRIAN: I don't really get it. I play fantasy with my friends and already make money.
> MARK: It's fantasy kinda like how u can play poker online for money. setting up a lobby like a poker site, where u sign up for leagues with different buy ins, scoring, drafts/auctions, players durations, etc.
> BRIAN: I do think the instant gratification is part of the appeal for online poker.
> MARK: It's online poker meets fantasy. But it HAS to be short duration.

Brian had also grown up creating his own versions of fantasy games for his friends. A hockey player from Long Island, Brian would tally all the stats using box scores from newspapers and then email the standings to his friends. His first instinct about Mark's idea was that it was brilliant. As fun as fantasy sports were, Brian knew just how frustrating, anticlimactic, and ultimately unsatisfying they could also be. In baseball's relentlessly long season, for instance, after that exhilarating draft in late March, you were unlikely to still be checking your team every day by Memorial Day, and by August, if you were out of the money, it was a miracle if you remembered that you still had one. The direct connection that Mark had made between poker and fantasy sports was what made the idea fresh and new and interesting to Brian: the short duration was key.

The ability to compete against other users whom you've never met, over the internet, will become extremely popular, much like online poker, read the presentation that Brian told Mark to put together for potential investors.

Having the same players all season and having to wait months for a conclusion and potential payout is not enough for today's fantasy players. Sports fans will love to reset every week, or even every day . . .

Playing blackjack, video poker, or betting on sports against "the house" is almost always a losing proposition in the long run. Like poker or stock-market trading, this will provide an opportunity for some of the most skilled players to make money over the long run . . .

The DraftStreet founders were sure they were onto something. They joked that they should all move to the UK, where sports gambling was legal and rampant, rent out a sweet flat maybe somewhere in London, a bachelor pad to end all bachelor pads, launch the company, sell the game, and move back to the US with their millions. While they all agreed it was a genius idea, it wasn't clear to them that a game like this could make it through the legal buzz saw — sports gambling, after all, was illegal in the United States — but the idea was just too damn good. Gambling was legal in many other countries, including the UK, and there were plenty of offshore sites that would operate a game like this.

Then one day everything changed. Mark, Brian, and their two other cofounders, had gotten together in New York one weekend to formalize a business plan. Sitting at his computer, Mark came across the home page of a website with NBA star Gary Payton splashed over it. "Win daily cash games playing daily fantasy," the site read. It was . . . *precisely* . . . Mark's idea.

"No," he whispered to himself as he stared at his laptop screen. He felt like a fool that it had never occurred to him that there might be another group of guys out there with his idea, having precisely the same conversations that they were having. Mark was crushed.

"Fuck!" he screamed, practically scattering the pigeons at the window of the conference room they'd taken over. "Fuck! Fuck! *Fuuuuuckk!*"

Mark was devastated. He thought they were done, finished.

Brian felt the opposite. To Brian, this was merely confirmation. The race was on.

MARK: So why hasn't anyone heard of these sites?

BRIAN: Question is, are those sites very young? have they not been doing good marketing? are the sites just not good products? or is there just not a big demand? I dont think it's the demand. bc none of us have heard about it.

MARK: All of the above. def not good marketing.

BRIAN: That means they're not hitting nearly enough of the market.

MARK: Like how have none of us heard of this. That's just bad marketing.

BRIAN: I think we'll need a lot of money to do this right, but we'll prob have to spend a solid $100k on marketing alone to start. i don't even think we need huge numbers to make a lot of money. bc there really won't be much cost after the initial push.

MARK: at least we know it's legal.

While the mere existence of other sites quickly allayed their fears about the game's legality, Brian had some lawyer friends in New York who explained to him the specifics of the legal protection. Fantasy games were separated from sports betting by an obscure piece of legislation called the Unlawful Internet Gambling Enforcement Act (UIGEA). The act was what had pulled the rug from under the poker industry, but fantasy games were deemed legal. It all did seem tenuous: some of Brian's lawyer friends called it a loophole, and others were adamant that the question of legality could be a serious problem if these games ever got big enough for anyone to care about them — but that was a bridge they would cross when they came to it. There was no time to waste, because it was clear that no one had to move across the ocean to get their idea off the ground. They now had a name for their operation: DraftStreet.

Mark then found that once you started really looking for sites like these, you could find them everywhere, sprouting like weeds. The site Mark stumbled upon was an outfit called DraftZone; a handful of others resembled high school computer science projects, and there were also "daily games" products tucked away within big media sites, like ESPN and CBS, that were operational but not advertised — instead of straight cash, they offered gift cards as prizes. It was as if the big media companies wanted to dip their toes in the daily games space, but not so deep that they couldn't flee the scene the moment anyone started calling these games gambling.

And then there was an odd site with a simple home page, a site that seemed to change the kind of products it offered almost every day; of all the other sites, the DraftStreet guys were most perplexed by these shape-shifters. It was clear that this startup didn't have a grasp of who they were, which was odd, because every other site seemed like a vanity project run by a dude making games for himself. With a little investigation, they also noticed that this site was doing some different things in marketing — such as partnering with local newspapers and radio stations in big sports-mad cities like Philadelphia, the kind of traditional outlets that the millennials at DraftStreet would never imagine working with. Most perplexing of all was the page on the site listing the founders and featuring classy black-and-white head shots that looked more like what you'd see on a bio page for a consulting group than one for a fantasy sports company. The bios of the founders listed credentials that were just as jarringly out of place in their world: a management consultant at McKinsey; a marketing executive at Capgemini Ernst & Young; a University of Cambridge graduate and PhD candidate at the University of Edinburgh . . . and then it occurred to them that these founders hawk-ing this new kind of game that was going to upend sports in America were . . . five Brits.

Five fucking *Brits??*

Beneath one origin story there was always another origin story.

And beneath the story of DraftStreet was a story belonging to a group of founders who would find themselves asking, over and over again: *How did we end up here?*

Their story begins one evening in the summer of 2007, in an audito-rium full of wannabe entrepreneurs with half-baked ideas, hanging on every word of a local startup founder. A postdoc sitting in an auditorium at the University of Edinburgh looked up to see a man in a suit and fancy glasses walk into a room of unkempt students. *What is that guy doing here?* wondered Tom Griffiths. *That guy must have an interesting story.*

Tom Griffiths was just out of college, twenty-five years old, an aspiring Mark Zuckerberg whose problem was that he was not in Silicon Valley but in Scotland — a wasteland for startups — studying machine learning as a PhD student. He grew up in a place as far away as you can imagine from an incubator like Silicon Valley: in a tiny farming town in Wales called Narberth. To become a successful entrepreneur from Narberth was as unlikely as a kid in Beijing becoming a NASCAR driver, and yet Tom, the son of a medical doctor and an English teacher, seemed to be on the fast track early on. He started coding when he was eight years old, on an old BBC Model B, and always put his entire allowance into up-grading his computers. In high school, he was the president of his class of one hundred, well liked by his classmates, but he also had his head buried in books and computers, was captain of the chemistry quiz team, and became the top student in his class, even setting a school record for highest exam marks. You'd peg him as an A-plus nerd if it weren't for the friend who was always at his side: Rob Jones, always the coolest *boyo* in the class, king of the jocks, captain of the soccer and rugby teams. Tom helped Rob with his chemistry homework, Rob helped Tom get girls.

They started a band together and used Tom's coding skills to start a web design company for local businesses. Tom and Rob learned that if you had an idea and showed a little initiative, people were willing to pay you money. Their first project was building a website for a local businessman in rural Wales. After getting paid over £1,000 for the project, they suddenly had all the drinking money they would ever need.

Tom attended Cambridge, where he studied computer science in the mid-2000s. Around then, YouTube was sold to Google for $1.6 billion, and Tom was one of countless young programmers across the world who took notice of the fact that YouTube offered no original technology — it was just a website. Suddenly Tom looked back at his time at Cambridge and Edinburgh, where he'd spent days and nights learning to create original technology and building intellectual property, as almost wasted years. He decided that encouraging students to patent their technology was a bit of a fallacy of entrepreneurship feeder programs in universities. The future was about building a product that consumers loved, could grow with a network effect, and were willing to pay to play. So he and Rob, whose aspirations to become a professional soccer player had hit a wall after a gruesome injury, reunited after their undergraduate years and holed themselves up in a tiny studio apartment, where Rob slept on the couch, for six months, developing a site that helped groups organize and meet up. Facebook was exploding in the United States, and Tom and Rob imagined that their site — called Groopit — could make them the UK Mark Zuckerbergs. As they prepared for Groopit's grand introduction to the world, they were looking for anything — a sliver of inspiration for a new idea, a chance meeting with an investor — that could help them to the next step.

It came that night in the summer of 2007 when Tom showed up at the talk for entrepreneurs at the University of Edinburgh. In a post-event meet-up at a pub across the street from the talk, Tom introduced himself to the mystery man with the fancy glasses. Nigel Eccles was a lean, sandy-haired thirty-two-year-old with a quick wit and an air of restless curiosity — someone with, yes, an interesting story. That night Tom learned the basic facts: that Nigel had grown up on a dairy farm in Northern Ireland; that he had served in Iraq as a consultant with the British army; that he had worked in a number of startups before spending four years at McKinsey; and that he now had an executive job at an Edinburgh media company that had led his family, his wife and son, away from London to this city. There was one other takeaway from the conversation: Nigel was utterly dissatisfied with his career. He, like Tom, was ready to create something of his own.

A few days later, half-drunk and wearing rugby jerseys that made them look like local hooligans, Tom and Rob arrived at a house with a blue door and black grime facade on a winding, quiet street near the University of Edinburgh. After the two hit it off that night at the pub, Nigel had invited Tom and Rob to his home to continue the conversation, and on a Saturday Tom and his partner stumbled in from a rugby match on the other side of town. The moment the front door of the Eccleses' house opened, however, Tom and Rob realized that they had made a serious miscalculation.

While Nigel had seemed like the kind of mellow, relaxed fellow who wouldn't mind if two drunk guys showed up at his home to commiserate about the tortured life of an entrepreneur, it quickly became clear that the woman at the door wasn't. Simply with the stern look on her face, Lesley Eccles — Nigel's wife — made it clear that she didn't have time for nonsense — and for two inebriated rugby fans with a half-baked idea. During their visit, which was to show Nigel their idea, Tom and Rob found themselves trying to impress not Nigel but Lesley, a former management consultant who, they learned, was in between jobs, with a one-month-old baby. After just a few minutes of listening to what Tom and Rob had to say about their prototype for Groopit, Lesley more or less said, *This is terrible. Now get out of my house.* Tom and Rob were not crushed; in fact, they were inspired. After six months of banging their heads and hearing friends say only "That's great!" honest, sharp criticism was refreshing. Lesley and Nigel, they would find out, had a way of cutting straight to the problem. The core point of Lesley's critique was that Groopit was a Frankenproduct, a mishmash of too many ideas and concepts. That was enough for Tom and Rob to see that Groopit needed much more work than they had thought. They returned to the Eccleses' house over and over again, but during long talks in the backyard, below a dimming sky, the four also discussed something that had been percolating in the house for months: Nigel's idea for a new kind of game.

The idea was a news prediction site that offered users virtual cash to wager on outcomes of real-life events. Users in the United Kingdom and the United States could make predictions about what would happen around a news story, and their wagers would give them a reason to come back to the site and check the story. It was a sound idea — a far more original one, Tom and Rob admitted, than GroopIt, which he and Rob were quickly seeing was the kind of site that programmers in dorm rooms across the world were coming up with and trying and failing at.

Tom and Rob had met with an angel investor, a prominent Edinburgh businessman named Kevin Dorren, who was impressed by the two young men, and Dorren had told them, "I'd love to work with you." Just days after that initial meeting, Tom and Rob went back to Dorren and said, "We have a better idea. And there are a few more of us." The five founders — Tom and Rob, Nigel and Lesley, and a fifth, a former classmate of Tom's named Chris Stafford — had teamed up for this new site, which they called Hubdub. They immediately began to see that, while their idea was inspired, the execution would be cumbersome and almost hilariously impractical. They hired a half-dozen students from the University of Edinburgh to sit in a room and watch the news in order to make judgments as to which predictions had come to fruition, and it was nothing short of a nightmare.* There was no business model to speak of,

---

* In theory, projecting the environmental targets hit by a certain country was great for an intellectual crowd, but to tell someone to put in a projection and come back in seven years to find out whether they were right . . . well, that wasn't going to do much to boost traffic between 2009 and 2016. There was also an unexpected problem with the pool of players they'd attracted. They talked all the time about "virality" — the need for people to spread the word. But they found that a good segment of the user base was made up of people who, to put it bluntly, were on the site because they didn't have friends. Nigel said, upon seeing the results of user data, "Well, then, this is the worst product ever!"

and as a free product, Hubdub had nothing that they could monetize. While they had partnerships with media outlets, they had nowhere near enough revenue from advertising to prevent their initial $1.2 million investment from running dry.

It was clear that they needed a new idea — at the very least, they needed to pivot to a new variation of their game. One thought was to offer a politics-based game, but that was too similar to the original idea. There was one topic area that actually did better than politics: sports. Sports, in fact, made up 60 percent of their traffic — far more than any other category, especially among their US users.

There was a bit of a problem, though: while they were aware that online sports games existed in the United States, none of them had a clue about anything regarding that industry. Early on, as the founders tried to get a handle on the subject, they began to have a series of conversations with sports fans they'd found from their database of users. As they talked with high-ranking business development executives in the fantasy sports space, the conversations revolved around the season-long fantasy sports model that Lex Nerenberg had started playing thirty years earlier and that over fifty million were playing now. A conversation between Nigel and a business executive in the fantasy sports space went something like this.

NIGEL: Okay! I'd like to try this out.
EXECUTIVE: Great! But . . . right now, you can't. It's February. At
    the moment we're waiting for baseball season. You should try
    it in two months.
NIGEL: Well, isn't there basketball going on?
EXECUTIVE: Yes! And there are leagues going on right now!
    But . . . it's too late to join any of them — the season started
    four months ago.
NIGEL: So if I can't join after the first week of the season . . . then
    I'm just out of luck?
EXECUTIVE: That's right.
NIGEL: Well, what are you doing at the moment?

EXECUTIVE: Waiting for baseball season!

NIGEL: And when does that start?

EXECUTIVE: In two months!

NIGEL (to himself): *And you call yourself a business!? What on earth do you guys do all day?*

Besides the odd factor of seasonality — being beholden to the schedule of the leagues — the Brits thought the oddest thing of all was that the only way fantasy sports could grow was virally, through word of mouth. No one could wake up one morning during the season and decide that he wanted to play and go to a website and start playing. They thought it odd that, in the season-long model, a player had to have a group of friends who were willing to be in a league with him if he wanted to start one. And then there were the other groups of people who clearly enjoyed being in the league simply for the one day of the year when they got together with old friends and drafted the team but who found it a chore to do whatever else went into maintaining a team during the rest of the season, because if you had a losing team, at a certain point you avoided looking at your team the way you avoided looking at your growing waistline.

After every conversation, the founders would find themselves asking, *And this is a $800 million industry? How?* For an industry that allegedly had become so popular with the mainstream, Nigel in particular was struck by how arcane the actual games were. When it came to how they were played, Nigel thought of the fourth law of thermodynamics: with all the various scoring systems and rules, it seemed as if the games always gravitated to the most complex solution.

"Let me show you — we've got the best system ever!" another eager demonstrator would say to the founders, who were desperate to fall in love with fantasy sports: "So we built this website going back fifteen years, and we have figured out the absolute best scoring system . . . based on our calculations, QB passing yards are worth 0.04 point per yard, or one point for every twenty-five yards . . . and since for the average NFL quarterback, the ratio of touchdowns to interceptions is roughly

three-to-one, then based on that ratio, each interception should sub-
tract two points from your quarterback's point total . . . But throw that
out the window if you are in a nonstandard scoring league, in which
case you . . ."

The Brits could all feel their heads explode.

With a startup, there is always an element of hubris lurking in the
belief that you are the one — the only one! — who can crack a puzzle that
others have attempted to solve but with no success. There is also an element of hubris at work when Big Ten bros think they have the idea that
will fundamentally change how people play fantasy sports. But five Brits
who have never played fantasy sports and who believe that they can offer
something utterly new to an industry that's been around and thriving for
decades? Well, that requires hubris drenched in a vat of magical thinking.

Fantasy sports seemed, on the surface, like a saturated market, impenetrable to any sort of outside disruption. Part of the reason, the founders discovered, was that the sports space was toxic to investors and thus
terrible at producing big startups. The scarcity could be explained partly
by the fact that the behemoth incumbents (ESPN, FOX, CBS, NBC) occupied one end of the spectrum, niche activity (bloggers working from
home) was at the other, and only a barren wasteland could be found in
between. The last startup of scale was ESPN, founded in 1979; more
recently, the content website Bleacher Report was an unlikely success
story, but otherwise, examples of startup successes were nonexistent.
The industry was starved for innovation.

If the Brits had learned something from their previous failures, it was
this: what separates the successes from the failures is the foresight and
the tools to recognize which parts of a plan are working and which are
not working and then — perhaps most crucially — the willingness and
ability to immediately change strategy. The Big Ten bros didn't know
what to make of the site operated by the five Brits, who ran their operation like a laboratory, constantly making adjustments to the product and
improving it, releasing new features on nearly a daily basis, and never
settling on one concept until they could validate their assumptions. This

approach, of course, required constant feedback from users, which the founders were happy to take, even if those users were telling them that their product sucked.

"No disrespect," a forty-something man with a thick Bronx accent said to Tom over the phone. "But this sucks. This looks like something that my twelve-year-old nephew would be interested in."

Tom, who was surveying users, was deflated. He had just pushed out the first version of their sports game, which was built on a Google spreadsheet. In their younger days, they would have been humiliated by this assessment. But Nigel's number-one rule was that the game be simple, and their game was simple if nothing else. A user picked a lineup of NBA basketball players from a pool of players and went head-to-head against another user to see which lineup would perform the best based on how those chosen players scored in a game. The winner was the one who had more points based on a very simple scoring system that took into account points, rebounds, and assists.

The product *did* look like an eighth-grade school project. While the natural instinct for a technologist like Tom in building out a product would be to begin coding, Tom was now going at it in reverse: he decided not to code but rather to build a prototype as quickly as possible to see if this idea actually could go somewhere. He wasn't going to make the same mistake of holing himself up in a room for six months building a product that no one in the outside world was interested in. Now Tom — as well as Nigel and the other founders — believed in faster iteration and constant customer insight. Tom often quoted Reid Hoffman, CEO of LinkedIn: "If you're not embarrassed by your first effort, you've waited too long." Tom figured he was on the right track because the product he'd designed was an embarrassment.

Still, Tom thought they'd stumbled onto something interesting when they'd come up with the format for this game, even if it looked terrible. But now Tom was on the line with someone who'd been recruited to test the product, and he was telling Tom something different.

Tom's conversation with the man from the Bronx had begun with the typical list of questions.

What problems do you see with fantasy sports? (*None*)

Do you think it's a pain to commit every week to pick your lineups?
  (*Yes*)

Are you looking for an alternative? (*No*)

And now this man from the Bronx was telling him that the product Tom had offered him resembled something only a twelve-year-old would be interested in.

"Okay!" said Tom. "But before you go," he asked desperately, "tell me — what could we possibly do to get you to play this?"

There was a pause. "Well, tell me, can I win some money on this?"

Tom was caught off guard by the question. "Yeah, maybe — sure," he said. "How about five dollars to maybe win . . . nine dollars?" he said, running the basic math in his head of the house taking a cut of a bet.

There was a pause. "Well, if I could put in fifty dollars to win ninety dollars? Now you're talking!"

Tom felt the lightbulb in his head go on.

Adamant that they needed to validate their hypothesis in a very disciplined way,* Tom put an ad on Craigslist telling players to pick from a list of baseball players and email him their choices along with $10 over PayPal. Tom pitted users against each other, and the user whose baseball players accrued more points would see $19 of winnings arrive in his PayPal account. He was blown away by the response: a half-dozen random people responded. *A half-dozen!*

---

* With Hubdub, they'd made every mistake in the book. They agonized over what in retrospect were meaningless details that seemed like make-or-break decisions at the time. They spent weeks, if not months, debating over a name for their site, finally settling on an inside joke. (Nigel and Lesley's three-year-old counted up to ten, then unleashed gibberish that sounded like "hub-in-dub-in-hub-in-dub-in.") During one lunch hour, Tom and Rob sat at a pub, scribbling names down on a napkin. They returned to work having settled on one for their idea for a sports game: FanDuel. It got to the heart of the idea of these games in which fans faced off against each other. The other founders thought the name wasn't terrible. It didn't matter: there was too much goddamn work to be done.

The first version of FanDuel was a snake draft format — in which participants drafted a player and took him off the board so his opponent would have to select from a smaller pool — built on a Google spreadsheet. The first interfaces were Craigslist and PayPal. It was embarrassing, and that was the point: the idea was to get it out there, to listen to the users about their experiences, and to change the product quickly based on feedback. They ran tests to see how well they hit their product market-fit goals, and the answer was clear: not well. In their initial surveys, only roughly fifteen out of one hundred users said that they would be "very disappointed" if FanDuel took the product away. Putting all their faith in the feedback — and again presuming they knew nothing — the Brits made changes, sometimes significant ones, to their product overnight. They noticed that competing companies did the opposite: those companies were religious about their beliefs about what a fantasy product should be. The FanDuel founders, entirely agnostic when it came to the religion of fantasy football, were true believers of the surveys and the numbers; having been told by the numbers that their product sucked, they had no reason to believe otherwise. After a few alterations, they produced a salary-cap-format game, and now just under fifty of one hundred people said that they would be disappointed if they couldn't play the game the following day. It was a sign that maybe, just maybe, they'd stumbled onto something.

When the five Brits presented this idea for an American sports game to their board in the United Kingdom, it was met, not surprisingly, with some dismay. But like most investors, the board had invested in the people, not the product, and even if these five failed, they would end up doing something interesting and maybe even impactful. For this particular product, there happened to be one big concern at the start: the legality. In every early meeting, the first thing an investor would ask was: is this gambling? There were plenty of funds in the UK that didn't invest in anything perceived as gambling. Kevin Dorren and the other investors joked that they liked to vacation in the US — the last thing they wanted was to end up in prison there instead. But the lawyers for the five Brits had come to the same conclusion as the lawyers for the Big Ten bros:

fantasy games were covered by the legal scaffolding of the Unlawful Internet Gambling Enforcement Act. The founders — cautious and meticulous — listened intently to every word that the lawyers were saying to the room full of investors as the collective group decided whether to move forward with this idea for a new kind of game. They all looked around and saw faces that seemed reassured.

One of the founders, deep down, was terrified. Tom jotted down his thoughts in a notebook, and during one meeting he scribbled down words that he felt he might need one day as a reminder, or a reassurance: *Odds of going to jail? Highly unlikely.*

At DraftStreet, Brian Schwartz's job, as cofounder and CEO, was to present a vision for investors and to raise money. Mark Nerenberg's job, as cofounder and head of product, was to develop the games. It was Mark's responsibility to come up with various ways of making them more interesting — from instituting smaller features, like the ability for users to swap players after the first set of games locked, to adding entirely new games, including golf. Early on, DraftStreet had distinguished itself from the competition by having more innovative games that seemed to cater perfectly to the users' preferences. That they were onto something was becoming apparent when other sites began blatantly copying what they were doing. DraftStreet had created a lobby on its site that was inspired by the poker sites they'd all once played on. Soon enough, other sites were doing the same. Later, FanDuel A/B tested a version of a site that looked exactly like DraftStreet's. The copying was so obvious that Brian had one of his lawyer friends send a cease-and-desist letter to FanDuel's office.

When he went into conference rooms to face potential investors looking to put money into the industry, Brian was sure to use these appropriations of their model to DraftStreet's advantage and declare, "We're the innovators in our space — and they're knocking us off!"

The fact that the DraftStreet games designed by Mark were superior to the competition's was giving them an early lead. But that wasn't enough. If they were going to last, if they were really going to get rich off this, they needed to figure out how to tap into the pool of casual players to give the company a lead big enough so that someone couldn't come into the space with a boatload of investment money and wipe out everyone else. They had to acquire customers faster than any other company. The problem with this space was that traditional user acquisition techniques were not going to work, because casual players had no idea what daily fantasy was. Brian imagined someone looking at an ad and saying, "What the fuck is this?" The money, ultimately, was what was going to attract new users, but the tournament prizes were small peanuts compared with the prizes of online poker in its heyday. They couldn't advertise a million-dollar prize pool because their biggest prize pool was $1,000 — not exactly an amount that was going to draw a great deal of attention. As they added players, though, the sites held bigger tournaments with larger payouts, and eventually DraftStreet got to a point where it could award a decent amount of cash.

In its first big NFL tournament, a player with the handle Hixville-Hunk turned a $60 entry into $60,000. Mark had an idea: to post an advertisement on the site Barstool Sports, an online blog that they all read, but to do so in an article format. Looking at yet another fantasy sports ad, a reader could easily feel his eyes glaze over, but this would read like any other column he would see on the site; he'd need to get through just three or four sentences of something like this to understand how to play the game and how to make money from it. The site had a feverish following — it wasn't a site readers visited purely for the headlines; they went in because they felt as if they knew the writers. Mark's idea was to ask HixvilleHunk to write a five-hundred-word blog post, which DraftStreet would pay for, to run on Barstool. The post was the story of a twenty-one-year-old at Elon University who saw a promo for DraftStreet on Barstool and ended up entering a tournament with one of his buddies and winning $10. He put another $50 into the account and ended up winning DraftStreet's $60,000 first prize.

They all came up with a headline: "Does Turning 60 Bucks into $9,000 on DraftStreet Get This Dude Laid?"

The night of their HixvilleHunk post on Barstool, the guys ordered pizza, brought out the beer, and gathered around a computer with a dashboard that tracked all the deposits coming in. Their offices were in a loft space in Union Square in Manhattan that had been turned into a frat house, with NBA posters plastered over the walls, a fridge stocked with cases of beer, and, in the middle of the room, a custom-made beer pong table — if anyone was going to find out whether a beer pong table could be custom-made, it was the Big Ten bros with a little bit of investor money to burn. Within an hour of the post, the dashboard began lighting up as they watched $20 deposits come in. The founders burst into giddy laughter, their drunken euphoria far surpassing any other moment in the company's young history. By the time they left that night, DraftStreet had added over three thousand new users in the course of two hours, and when they staggered out into the New York night, they felt as if anything was possible for their little startup.

As much time as the Big Ten bros spent arguing over whether the football product should include a kicker, or whether a stolen base in baseball should be worth more than a walk, or whether players should be allowed four or five members of the same NBA team in their lineups, Brian began to see that to some degree all those discussions were noise. He began to realize that the war between all the daily fantasy companies, the battle to gain an edge over the others, wasn't at all about product differentiation. He believed that DraftStreet's product was superior to others, superior to whatever clunky game NBC Sports was half-heartedly pushing, or the latest iteration the five Brits were coming up with — but all of that was moot. Brian now saw that this war wasn't going to be won over product, or design, or even innovation.

This was going to be a marketing war — a battle, simply, to acquire users.

On Tom Griffiths's computer was a spreadsheet listing the daily fantasy companies that had entered the space since his company's founding in the spring of 2009. What began as a serious and painstakingly meticulous catalog of all the competitors that were springing up became a list of ninety-six startups within just years, at which point the founders stopped bothering to count. There were now so many outfits dipping their toes into daily fantasy that if you were a media company even tangentially related to sports and you *didn't* come up with your own daily fantasy product, you weren't doing your job. If you ranked those operators in order of how big a threat they posed to the two leaders, DraftStreet and FanDuel, at the top of the list were the sites that had stuck around simply because they were backed by big money, and even those were dubious operations. At the bottom of the list were fly-by-night sites, including one that was a porn company.*

"That's a problem for us," an image-conscious FanDuel investor said to Nigel. To which Nigel replied, "And what do you want me to do about *that*?"

There was a reason why not just anyone — a porn site, for instance, or a high schooler looking for a computer science project — could wake up one morning and decide they were going to start a daily fantasy company and turn into an overnight success. The reason was simple: liquidity was paramount. Liquidity was the reason why a behemoth like ESPN or Yahoo! would have second thoughts about entering the space. Unless a company had high liquidity — a big pool of players and money flowing in and out of the ecosystem — it simply wouldn't last longer than a tadpole that had washed ashore. By 2012, no one was capable of catching the two leaders in the space, DraftStreet and FanDuel, which had spent years building up their user bases.

Later, the daily fantasy war would be cast as a story of excess and greed, but the early brilliance of the two companies was that they were lean startups before the lean startup rage in Silicon Valley. FanDuel's founders were so obsessed with the bottom line that they strived to break even at the end of every month. DraftStreet was growing, with only eight

---

* "Fantasy sports and naked girls have a lot in common," proclaimed the cofounder of Vivid Entertainment, one of the world's largest adult film companies, in the announcement of a new daily fantasy product. "They're very popular with a certain segment." Alas, Sports 4 Money never got off the ground.

employees, and it even experienced a stretch of profitability in 2012. In fact, neither company saw the battle as a zero-sum game. The way Brian saw it, both companies could fight over customers, but they could also co-exist. Brian had big dreams for DraftStreet, but even those dreams were modest by later standards — in the most bullish of his projections, he saw the potential for daily fantasy as maybe in the millions within a few years.

The expectations of early FanDuel employees were intentionally tempered: the founders told new hires that in a best-case scenario, the company would be sold for a nice sum — how big would vary depending on which founder you asked — within a few years, allowing the founders and employees to move on to the next thing. DraftStreet and FanDuel were neck and neck; there were moments when DraftStreet, which focused more on its basketball and baseball products, held the lead, only to be overtaken during the NFL season, which was the focus of FanDuel. But by 2012, as the capital markets began to open up and investors emerged from the wreckage of the financial crisis, real money started flowing into the industry. That year Brian raised nearly $2 million, only to learn that, months later, FanDuel had raised $12 million. Brian began receiving offers from offshore casinos and then, finally, from big media companies in the United States. One was the media conglomerate IAC.

Brian and the founders were looking to raise money to keep up with FanDuel, but they weren't looking to give up the company, and they certainly were not looking for a deal where a conglomerate like IAC would buy out all the existing investors and take over the majority of the company. But something was making the deal harder to refuse in the end: FanDuel was pulling away from DraftStreet, acquiring customers at a breakneck pace. Not only were they raising more and more money, but, most surprising to Brian, they were proving to be more effective at what was classic direct marketing: advertising a product with a measurable result. From afar, Brian saw FanDuel marketing in local newspapers and even putting resources into an aggressive radio campaign. But there was something else going on in the marketing war that Brian couldn't exactly put his finger on. The only thing that was clear to him was that they were losing that war, and it ate at him that the Brits were beating him at his own game and he couldn't figure out how.

On the night that Mark phoned home with the news that DraftStreet was being acquired by IAC, Lex Nerenberg could hear the rush in his son's voice. Mark was staggered to see that his idea for a new kind of game had taken on such a life of its own that an entity like IAC was willing to pour money into it. Mark's life wasn't going to change overnight, but he now had enough money to buy an engagement ring for his girlfriend and move into a nicer apartment in the city. He also now had the satisfaction of knowing that, having once felt adrift, with no apparent place in the world, he'd had a hand in creating a place in the world that he could now call his own.

Tom Griffiths moved from Edinburgh to New York City, where FanDuel had opened a US office in Union Square — just a block from its fiercest rival, DraftStreet, which was now backed by a media conglomerate and had new momentum to challenge FanDuel as the top daily fantasy operator. But something was happening to change the dynamics of the game: a new entrant. It had been around for months, had even appeared on Tom Griffiths's spreadsheet when it arrived on the scene in 2012, but seemingly overnight it had become a competitor worth paying attention to. For starters, the company, called DraftKings, had raised $11 million, an eye-opening amount for a company that barely had a footprint in a nascent, unproven industry. In a short period of time, it had developed a relationship with the most prominent daily fantasy content website, RotoGrinders, which instantly gave the company street cred with high-volume players who were beginning to make enough money off daily fantasy that they were quitting their jobs to play full time.

Most notably, this startup was clearly burning through its cash. At DraftStreet, the guys had built a scraper to mine data from this new rival's lobby, to track exactly how many leagues and players the site had each night, and at the end of every night they pulled up spreadsheets and knew exactly how much the company made that day. It was a simple math equation, and there was no way around it: because their tournaments, with massive prize pools, weren't filling out with enough entries, the site was losing boatloads of money. It wasn't just that it was losing money; it was losing money in the one area in which a daily fantasy operation was supposed to be making money: on players entering tournaments. It was unsustainable, and, Brian Schwartz thought, reckless and destructive. There was a reason some in the industry called them the suicide bombers.

"There's no way this is going to last. This is so stupid," Brian told the others as they watched the site put up tournaments with massive prizes night after night that didn't fill out with enough entries to cover the cost of the prize money.

At last, the founders at DraftStreet and FanDuel could agree on something: they both despised these guys in Boston who were taking *their* idea. "This isn't a way to run a business," said Brian. "No investor is going to be stupid enough to keep putting money into these guys." The reaction was the same at the FanDuel offices. No one was taking this new player in the daily fantasy war very seriously. No one except for the head of marketing at FanDuel, who was on the front lines of the battle to acquire customers. The woman who, in 2013, from her office in the FanDuel headquarters in Edinburgh, saw all the pieces in the escalating battle and, calling attention to this upstart company in Boston, began to type out a warning to her cofounders.

These guys are the ones to watch out for, Lesley wrote.

Get ready for a war. We will *win.*

2

TALE OF THE UNICORN

Boston, Spring 2013–Summer 2014

What are you doing? You're going to run this company into the ground!"

The cofounders were at each other's throats, again. "These people are going to lose their jobs!" Paul was now almost screaming at Jason, gesturing toward the open space where rows of employees hunched over their desks.

Outside their office walls, they were the rogue startup with the singular mission to acquire every single customer, even if it meant blowing up an industry in the process. They occupied a third-floor space in a seven-floor redbrick building that crouched on a bustling street corner in the heart of Boston, inside a room with windows that overlooked the tops of the plush elms that lined the sprawling downtown park below. The space was modest, the walls bare, but as makeshift as it could appear to an outsider, to the three cofounders of DraftKings the office was a beautiful miracle. Just two years earlier, the three of them — Jason Robins, Matt Kalish, and Paul Liberman — were midlevel analysts at a company in the suburbs of Boston spending nights after work and weekend mornings working out of a spare bedroom in Paul's town house, trying to crack the puzzle of daily fantasy games. Within months, they moved into a closet-sized space in the Boston suburbs — now here they were, armed with more than fifty employees, an odd concoction of former poker sharks and Ivy League quants but a full-blown company nonetheless, bulldozing ahead with a bravado and brazenness that astonished FanDuel and DraftStreet, the two operators that had watched countless fly-by-night operations come and go like fruit flies but had seen nothing that rivaled this upstart's hyperaggressive marketing strategy.

Still, despite DraftKings' efforts, the top of the daily fantasy hierarchy bore a striking resemblance to what it had been over the last two years: FanDuel at the top of the heap, DraftStreet a close second. Now the 2013 NFL season was months away from starting and the clock was ticking on DraftKings, the third horse in the daily fantasy race, to make its move. Paul, the 27-year-old chief technology officer, just didn't believe that burning through all its millions on TV ads was the way to do it. "This is crazy," he said.

"We *have* to do this," Jason, the CEO, shot back. "Are we *all in*, or not?"

From the start, Jason had a way of getting others to see things his way. The company was already growing every month, and the way Jason saw it, there was no reason why it couldn't continue to grow at that rate for years — no reason, in fact, for it not to grow at a much faster clip. Jason and Matt were poker players with an appetite for risk, but Jason was by far the most aggressive founder with his approach. Jason was never interested in hearing the downside scenario. That mentality often clashed with his CTO's. Paul, before he started at DraftKings, had never stepped foot in a casino. But he was the one individual at DraftKings who could stand up to the CEO, and he and Jason battled constantly. "The endurance of the two of them to fight about seemingly meaningless details of the product was astounding," says an early employee.

On this day, however, the direction of the company seemed to hang in the balance, and Paul could already sense that he was on the losing side of an argument. The three founders had been *all in* on this together since they decided the year before that they'd walk away from their positions at Vistaprint even though none of them had any experience running a business. The three of them put in nearly $25,000 to get things off the ground — Matt, for instance, took out every last dime of his bank account: $9,600. From the start, Jason was the most aggressive: he had no desire to be just another startup to come and go. Two years earlier, not long after they set up desks and a whiteboard in Paul's apartment, they began scraping the numbers publicly available from FanDuel's site — the size of their tournaments, the number of customers putting down entry fees each night. Jason had sat his two cofounders down. He presented them with two spreadsheets. One was their old budget — $500,000 of spending over a year. The second showed how much Jason believed they needed to spend — on tournament sizes and marketing — to make a dent in the industry, to possibly catch those Brits, who at that point in early 2011 had raised $1.2 million. The number that Jason presented was nearly three times as much as their old budget, just under $1.5 million.

Back then, to wannabe entrepreneurs in a lonely town house, the number was startling. *One and a half million?* But it would take them less than a year to nearly burn through what they had raised from their initial investor, the Boston venture capital firm Atlas Ventures. They had closed on their seed round in April 2012; by year's end, they were broke, taking bridge financing while out trying to raise more money. At the start of 2013, FanDuel announced that they had closed an $11 million Series C funding round. At the time, DraftKings had been incubating in Atlas's "seed program," in which the Atlas VCs would watch founders go through their early trials while latching onto an identity. Eventually, Atlas would graduate young companies from its program and help founders put together a Series A round. For some startups, Atlas would offer eighteen, sometimes twenty-four months of runway; some fledgling companies died before even emerging from their spare town house rooms and reaching the next level. In the spring of 2013, however, the Atlas VCs deemed its fantasy sports baby ready for its Series A, and a $7 million round was announced.

Now the question facing the founders was, *What to do with that money?* It was clear that they would devote the vast majority of those resources to customer acquisition — but how? By 2013, FanDuel, Draft-Street, and even DraftKings had built up significant digital presences. But scaling up would require cracking open a *new* channel. FanDuel was just beginning to dip its toes into ads on a new channel that would raise the stakes: television. For a company chasing customers, TV was an obvious play — an effective channel. There was a reason why even FanDuel was cautious, though: TV was expensive. Jason had presented his plan: TV was going to allow them to close the gap in the market, and he was proposing to spend about 70 percent of its budget on TV. If they were going to make a mark on this market, they had to go big. To go big, they had to spend big — bigger than anyone else, even if they were the third horse in the race. *Especially* because they were third in the race.*

"You're going to bankrupt us," Paul said. "You're going to run this company into the ground."

"We don't have a choice," Jason replied.

"This is a crazy way to run a business," Paul said.

For a startup with a completely unproven product to raise boatloads of money, seemingly overnight, and then to burn through it all even faster — it *was* a crazy way to run a business. Unless, of course, there was always more money to come.

In the aftermath of the 2008 financial crisis, as an obscure creation was having little success getting off the ground out of an office at the University of Edinburgh, money had dried up for startups everywhere; it had become nearly impossible for companies to pull off initial public offerings of stock. Without the possibility of IPOs, venture capital firms were never going to see a return, and funding, as a result, vanished. Venture investment was frozen. Between late 2008, when FanDuel raised its first $1.2 million, and September 2011, when it received $4 million in funding from the London VC firm Piton Capital, Nigel Eccles walked into eighty-seven different conference rooms and eighty-seven times got a no. For nearly two years he was unable to raise a dime from new investors.

---

* Paul Liberman had a reputation as one of the sharpest young quants at Vistaprint. But the way Jason saw it, Paul had carried away a bias against TV from his days at Vistaprint, a direct-marking company that had put almost all of its marketing budget in digital and largely ignored TV. That is, until Jason helped lead Vistaprint's first TV marketing campaign.

The tide turned, however, in late 2011, when the capital markets began to open up: foreign money, crossover, and public investors who were creating sections of their funds to invest in pre-IPO businesses were suddenly in abundance. The unprecedented sums of money that flowed into the venture world would soon make bets on Wall Street in the 2000s seem like wagers at the $5 blackjack table. Startups like Zynga and Groupon enjoyed the biggest IPOs since 2004, when Google went public, and the following year saw Facebook enjoy the biggest IPO in the history of the tech industry, creating a climate in which investors were tenaciously trying to find the next "unicorn" — in Silicon Valley parlance, a company valued at over $1 billion. Soon enough, there was money everywhere, and any college dropout riding around on a scooter in a $90 hoodie toting a half-decent idea suddenly could raise hundreds of millions in venture funding: a $700 machine that made eight ounces of juice, a bathroom scale that posted your weight on Twitter, a business hawking scooter rentals and grilled-cheese-sandwich makers . . . no idea was too out there. It was a frothy environment, not just because it was fueled by the kind of magical thinking at the root of the bubble of the early 2000s but also because, with the Federal Reserve printing more money in the aftermath of the financial crisis, there was easy money around. Stock prices were skyrocketing, the value of endowments and pensions was rising, and money was gushing into venture funds like a great flood into a desiccated plain.

The second VC boom was taking off in Silicon Valley but also beyond. While Edinburgh, even in 2013, remained infertile ground for startups, Boston was a hub of innovation, where the VC world was uniquely ferocious and Machiavellian. In venture capital investment per capita, the Boston metro area ranked third behind only northern California. "There's a lot of jealousy, and there's a lot of 'I'm just as good as that guy and I'm going to prove you wrong,'" says one prominent Boston venture capitalist about his city. "As a result, it's an absolutely cutthroat environment, where the big boys' club is maybe just a dozen firms. You have a dynamic that is just . . . *insane.*"

The coworkers who'd never started a business found themselves inside this crucible. They knew that the odds were stacked against them. For starters, none came from any real money. Jason was from South Florida, the son of educators. Matt, a local kid from working-class Lowell, was the first in his family to go to college — his dad worked at a prison and his mother was a hairdresser. Paul, meanwhile, was five when he came to the United States with his family as part of a wave of refugees leaving Russia. Bringing just two bags with them, his family eventually settled in Rhode Island, where for a time they lived off food stamps.

The three were, in short, outsiders. There is no greater currency in the startup world than access — access to other businesspeople, who give you access to venture capital, which in turn gives you access to capital, the essential oxygen for a startup company. The three had none. At the start they asked friends, friends of friends, parents of friends, for any word of advice. They cold-called people in the Boston business world for a lead, an introduction — anything to get them in the door.

"Sure! I'd be happy to help," said one lawyer Jason had reached out to. "But I don't know how big of a help I'll be. I'm a *divorce attorney!*"*

Armed with laptops and a slide deck, the cofounders walked into conference rooms, trying to persuade potential investors to arm them with capital.

THE FUTURE OF FANTASY SPORTS read the first slide of their presentation, followed by WHAT IS DRAFTKINGS?

---

* Jason would later marvel at the chain of fortuitous events that propelled them forward: how he happened to have a conversation with one lukewarm investor one morning over the phone . . . an investor who had happened to be having drinks that very night with a venture capitalist from Atlas, and said he could float Jason's idea . . . and how Jason happened to be free that following night to have beers with the two of them . . . and how he and the Atlas venture capitalist hit it off, talking sports. Jason, though, also happened to be starting a conversation with another firm; now, with the Atlas investment, Jason had two firms he could play off against one another. Suddenly, this peculiar daily fantasy sports company was even more interesting to any potential investor, which made Atlas even more interested in locking up an investment — a $250,000 investment from Atlas was suddenly a $1.4 million term sheet.

"Daily fantasy sports is the fastest-growing segment of the massive fantasy sports market" . . . "The DraftKings experience is an à la carte fantasy game" . . . They zipped through slides that flashed numbers showing the potential of their product: customer spend was high and climbing, as were monthly entry fees per active user and revenue. The trends, even the most skeptical potential suitor had to admit, were impressive for such a new company.

The presentation continued: RECENT LEGISLATION HAS PAVED THE WAY FOR INNOVATION IN THE FANTASY SPORTS GAMING MARKET, read a header on a slide. "Gaming" was an intentionally ambiguous term used in place of "gambling" within certain circles. Casinos liked using the term because it didn't come with gambling's stereotypes; daily fantasy operators liked it because it did. The very reason that daily fantasy companies could exist was that, of course, they weren't considered gambling operations: the Unlawful Internet Gambling Enforcement Act, Jason would explain to the room, specifically exempted fantasy sports from antigaming laws since it was considered a game of skill. Other games, such as sports betting and poker, were classified as games of chance and banned.

REAL-MONEY GAMING LEGALIZED IN FANTASY SPORTS, continued the presentation: "UIGEA paved the way for real-money gaming in fantasy sports while also dealing a major blow to cash-based chance gaming. In 2011, most of the major poker and sports book sites were blocked from doing business in the United States in what became known in the industry as 'Black Friday.'" The slide was referring to the day the US Department of Justice unsealed a fifty-two-page indictment against the nation's most popular online poker sites, which immediately ceased serving poker players. By mentioning the moment the rug was pulled out from under the poker industry, the DraftKings founders were subtly pointing out a significant fact: millions of dollars of liquidity were up for grabs, with poker players with fat bankrolls looking for a new game to put their action into. The poker comp was a key, but not exactly a groundbreaking one; even if FanDuel had never been nearly as overt as DraftKings about poker's role in bringing liquidity into the daily fantasy ecosystem, the DraftStreet founders had made that connection from day one, and anyone who'd ever been to an online poker site could quickly see that a daily fantasy operator's lobby was essentially a carbon copy.

Even though FanDuel and DraftStreet had proved to a certain extent that it was possible to raise money in the fantasy sports space, it was still an open question as to whether an investor was going to pump serious money into an industry that had largely failed to produce successful startups.* In the end, for a VC, it was about the founders — it was always about the founders. In this case, it was simply a question of why to believe in this particular group of rookie entrepreneurs.

They were always aware of how they were perceived: the rogue operators who were intent on blowing up the industry. They embraced the role as they gunned for a market leader that was four times as big as they were. "We loved competing with FanDuel," Matt says. "We loved putting up big tournaments and that people thought we were crazy. We loved coming up with an offering that was different, or rewards that were attractive. The mentality was: We have nothing to lose."

It was a mentality led by their CEO. From the start, Jason took the lead in pitches, explaining to a room full of investors why they were the group that was going to win the daily fantasy battle.

Jason wore his restlessness on his face, with sharp, darting eyes, short brown hair. He spoke in long paragraphs that went on and on and seemed like meandering monologues but actually were laid out like a scripted business pitch. He dressed in loose-fitting khakis and sports coats that seemed a size too big. "It's like he's put on his bar mitzvah suit," one DraftKings employee would later say. "He walks into rooms, and

---

* In 2012, the larger venture capital world was still mostly clueless about fantasy sports. "There always existed a disconnect between the capital markets and fantasy," says one venture capitalist who considered investing in daily fantasy in the early 2010s. "There was not, within the VC circles at least, any broad understanding of what fantasy sports was. It was like Dungeons and Dragons, or Minecraft — you'd heard about it, but you didn't know shit about it."

he never introduces who he is. People assume he's some sidekick or an assistant. You're like, no — this is the CEO and founder of DraftKings!"

But once he stood in front of a room full of investors, Jason knew that, in the end, bullet points and figures on a slide were meaningless. He knew what he was there to do: to tell a story — one that was bigger and grander than anything that had ever been heard about the story of fantasy sports.

From the start, in fact, he'd always reminded everyone at DraftKings that they were all telling a story. The one being written now, up until this moment in 2013, was just strange, wasn't it? This story of fantasy sports in America was led by five Brits who didn't even play fantasy sports? Who weren't even sports fans?

Jason believed that his startup owed it to the world to reboot this story. He would later say, of his sense of calling, "I felt like we were almost letting people down. Because this was our story to tell."

It was their mission: to take this story and make it their own.

To understand the story of DraftKings, you had to know the story of the CEO, and the story of Jason Robins — as a fan and as a sports nerd — begins many years earlier. It begins with his first hazy memory, dating back to when he was a young boy, when his father took him to a college football game and he found himself sitting in a sea of orange in a strange oval propped up by concrete pillars and everything around him was huge and overwhelming, including the rumble and roar of the crowd of eighty thousand that would become an unshakable part of his youth. Jason grew up not unlike any young fan in South Florida in the 1980s and '90s, madly in love with a great juggernaut of a football team that steamrollered every opponent in sight, and through high school he would miss only three of nearly one hundred football games at the old Orange Bowl, feeling pure ecstasy when the 1991 University of Miami football team clinched their perfect season — and pure agony when his quarterback threw an interception in the national championship game the following year. As a boy, Jason sat in the stands for even more Hurricanes baseball games, and his dream was to be one of those gods on the field, awash in the cheers. Then reality set in when he began to understand there was a reason why his Little League baseball coach always penciled him in to right field and at the bottom of the batting order.

The hidden side of the games he watched pulled him in deeper. Every morning he raced to the kitchen to open the newspaper at the table, take out the sports section, turn to the back pages with the box scores, and discover all over again the strange thrill of memorizing the numbers inside them. Every morning he played a game in which his mother or father would quiz him on the numbers — "How many RBIs for . . . Cal Ripken Jr.? . . . Right, okay, now finish your breakfast!" — and he began to see that he could find as much joy in memorizing and calculating statistics and probabilities as he'd known in watching and playing the game itself.

His obsession with stats and strategy only increased, and then with the rise of the internet and the launch of fantasy platforms on Yahoo! and CBS Sports, he saw fantasy games as just an extension of video games that had allowed him to feel as though he had some say and stake in the games on the field. He discovered a website that offered something called salary-cap fantasy games, where you could pick and choose your players and compete against total strangers, and he found himself playing in more than one hundred of these public leagues, with strangers, all at once. "It was love at first sight," he said of this magical realm he'd stumbled into.

Every new innovation through the years was a miracle bringing him even closer to the games on the field. It was a miracle how he could sit on his couch on an NFL Sunday and watch a channel that would toggle to any game when a team was inside the 20 yard line threatening to score. It was a miracle how he could, with a few taps on his phone, transport to any baseball game in the country and watch the game anytime, anywhere. And it was a miracle how he and any fan could, while watching any NBA game through à la carte streaming packages, post highlight clips while texting old college friends, colleagues, even his old bosses, to connect, to share in their anguish, and, of course, to talk shit.

But as a fan and a nerd, he could also see all the problems and shortcomings, even with fantasy games. He believed that as thrilling as it could be watching football on a Sunday and following how your lineups were doing, it was still impossible to understand your equity in a real-time sort of way — to keep track of big moments in multiple games while knowing just what you needed in your lineup to win your head-to-head season-long fantasy opponent, or to cash in on a massive daily tournament. He believed that the future would be a completely hands-off, fully automated sweating experience tailored to a fan's lineup, a product that could, say, flip to Cleveland when a team was at the goal line, about to score the points that would put him in position to win a weekend duel with a buddy or maybe, just maybe, a million dollars.

Daily fantasy games were simply a bridge — from a fan's nostalgia-soaked past to a new world. The games they were creating were how they were going to get to the future. And that future was inevitable. Because even though daily fantasy companies were cast as disrupters, there was a difference between them and a disruptive tech company. Typically, with disruptive technology, there were clear losers — retail stores in the case of Amazon, Big Taxi in the case of Uber. Fantasy gaming, meanwhile, was a virtuous circle. There were no losers. Fans, leagues, networks, advertisers, investors: *Everyone* was a winner in the story of DraftKings.

Everyone, that is, except for anyone who stood in DraftKings' way.

Not only could Jason Robins tell you the name of every VC or potential investor who had ever told him *no* or hadn't returned his call, but he could tell you where they were vacationing when they ghosted him. "They're all in here," he would say, tapping at the mental list of names behind every slight and rejection he'd received. If needed, he could reach back and retrieve the name of the founder who turned him away when, as a bright-eyed recent college grad out of Duke, he knocked at the door of a startup, wanting entry to an exclusive club, only to have that door and then later many others shut on him. He could give you names from the fifty firms he'd pitched to and been told *no* by as he and his DraftKings cofounders went to conference rooms across Boston begging for initial seed money. He could gleefully rattle off the names of the potential investors, and, most delightedly, FanDuel board members who scoffed that they'd never catch the industry leaders. Jason Robins's defining trait, those who worked with him said, was his unwillingness to take *no* for an answer, his stubbornness, and his certainty that his vision would propel them to win the daily fantasy war and that anyone who didn't see that would be proved wrong.

Jason's admirers cited his aggressiveness and abrasiveness as strengths; his detractors found him aloof, arrogant, hot-tempered, and calculating. "A total conundrum," says one DraftKings employee. "He has one of the worst tempers I've ever seen. He can be totally unreasonable and irrational. You get off the phone with him after he's been screaming at you, and you think, *I don't want to talk to him ever again.* And I consider him a friend." He wasn't necessarily a boss you wanted to vacation with on Cape Cod, but even some of his staunchest critics would agree that he was *precisely* the guy you wanted as CEO of your company: the CEO who had a bigger and grander story than anyone else and would do what it took to make that story a reality.

Massive tournaments with prize pools that were bigger than anything offered at FanDuel and DraftStreet; partnerships that pushed the envelope; hyperaggressive advertising on channels, including TV — Brian Schwartz saw how Jason ran his company and came to one conclusion. "He saw it as a winner-take-all game," Brian says. "The thing is, we never thought that if we win, it means they lose. We were growing, all of us: I saw them growing, but we were growing as well, so I was just like, *It's going well for everyone.* We stayed pretty lean — we were pretty smart marketers, we thought. We figured out ways to acquire users easily. We never spent on an area that we didn't think was profitable. But the way they were behaving at DraftKings — aggressive, aggressive, aggressive — it was as if there could only be one winner.

"For the first year they were just getting people to go to their site, and that bothered us. We're like, 'Fuck this,' we'd worked so hard to grow the space and now they're just taking our users with partnerships and giving insane prize pools away."

Raising vast sums of money and pouring it directly into a barrage of ads and into massive tournament pots that likely weren't going to fill out: that was one way to run a business. Just not the way Brian would choose to run one.

"They're burning money, that's all they're doing," Brian said to his co-founders. "It's crazy. Unless . . . there's more money to come."

As it turned out, there was. Jason's story of how an obscure fantasy sports game was going to change the entire sports industry was taking hold with investors. In late 2013, in fact, on the heels of a successful early NFL season fueled by an ad spend that was 70 percent TV, DraftKings announced a Series B funding round of $24 million, led by Silicon Valley VC group RedPoint Ventures. A group of fledgling daily fantasy companies on the fringes began to see the writing on the wall: in no reality would they be able to compete against a company with a war chest like that. The second-place horse in the race, one that was quickly losing its lead on the pack, was one of those companies that knew its days were numbered. Even if they did have access to that kind of capital, the Draft-Street founders, at the end of the day, didn't have the stomach to burn through the enormous piles of cash that it would require to stay in the game. More important, IAC, which had become DraftStreet's largest investor a year earlier, had no interest in being part of an industry where the stakes increased at breakneck speed.

From the moment the company launched four years earlier, Brian had kept an open mind: he never viewed it as his destiny to be the CEO of a fantasy sports company; if the right offer came along for DraftStreet, he wouldn't hesitate to take it and move on to his next venture. He and the founders, though, had only so much say in their fate: when the company was acquired by IAC in 2013, they'd given up majority control to a board that, in 2014, seemed very interested in selling the company to the highest bidder. Suitors lined up quickly. Among them was FanDuel. Eyeing DraftStreet's customers, Nigel had talks with Brian, but Nigel simply didn't see value in an acquisition, not if his company estimates were correct and they were only going to get roughly 20 percent of DraftStreet's users from the deal. But there was another interested party. DraftKings wanted to talk.

Even though he viewed them as a rival and loathed their approach, Brian could respect what the DraftKings founders had accomplished. No entrepreneur could dismiss the growth this company had seen in just a year. Brian had to hand it to Jason: He didn't make the mistake they all had of thinking it was all about product differentiation when in fact user acquisition was the key. Brian thought the DraftKings product was just a clunkier version of his own in the beginning, but it didn't matter, because DraftKings had figured out how to acquire users, albeit in a way that was dependent on tens of millions of dollars' worth of spending. Brian could acknowledge that there was a twisted brilliance to the DraftKings strategy: with night after night of tournaments with massive prize pools that might or might not fill out, as well as the aggressive advertising, they had the appearance of a big company even if they weren't.

Brian accepted the invitation to visit the Boston offices of DraftKings, and the moment he stepped inside he could see that his suspicions were true: he and this company existed in entirely different realities. The downtown offices, the staff that was at least six times the size of DraftStreet's: Brian thought to himself, *This is a daily fantasy operation?* The offices seemed more like the company DraftKings believed it would someday be than the company it actually was. The different reality of this world became even more pronounced as he got a closer look at the business. It was not just the vast open office space or the corporate vibe or the surface differences between the personalities of Brian and his cofounders and the Boston nerds, who shuffled around in button-down shirts and khakis; it was also what seemed to Brian to be their wildly aggressive projections. In a meeting, one of the DraftKings executives talked about the lifetime value — the LTV — of the daily fantasy customer. The LTV was the holy grail of the industry operators, a figure that was elusive because fantasy players were an impossible demographic to pin down.

Knowing a customer's LTV is essential for any startup trying to predict the long-term profitability of a business. It must know if customers are worth more than what it costs to acquire them. The DraftStreet founders' best estimate of the LTV of a user was somewhere between $200 and $400. And *that* was being generous. When the DraftKings executive told him their LTV figure — more than double their highest estimates — Brian just began to laugh.*

In a broader sense, Brian had become mystified at what he viewed as ignorance on the part of some investors who, without any understanding of the nuances of how daily fantasy worked, were willing to take things at face value and not ask more questions, even though it was a complicated business. There were, for instance, two primary levers the companies could pull to jack up their contest sizes. The first lever was direct spending on marketing to bring in new customers, which would allow the operators to run bigger contests. The second was "overlay," which was posting larger contests than their current user base could support. Overlay was essentially a sale for existing customers to get them to buy in more. Overlay didn't create earnings and was actually a cost. Some companies viewed it a marketing expense. The size of the marketing and the overlay that each company was willing to swallow were both dictated by how aggressive it was in going after market share.

Brian was surprised at how some investors, clearly not understanding the basics of the business, were willing to regard overlay as revenue when in fact it was clearly a cost for the daily fantasy operators. "It's scary talking to investors how little they know about the company that they're even invested in," he says. "If you wanted to, you could skew numbers any way you wanted."

But none of that mattered now, because reality was setting in: the company Brian despised was going to take over his baby. It became of-

---

* LTV estimates in daily fantasy would continue to vary wildly. "DraftKings CEO says LTV for user varies by sport but sees it at $600–$1000 . . . (Part of reason why VCs have been investing so aggressively)," Adam Krejcik, principal at Eilers and Krejcik Gaming, tweeted in 2015.

ficial inside a cavernous, glittery sports bar in downtown Manhattan, where the Big Ten bros showed up to their own funeral. They sat down, across from the nerds from Boston. Plans were already in motion. A New York office of DraftKings was going to open, offering a home to all the DraftStreet employees. The four founders of DraftStreet would share the buyout money in a completely even split. Each of the founders was also going to be offered a cushy position at DraftKings.

Mark Nerenberg would become the most senior executive for Draft-Kings in New York, leading a young, hungry staff of engineers. It had been seven years since he first sat down and put his idea for a new kind of game into an email, five years since he sent his pitch to Brian. It was a fantasy then, and in his wildest dreams he never imagined his game to take hold like this. Still, in the moment he became the new vice president of operations at DraftKings, a part of Mark was crushed. On his first day at his new company, Mark, the new vice president of game operations at DraftKings, would show up in mesh shorts and a black T-shirt emblazoned with the word DRAFTSTREET.

Brian was offered a position to head up DraftKings' fledgling efforts overseas. He was dangled a nice salary on top of the chunk of cash he was receiving from the acquisition — but he was genuinely torn about what to do. Brian couldn't possibly predict what was next in the daily fantasy story, given the roller-coaster ride it had already been up until this moment. He couldn't know then that DraftKings' acquisition of DraftStreet would be a turning point in the war. He couldn't know that Nigel had made a gross miscalculation: the percentage of users that DraftKings would acquire from the deal would be nowhere close to the 20 percent that the FanDuel team had estimated; in fact, nearly 80 percent of Draft-Street's customers would move over to DraftKings. Nigel would later call his miscalculation one of his biggest mistakes in the war. Overnight, on the heels of the deal, the Boston-based company would now be a true rival to FanDuel, not just in fund-raising dollars but also in customers. The monster was about to be unleashed.

As Brian spent more time at the DraftKings' offices, his decision became clear. From the start, the dream of the DraftStreet founders was to build and create something new — something that was *theirs*. To continue on the rocket ship after it was taken away from him would be as much of a sellout as staying in a well-paying desk job in finance. Brian saw the young DraftKings employees, fresh out of college, whip-smart Ivy League grads who'd turned down finance jobs to chase a dream, bouncing around the office with an energy that he envied. Then he saw the CEO huddle up with his cofounders for a conversation that he wasn't a part of — that he would never be a part of.

It was not until he sat down with Jason and his cofounders, as the ink was drying on DraftKings' acquisition of DraftStreet, that Brian could begin to see the true scope of the story that his rival CEO had imagined all along. It was then that Brian Schwartz saw that while his story in this world was ending, a larger story was only now beginning.

"We're building a billion-dollar company here," Jason said.

And Brian thought to himself: *A billion dollars? You are out of your mind.*

3

LESLEY'S PROMISE

Edinburgh, Summer 2014

I t was Lesley's friend Lucy who invited her to the weekly scrapbooking club, which gathered at a home tucked away on a winding, tree-lined cobblestone street. A small group of mothers arrived clutching boxes of old photographs and craft supplies, desserts and bottles of wine, seeking a night away from their breathless city lives. *This will be good for her,* Lucy thought, because if anyone could use more wine in her life, it was Lesley.

In the group, Lesley was always the odd duck. For starters, among lawyers, teachers, and stay-at-home moms, Lesley had a job that no one quite understood, other than that she was an entrepreneur. As the women cut and pasted photographs and other keepsakes into albums while Lesley talked about this new company that she and her husband had started — something to do with online games in America — the others in the group did their best to avoid staring at her as if she were a circus carny. *What, exactly, was this American thing called "fantasy sports," and how on earth did someone like Lesley get roped into it?*

Lesley was also not into crafts like the other mothers, nor was she as naturally artistic as they seemed to be; still, she always looked forward to the nights out and to trying something new, and despite barely being able to find time to shop for groceries, she made sure to fit this group into her schedule. Soon after Lesley joined, the group's leader suggested an activity she thought could add some spice to the nights through a fun, harmless exercise: a little competition in which all the mothers would have thirty minutes to create a page inspired by a theme — vacations, holidays, children, Disney characters, and so on. They would vote on a winner, and the winner would receive a set of spanking-new scrapbooking supplies.

When the competitions started, the others chatted on about kids and the latest new restaurants and the books they were reading, but Lesley put her head down and went to work on her book. If they'd looked over at her, the others would have seen someone intensely focused on the task at hand, but they couldn't possibly know just how much winning meant to Lesley. They couldn't know that to Lesley free craft supplies were in fact a very meaningful reward, given that she had three little ones and her family had been in such a bad financial state in the early years of the company that she hoarded coupons and shopped at secondhand stores and was too afraid to even glance at the monthly bank statements, so that she could avoid the reality of their lives: after pouring all their savings into this hopeless startup of theirs, she and Nigel were flat broke.

For Lesley, there was another motivation: the competitions were a chance for her to prove that she belonged in the group, to show the others that even though she had joined as an outsider, she'd become a worthy member of this club who in fact was just as skilled as the others in the art of scrapbooking — and after weeks of honing her craft, maybe now even *better* than any of them. And so when time was up, Lesley's albums were always the most complete and comprehensive. The odd duck in the group won the weekly competitions just about every time.

Then one day the leader of the club reached out in an email to tell Lesley and Lucy that the club would no longer be meeting. No explanation was given.

A few weeks later Lucy received a phone call from the mother who had led the group, telling her that the club had actually started meeting again. But there was a catch if Lucy wanted to rejoin: at the behest of the others, Lucy couldn't bring along any acquaintances this time around, and she couldn't bring Lesley.

When Lesley was back home on Wednesday nights — and back on the living room couch with her laptop, working, as she faced her impossibly endless list of daily responsibilities head-on — Nigel was disappointed for her because, for the first time, she had found an outlet from her new job. Then again, the truth was that when Lesley had begun to talk about these competitions they were having at the club, Nigel had begun to sense trouble. They'd been married for nearly ten years, but in these last few years since they'd started the company together, Nigel had seen new layers to his wife. It wasn't just that she had turned out to be a shrewd entrepreneur in her role; he also saw a resilience and determination and, yes, a cold-eyed competitiveness that he'd never seen before.

Nigel, more than anyone else, knew that whoever got into a winner-take-all game with Lesley sooner or later found out what, exactly, they were up against. Nigel knew that Lesley was always going to do everything in her power to win, and it didn't matter whether it was a weekly scrapbook competition or a race to become a billion-dollar unicorn.

They made the walk together every morning, from their house with the blue front door and past the black sandstone facades that always made it feel like dusk in this city, over the ancient bridge and through the park called the Meadows, along the paths lined with cherry blossoms. Just beyond the trees was the room in the university building where the founders assembled every day and attempted to crack the puzzle of fantasy sports, but every morning, before Lesley and Nigel walked into the building and joined the others, they stopped at the red corner café, took a table by the window looking out onto a quiet street, sat down with their bacon rolls and tea, and just as they did on this late summer morning in 2014, planned out the day.

But this day was different from the others. A month had passed since DraftKings' acquisition of DraftStreet, and it was now a race between two companies, weeks before the start of NFL preseason games. Word was getting around that Nigel was about to make a countermove, that a monster Series B, led by Shamrock Capital, was imminent. Within the investment world, a number had been going around, a guess as to how much money Nigel had been able to raise. The rumor was $40 million. Before that round was finalized, DraftKings made a splashy announcement of the amount they'd raised, in the aftermath of the DraftStreet acquisition, from venture capital firm Raine Capital: $41 million.

Nigel laughed. *You have to hand it to them, it's a pretty fucking good troll,* he thought. Others shuddered. The number was a warning shot.

This day was different for Nigel and Lesley because a meeting of the FanDuel board would soon convene inside the Edinburgh offices to set out a game plan for the upcoming season and, specifically, to get approval for the ad spend for the rest of the year. As their deal was closing, Nigel had given Shamrock a number that represented the projected ad spend during the NFL season. In Edinburgh, with everyone in person, they would finalize their plan.

Six years had passed since their lives changed completely, when Nigel decided to quit his job to start a company with Lesley. One morning in 2008 the two of them were in the car together and Lesley looked over at Nigel and saw a miserable human being. Nigel had been like this for years. Stuck in a consulting desk job that didn't inspire him, Nigel would sit at home with the *Sunday Times,* read a fluffy profile in the business section about the latest success-story entrepreneur, and growl, "I could do *that!*" Nigel was like a tortured writer who always talked about penning a great novel but never actually sat down to write a sentence. After a decade in London, where both he and Lesley had worked for most of that time as management consultants, they had relocated to Edinburgh to less chaotic environs. They immediately felt at home, but in one critical way nothing had changed: Nigel was still a ghost. The downside of Nigel's walking away from his high-paying job would be immense, as they'd just cleared out their bank account for a massive mortgage on a new house and Lesley was on maternity leave, having had their second boy months earlier. But there were worse things than financial insecurity.

That morning in the car, Lesley looked over at Nigel and decided she couldn't take anymore. "Just do it," she told him firmly. "We're going to be here ten years from now, with you giving me that look that *I* was the one that stopped you. So just do it."

Now, their jobs remained as they were at the start. Nigel's job as CEO was to raise funds. Lesley's job as head of marketing was to spend them. Nigel went into rooms full of investors asking for money. Lesley went into rooms to tell investors how she intended to turn the money into paying customers. Working in tandem like this was never part of a grand career plan — they were the type of couple that was utterly incapable of planning a vacation more than a week in advance. Not that they had time for any vacations. Things were moving at a dizzying speed: after years of banging their heads against their desks, trying to crack the puzzle of daily fantasy, they suddenly had thousands of customers and tens of millions of dollars of funding.

The upcoming 2014 NFL season would be their chance to pull away from the growing number of competitors in the space. "Okay, let's do this," Lesley said to Nigel as they finished up in the café, and now, on this day in August, it was time to present their plan to their new investors.

The number Nigel had given to Shamrock only two days earlier of the projected ad spend for the upcoming NFL season was different from the number that Lesley now had in her head of how much she needed to crush their rivals. Nigel knew that the board, led by a group of private equity sharks from LA, was going to fight Lesley on that number.

But he also knew that these sharks had no idea what they were up against.

A month earlier Lesley had been feverishly preparing for a biannual marketing meeting — where she would present plans to the whole team in New York and lead a brainstorming session of new ideas for marketing during that upcoming NFL season — when she put aside her work to spend the weekend with her parents in her hometown of Forfar, where her mother was undergoing an operation. The drive north from Edinburgh and into farmlands and to Forfar snaked through the land's gray rocks and verdant hills and iron bridges over the rumbling waters of the river Tay and into the small town, where rows of brown shoebox stone houses lined narrow cobblestone roads. The journey always took her away from one world and brought her back to another. With each passing mile away from the city, she felt herself detaching from all the work drama as the memories of childhood came rushing back: of growing up in a household where every penny was counted and saved; of hiding behind the sofa with her younger sister when the bill collector came; of having had a sense of never wanting to live a life controlled by uncertainty and fear. The daughter of a carpet salesman and a stay-at-home mother, Lesley was naturally an introvert, but she recognized early on that things were not given to people in this world, that if she was going to get anywhere, she would have to push herself out of her comfort zone. And she did, in ways that surprised even herself, as she went out for the school play, ran for student council, and then was the first in her family to go to university. At St. Andrews, she majored in languages and spent her days in libraries with her head buried in ancient German texts — Hartmann von Aue, Goethe, Brecht. Her senior year she sat in the career services offices wondering what one does with a modern languages degree, and she felt lost, unsure of what she was now going to do with the rest of her life.

It was at St. Andrews that she met the tall, lean captain of the shinty team. This was not love at first sight, not for her at least. The night they first met, at a ceilidh, a traditional Scottish dance, Lesley saw a problem from the start: this boy Nigel was, for one thing, much too young. Two academic years younger, to be precise, and Lesley could sense instantly that he was a restless twenty-year-old with commitment issues. But there was something about this young man she'd been introduced to through a friend that she found magnetic. Nigel — sarcastic, wry, charming, with short-trimmed blond hair and boyish looks — spent his days diligently working toward top marks as a math major and spent his nights and weekends playing sports and holding court at the pub. She found herself excited and elated by the differences between them, but it would be their similar worldviews that sustained them past their second and third dates.

Nigel had also grown up away from the city, on a dairy farm in county Tyrone in Northern Ireland, the youngest of four brothers, and he too had a seemingly innate understanding that there were no guarantees in life, no safety net. Nigel's father passed away when he was five. He had no memory of Sam Eccles, only the hazy image of eating cake at his funeral. What he would never forget were his early memories of his mother, who was left to raise him while still overseeing the daily operations of the farm and working a day job as an elementary school teacher to make ends meet in a house bursting at the seams. In those early years of Fan-Duel, Lesley often thought about Nigel's mother on the farm, how she was able to somehow make it work. Lesley thought of her own mother too. Not only the way her mother was there for her every moment of her childhood, but also how she and her father, after Lesley had gone off to college, opened up an inn outside of Forfar, to make ends meet for their family. Early in their relationship, Nigel and Lesley spent nights during weekends and holidays working the front desk at the inn, seeing first-hand the day-to-day grind of running a small business.

Her parents couldn't tell you the first thing about fantasy sports in America, only that they were immensely proud of their daughter's business. Bruce Tyrie saved every newspaper clipping in the *Scotsman* and the London papers through the years and called Lesley whenever he saw FanDuel signage in the background during sporting events on TV. Her mother, Beryl, was proud of the kind of mother Lesley had become. The couple's decision to stay in Scotland had delighted Lesley's mother, who was always worried about how far Lesley would push herself in her career, working those unsustainable hours.

Soon after she and Nigel arrived in Forfar, she knew that she would have to cancel the trip to New York for that biannual marketing meeting. Something had gone wrong with her mother's operation and she had taken a turn for the worse. Over the next four days Lesley didn't leave her side as she, her sister, and her father watched her mother struggle painfully, and in delirium. Lesley felt like a child again, helpless against the larger forces at work. They turned off the machines at eight in the morning on a Friday. Lesley buried her mother the next week. Devastated, Lesley took two weeks off. Nigel assumed that she'd need more time to herself when the Shamrock investors were due to arrive.

"No, I'm coming back," she said, in a voice that seemed even more resolute than ever. "We have to do this. *I* have to do this."

Lesley was back at work in the Edinburgh office. With the NFL preseason fast approaching, with DraftKings coming after them at full sail after their new acquisition and a round of fund-raising, and with FanDuel's war chest now full of funds to deploy after locking up their deal with Shamrock, what was Lesley going to do — just curl up into a ball and disappear?

Not now.

There was a war to be won.

They blustered into the offices, the private equity sharks from America who were here in Edinburgh to meet their new partners. Shamrock was a private equity firm focused on media and entertainment, and as a business on the lookout for areas with growth potential, they'd always been big believers in sports. They believed, specifically, in the value of sports content, because in this new media world advertisers were beginning to move toward live events, one of the few remaining places where viewers were willing to sit through commercials in order to partake in the live viewing experience. Shamrock saw fantasy sports in particular as the future, because they believed that the explosion in popularity of fantasy games had made the NFL, the biggest sports league in the universe, what it was today. Shamrock, which once had a stake in the Harlem Globetrotters and in the past had flirted with the idea of buying a professional sports team, had long been looking for a way into the fantasy industry, but until now it had been an industry that was barbelled: at one end were the behemoths — Yahoo!, CBS, the NFL, ESPN — and at the other were guys in their basement blogging about whether you should start Tom Brady without his top receiver in a matchup against the top-ranked defense in the NFL on the road in a snowstorm in Denver. Now things were changing with the arrival of daily fantasy — fantasy sports on steroids.

The Shamrock partners had always believed that sooner or later their search for the next big thing would lead them to fantasy sports — they just didn't think it would lead across the ocean, to this ancient city, to a table surrounded by Britons. Mike LaSalle, one of the Shamrock partners who'd made the trip, had also visited DraftKings on a scouting trip, and that office made sense: when you stepped inside their open Boston space, you felt as though some designer had come in and created a set for what a fantasy sports company should look like, complete with employees whose faces said, *Holy shit, can you believe we work here?* That office embodied Jason Robins's vision — it represented what he thought the company would be in four years. In FanDuel's Edinburgh office, you could barely fit a dozen people in the room.

And yet LaSalle had no second thoughts about Shamrock's choice of horse to back in the daily fantasy race. "Nigel, he's not like Jason," LaSalle had told his partners. It wasn't exactly a knock on Jason; when he met with Nigel in New York, LaSalle simply felt more aligned with Nigel's cautious, analytical approach. They weren't venture capital guys who could throw fifteen darts at a target and just need one to hit the bull's-eye. A private equity firm like Shamrock had just five darts and could only afford to miss once. They wanted to see a pathway to profitability, and soon. But Nigel had clearly found a successful business model. "In 2011," says Paul Martino, partner at Bullpen Capital, FanDuel's first U.S. investor, "these guys were making a million-dollar a year run rate with only 10,000 registered users. They were acquiring users for $35. I'd never seen anything like that."

FanDuel in the early years had been a brilliant model of efficiency: they counted every penny and cherished every additional user. But they'd decided that they needed more financial capital to grow into the company that they believed they could become. Shamrock would give Fan-Duel — and the entire daily fantasy sports industry — legitimacy, which was huge for an unknown startup with an unproven product. Countless professional investors played key roles in building wildly successful startups, allowing for big IPOs and founders to exit with sweet paydays. But the downside to taking on VC or private equity investors was not insignificant. Through each funding round the founders decreased their ownership percentages; by the C round, investors usually owned more than 50 percent of the company. The founders lost more and more control of decision-making as well.

They knew the risk: the moment they let these private equity sharks in their door, there was no turning back from what was a grow-grow-grow strategy in a race to become a billion-dollar company. The move to bring in private equity investors didn't necessarily clash with the founders' initial vision of the best-case scenario for their plucky startup: in job interviews for their earliest hires, they told would-be employees that they were all in — for a few years at least, until they could sell their company or reach an IPO.

The Shamrock investors were also in the game to win it, and they'd assembled in Edinburgh to make a game plan. The big question entering the fall was the ad spend, and when he stepped into the offices of FanDuel, LaSalle had a number in his head of how much the budget was going to be. That number, much discussed with Nigel days after the funding round had closed — only days before this meeting — was just over $21 million. This was a staggering figure for a private equity firm typically uninterested in unprofitable businesses. But from the beginning Shamrock knew its investment in FanDuel was unusual for them because, initially, the business was going to show losses. It was something they were willing to swallow if the upside was as high as believed.

The founders and the board, which included Martino from Bullpen Capital, all settled into their seats in the conference room. After a few words from Nigel, Tom Griffiths and Rob Jones — the two genial and sharp tech geeks who were clearly passionate about their sleek product, which by then had already been showered with awards — spoke next, introducing the product's new features for the upcoming season. Then it was the chief marketing officer's turn to take the floor to present the ad spend for the NFL season.

Mike LaSalle had never met Lesley Eccles, but on this day he was about to become well acquainted with her. Lesley began to tell the room how the daily fantasy world was changing. She painted a picture of the unique dynamics of this particular season: after years of staying away from this space because of the legal concerns, ESPN was going to open the category — the biggest advertiser in sports was now in play. There was a second factor: the emergence of DraftKings.

"We're going to have to be aggressive here," Lesley said, then changed the slide, which presented a number for the ad spend: $43 million.

It was more than double what the Shamrock partners had expected. After LaSalle processed what was happening, he spoke. They could go up from $21 million — but surely, he thought, there was a compromise between that and the $43 million that Lesley was proposing.

Lesley looked at him and said simply, "Forty-three million. It has to be $43 million." There was a stunned silence in the room. Then back-and-forth. As they ran the numbers, the board's demands inched up to meet Lesley's.

At one point the two sides were negotiating over $1 million. But Lesley wouldn't budge. From his seat at the table, Nigel shot Lesley a look: Are you really going to do this?

"There's no negotiation here," she said. "It has to be forty-three. We have to do this," she said. "Not a penny less."

Money and time: this is what Lesley always said she needed to win the war. Money and time. It had taken her six years to get to this point. Six long, maddening years to create the machine.

She needed the money: $43 million. It had been Lesley who had built the machine, she who knew better than anyone else in that room about the customers up for grabs, she who knew better than anyone how to acquire them: $43 million. That's all the board needed to know. Sure, she could have told them *why* $43 million — she could have told them that

Brian Schwartz's realization had always been correct, that it all came down to customer acquisition, that no company, up until now, had been better at customer acquisition than FanDuel. What Brian saw as a weakness of FanDuel was in fact a strength, an advantage in this battle over customers. Being a sentimental fan caused him to be blind to the products' obvious problems. Lesley, clinical in her approach, saw the world with fresh eyes.

She could have explained the details of why every penny of that $43 million was absolutely essential. She could have begun with the nitty-gritty basics of the cost per acquisition model that she had spent years banging her head against the wall over, the basic model that others learned in Econ 101 while she was off reading Goethe, the basic model that was one of many she learned from Google or one of the many books she would read late into the night in her crash course in marketing. The CPA model explained that you had to pay a certain amount of money to acquire a customer; that CPA was just the start, the foundation for everything else; and that there was also the LTV, the lifetime value of the user; and that as long as your CPA was lower than your LTV, then you would make money. She could have also explained that that model was impossible because LTVs were impossible. Because fantasy players were unlike other customers in other industries because every year players came back. (In surveys, when players were asked if they expected to give up fantasy, the most common answer was *never.*) And daily fantasy was not like, say, a cable service, where everyone was largely of the same value; instead, it had one of the most enormous spreads in customer value of any industry in the history of the world, because high-volume players were worth so much more to the business than hundreds and maybe thousands of players who were going to click on an ad and on a whim play once or twice, which is why finding and then catering to high-volume players was of paramount importance to survival.

She could have gone on to explain how the machine she built was fueled and how it hummed and operated. How radio, at the start, was her secret weapon in beating DraftStreet, and how she cold-called countless so-called expert consultants, so many that Tom kept a running list of them on a whiteboard as a joke and crossed them off when Lesley would inevitably declare them useless. Eventually she began working with a consultant in the state of Maine, of all places, who taught her the ins and outs of radio, a man who didn't have one hundred thousand Twitter followers but actually knew what he was talking about and who showed her the secret passageways of radio marketing. She tested relentlessly, changing messaging within the script based on these things called promo codes, setting out three or four different ways of describing what FanDuel was but always making the same offer, each time with a different promo code: megabonus, NFL2014, bearclaw, or any of the hundreds of promo codes that showed them which ads worked, and at what time of day, and which ads didn't. With that knowledge, she deployed ads on a turn-on, turn-off basis, like a spigot, so that they weren't committed over a long period if they weren't working one week; the ads could either be quickly shut down or revved up when they brought users rushing out like water from a hose. She could have explained to these investors that radio shaped the company's marketing ethos going forward, that they were slaves to the numbers and analytics and relentless testing, that the promo codes would be used on TV. She could've shared all the odd quirks and surprising preferences of customers, what worked and didn't work: that female voices always tanked and male voices always performed better; that cities in the Northeast were particularly strong, California was less so, and many of the southern states, like Texas — the heart of football country — were complete duds; that on Facebook everything hinged on the image and not the words, black and white was always a disaster, and nothing worked until a silly little image in one of the Facebook ads of a pig that was a football somehow brought users to the site in droves. She could have showed them the power of carpet-bombing during preseason and the first few weeks of the NFL season — a concept that the DraftKings guys had totally dropped the ball on — and explained why advertising outside of those first few weeks was like selling Christmas trees in June. She could have told them how she was just beginning, now, to understand TV, and how focus groups and ad agencies might love the more cinematic approaches but even if you got Martin Scorsese to direct your brand ads, nothing drew customers in better than those confessionals that looked like Hair Club for Men ads, which she agreed looked like cheap ads, but what did it matter if, as the data was telling them, they worked like gold?

She could have told them what it was like to be a woman in Scotland writing radio scripts for guys named Opie and Carton to read on the air to their rabid listeners. Lesley got so good at channeling the preferences of football fans in the Deep South, creating scripts that were so authentic and pitch-perfect for this demographic, that she received a cease-and-desist letter from Jim Rome's radio show in the United States for trying to impersonate him, which of course was preposterous. She didn't have the slightest clue who Jim Rome was.

But there was no need for Lesley to explain anything to anyone — because now it was about money. It was about $43 million. Her promise here in that moment was that if they gave her the money, the machine would do the rest.

Just a few weeks after that first meeting with the Shamrock partners, the founders and the board reconvened. They sat in their same seats but this time it was Lesley opening the meeting.

It was just a few weeks into NFL season, but the data told tell them how much money they were going to make through September. The first slide in her presentation would show the customer acquisition costs, over digital and TV. The numbers matched Lesley's projections almost perfectly.

But before turning to that slide, Lesley took a moment to look at one of the board members at the table — the man who was becoming her biggest foil. Before turning the screen, she said, "Mike, this slide is for you."

Later, Lesley would often think back to a moment before the war erupted, a moment during one of her daily walks to the office. It was 2010, two years after they'd given up everything for this idea for a silly little game. As they kept trying, unsuccessfully, to attract users, the company's funding was beginning to run dry. They raised $1.2 million in November

2007. It would be another four years before they raised another dime. For seven years they'd slaved away in that room, on the University of Edinburgh campus, with vomit-colored walls. On Fridays, they went to all-you-can-eat curry, flashing their university IDs for the extra discount. During the winters, the landlord would inexplicably shut off the heat, and they'd all work in fingerless gloves in frigid rooms. The mice they could deal with; it was when the mice died that was a problem.

At the beginning there was no way for them to know what their life would become: that their entire savings would be put into this venture; that neither of them would take a salary for a year and a half; that Lesley would be saving coupons and shopping at thrift stores; that when they'd get to the most desperate times, Nigel, like a sad character out of a Dickens novel, would go to the bank to sell off another Krugerrand coin he'd collected as a boy growing up in Northern Ireland, just so that they could make payroll.

She felt like a fool: to think that their silly little game would amount to anything, to think that they — a group of Brits of all people! — could transform the $600 billion American sports landscape, to think that she — a woman living in Scotland! — could crack the puzzle that countless others in the US who lived and breathed this stuff had failed to do. If you'd asked her in that moment, she would have told you that she would be happy to just get their money back, to simply break even on this misadventure. But on this day in 2010, even that seemed like a long shot. She felt as if she were standing at the edge of a beach, and the ocean was moving in toward her, and she was trying to push it back before becoming swallowed by it whole.

Another futile day awaited her, another day of trying to figure out how to attract users, but first Lesley took a rare moment for herself. She stopped, sat down on a bench, and felt herself begin to cry.

A figure approached; it was Nigel, who'd come looking for her. A cold wind whipped through the air; in springtime the Meadows could be the most beautiful place in the world, but now, in the dead of winter, the park felt desolate and lonely.

Nigel sat down next to Lesley. "We'll be okay," he said.

"Will we?" Lesley asked.

"This is what we wanted," Nigel said. When things were bleak, Nigel often repeated those words to Lesley, as a reminder not just that they'd made this choice, but also that it was up to them to make it work.

"Two users a day," he said. "We just need two users a day, and we'll be okay."

In later years, she thought back to that morning as a reminder of just how far they'd come. By 2014, after Lesley's machine was fed and unleashed, they were now adding half a million new users — on one NFL Sunday. Lesley's machine worked so brilliantly that the $43 million ad spend became a $70 million ad spend during the season. They closed the year just above $57 million in revenue, up from $14 million in the previous year. Every cent was worth it. Time and money: Lesley was right all along. The markets did open up, and DraftKings, despite their $41 million warning shot, had not made a dent in FanDuel's market share lead. In fact, FanDuel's lead expanded over the course of the season. By the start of the next year, FanDuel was nearly twice the size of DraftKings, with a 65–35 market share lead.

When the season was over, Mike LaSalle called Nigel. "We won't doubt you guys again," he told him. "What you guys did was brilliant."

In 2014, across the United States, just over fifty companies had joined the unicorn club, including a car-service company called Lyft, an e-cigarette outfit named Njoy, and a solar-panel manufacturer, Sunrun. Within the startup world, there was new buzz that a fantasy sports company was to join that list in 2015. The world was taking note, in the United States and beyond. A headline in the *Belfast Telegraph* read: "Tyrone Man Nigel Eccles Will Soon Be Northern Ireland's Newest Billionaire."

The next time all the top executives at FanDuel — the founders, the investors, and the board — met again, it was in New York City, as another football season was approaching. They were having dinner together when one of the board members sitting next to Lesley leaned over to her.

"Do you realize how rich you and Nigel will be?" he asked.

"Excuse me?" Lesley asked.

"You guys are going to make $100 million off this."

The board member leaned in closer.

"Me? I'm going to buy a castle," he said.

"A castle?" said Lesley.

"With the money we're going to make together," he said, "I'm going to buy a castle on an island.

"But you, you and Nigel, will be able to buy the *entire island*."

4

WHERE ARE ALL THE GROWN-UPS?

Las Vegas, Summer 2015

From the very start, the new fantasy sports game that the founders at FanDuel and DraftKings had turned into this bright, shiny world was a beautiful, magnificent, truly unbelievable thing, Cory Albertson thought, because if someone had come to him and said something existed that was even more of an exhilarating thrill ride than his true first love — that chronic disease called poker — and that this thing was perfectly, 100 percent legal *and* something you could make boatloads more money from than grinding your face off each day on one of those offshore poker sites, he would have laughed whoever was peddling that fantasy out of the room. But now he's looking at the ballroom around him — the cinema-scale TVs flickering like the video screens at Times Square, the guys sprawled on the couches downing their beverages at a frat-house party pace, the bros who speak in the beautiful language of stacks, fades, value plays, and FPPGs and rattle on about the insane ROI of Clayton Kershaw and how anyone who overthought things and doesn't have a Rockie playing at Coors Field today might as well hit the craps tables downstairs — and Cory feels as if he's found a world that has been conceived and built solely for him.

Though his head is already in a fog, which might have something to do with the cocktail in his hand or the game broadcast blaring on the sound system so loud it's hard for him to decipher what's being said or that another $1 million is within his grasp. There is a detonation of cheers, and it's impossible to know if it's because of the single at Yankee Stadium just now on one broadcast or the walk at Coors Field on another, but either way he has one eye on the screen over the stage that is blinking and reshuffling every few seconds, like an arrivals and departures board, with updated standings of the fantasy players in this room. The FanDuel Fantasy Baseball Championships are in full swing at the Cosmo casino on the Vegas Strip, and the name at the top of the screen is "Rayofhope."

Cory, aka one half of rayofhope, is standing in the middle of this dimly lit ballroom wondering what color he'll choose for the new Ford F-150 he's going to buy with a chunk of that million, the thought racing through his head while he's talking to God — two gods, that is.

The first god is the one he prays to every day when his partner, Ray Coburn, the second half of rayofhope, clicks his laptop a final time a minute before lock, the god who had told him this morning to play one of their four lineups in this event loaded with New York Mets, resulting in a lineup that ended up like this:

P — Carlos Rodon, White Sox @ Mariners
C — John Jaso, Rays @ A's
1B — Paul Goldschmidt, Diamondbacks @ Reds
2B — Anthony Rendon, Brewers @ Nationals
3B — Juan Uribe, Mets @ Rockies
SS — Troy Tulowitzki, Blue Jays @ Angels
OF — Yoenis Cespedes, Mets @ Rockies
OF — Michael Cuddyer, Mets @ Rockies
OF — Juan Lagares, Mets @ Rockies

And now Cory has his other eye on the screen, a late August ballgame that is largely meaningless to the world outside of this ballroom, and he's watching three Mets all reach base consecutively and earn their keep.

The second god he's talking to is the man next to him, the rotund forty-something man wearing blue jeans and an oversized black T-shirt over his boulder-shaped torso, a shirt bearing the name of the company that's throwing this bacchanalia. This man looks as if he's not entirely sure how he ended up in a room of twenty-something drunk white dudes who weren't born yet when he was the biggest sports star in the universe.

Cory has showed up to the event wearing a baby-blue Bo Jackson Kansas City Royals jersey purchased online, figuring it will be the perfect ice-breaker when he introduces himself to the host of FanDuel's season-end baseball live final, which will crown the best daily fantasy sports player, and players, on the planet — or at least the luckiest.

"Having a good time?" Cory says.

Bo looks over at the tall redhead standing next to him, and his eyes narrow. "You know, that's a fake," he says.

"Pardon?"

"That jersey you're wearing — it's fake," Bo says.

And so Cory's plan to impress his childhood hero has failed, miserably, and while he's crushed, he also knows as well as anyone that surreal and awkward interactions like this, like plates of prime rib stacked high and seven-and-sevens flowing everywhere, are staples of these live final tournaments at which he's become a regular attendee. Swirling around him now as he tries to salvage his precious minutes with his childhood hero are more roaring eruptions, and it's not clear whether the room is cheering or booing the José Reyes home run in Colorado that is the cause of the ruckus, and all he knows is that the scoreboard is flickering and rayofhope's once cushy lead has evaporated because José Reyes is one of the Mets he and Ray *didn't* slot into their lineup in what was projected by everyone in this room to be the highest-scoring game, by far, on this evening slate and thus the source of the most players selected in lineup entries. As he watches his lineup tumble in the standings, the blood washes from Cory's already pale face, and now the new Ford truck that was in his driveway is rolling back to the dealership floor, and he's starting to get that sickening feeling that he's felt before: when he lost $500,000 on one hand at the World Series of Poker. Cory turns to Ray, who's wearing a blue T-shirt that says ENJOY YOUR BURRITO and a Yankees hat that looks as if it maybe hasn't been washed since 1993.

Maybe the best way to tell the sharks from the minnows is to look around the room and see who is cheering and cursing and fist-pumping and who is standing there emotionless and expressionless. Cory and Ray amassed over four million in winnings while playing daily fantasy, which made them one of the half-dozen or so most successful professional daily fantasy players on the planet. Just ten months earlier, in another fantasy football contest, run by DraftKings, Cory and Ray took home a $1 million prize. Today Cory and Ray have a real chance at that second big score, a shot at becoming the first players to win *multiple* $1 million live events — an achievement, they believe, that would say a little something about the hierarchy of the top players in the daily fantasy universe, and they've been through enough to know better than to burn too many calories cursing a José Reyes home run because there are inevitably more swings to come. Having attended a half-dozen or so of these tournaments, everywhere from Los Angeles to New York to Toronto, Cory believes that few events in the history of man have triggered the emotional oscillations of a daily fantasy live event.

He and Ray had determined, in the days leading up to the event, that in order to gain some edge over all the sharks in the room, they had to go with bigger long shots in their lineups and that it would be more important than ever to differentiate their lineups, because every shark in the room would know the right plays, making it impossible to find an edge without taking a few bigger gambles — and so while they were going to go all in on the Mets in Colorado, they were also going to go all in on a high-priced player who was far from an obvious choice: Paul Goldschmidt, first baseman for the Arizona Diamondbacks, mired in a .208 slump in August, homerless in nearly a month. Going all in meant shelling out big dollars on a premium player, leaving a smaller piece of their allotted salary pie for the rest of the lineup. To Cory and Ray, it was a value play — Goldschmidt's performance over the last month had suppressed his salary, which, like every player's changed every day; he was due. When that big game was coming — today, tomorrow, next week — they didn't know. Sometimes, Cory and Ray thought, you just have to take a leap of faith. They were in their hotel room at the Cosmo, about to head to the ballroom, tuning in to the Diamondbacks game in Cincinnati, when they saw their faith pay off: in Goldschmidt's first at bat, he homered, and in an instant rayofhope was the team to beat. Until that later José Reyes home run, that is, and they weren't.

There is always an odd dynamic in these events: all the action of the event is restricted to the action on the giant screens above the contestants in the room. There's been talk of ESPN airing a live daily fantasy event hosted by its new partner, DraftKings, but whoever made that proposal has clearly never actually stepped foot in a live daily fantasy event. Because inside the actual room itself, grimaces, belches, trips to the buffet table, people checking their phones for updates, people *watching* the broadcast: these would have to qualify as highlights in a theoretical broadcast. But then there are the occasional moments when the stakes are clear and can be distilled into a single moment on the field. A moment, late in the evening, like this: Rayofhope needs another home run to lock up first place, and now Paul Goldschmidt, with one home run on the night already, is stepping up to the plate. Goldschmidt has played in 583 career major league games up until this one, and over those 583 games he has homered twice in a game only six times. Goldschmidt is three-for-three on the night, and over his 583 career games he has notched only ten four-hit games. The odds, in other words, are against Cory and Ray. But then a pitcher named Pedro Villarreal unleashes a pitch to Goldschmidt, on an 0–1 count, and the swing looks good on the broadcast, the ball off the bat a laser to right field, and when the screen cuts to the shot of the Reds right fielder, he's moving back toward the fence and looking up. As he watches the action on a big screen in the ballroom, as he watches the baseball drop into the picture, Cory's heart stops.

A few moments later, he and Ray are standing on a makeshift stage with Bo Jackson. The team known as rayofhope is holding a check — pay to the order of WORLD FANTASY BASEBALL CHAMPIONSHIP 1ST PLACE, for $1,000,000 — signed, in a lavish font, by the man who is footing the bill for the bash: *NIGEL ECCLES*.

Cory looks around the room. With each live tournament he attends, the size of the ballrooms and buffet spreads and prizes, and therefore the emotional swings, gets bigger, bigger, and bigger. At every one of these events he sees the familiar faces, faces that he sees only at these events that are a unique and weird cross between a high school reunion and a fight-to-the-death cage match. Because, while the rooms include minnows who lucked into an entry, mostly they are sharks who have become both, in some cases, his friends and his fiercest rivals. Sharks like the best friends in Denver — Condia and 1ucror, they went by — who unapologetically hunted inexperienced minnows; or the Amherst grad who goes by the handle Maxdalury and who quit his day job as a computer programmer and within months used his daily fantasy winnings to buy a downtown Boston penthouse whose previous owner was a Boston Celtics star; or the affable poker shark Cal Spears, aka Brasky, who used to run an online forum for poker strategy and now runs the biggest online forum for daily fantasy strategy, called RotoGrinders; or the personality who won the industry's first six-figure prize a few years back, a world-class oddsmaker named Peter Jennings — CSURam, he goes by — who would buy you a cocktail with a smile and, if you weren't careful, shake you down for a few thousand dollars by the second cocktail.

They are misfits, troublemakers, and outsiders with little in common other than the fact that they are all perfectly suited for this odd world and somehow not quite right for the world on the other side of the doors. Included in this group is the dude standing next to Cory. Ask Cory what Ray Coburn would be doing if he were not a millionaire professional daily fantasy sports player, and Cory would reply: "He'd be in trouble." Ray was kicked out of college after two semesters for his tremendously terrible grades, and he lived at home, where he took care of his ninety-year-old father. Years earlier, Ray had become something of a cult figure within the poker community. Back in 2006, before Black Friday, the website PokerStars had a leaderboard that ranked the most profitable players on its site at the end of each month. One month the name of a complete unknown was at the top. It was not necessarily odd that this was a player no one had heard of; what was odd — spectacularly odd — was that it was a player who had bet only microstakes, $1, $2, and $3 contests. A no-name from the Jersey Shore had somehow managed to win the whole damn tournament playing just the small stuff.

Cory, himself a professional poker player, reached out to the mysterious savant simply because he wanted to know more about a guy who was such a freakishly good poker player that he could pull off such a feat, and over the next few months, over chats and texts, they got to know each other. Ray had a dogmatic, almost orthodox need to understand everything from a mathematical point of view. He was the shrewd analyst, mining the numbers, while Cory was the executive manager, directing and looking at the larger picture. They teamed up and have been working together ever since, Cory from his living room in San Francisco and Ray from the house in New Jersey where he grew up, where his room was still decorated with the Yankees paraphernalia he'd collected as a boy.

Now they are two of the top pros in the industry, and after winning another million, still dazed from the evening, they walk out onto the balcony at the Cosmo. There is a word for the top prize at these tournaments — winners call it "life-changing money" — but Cory's and Ray's lives tomorrow will look and feel more or less as their lives did this morning: Cory's splurge will be that $40,000 Ford truck, not exactly the kind of sexy big-ticket purchase FanDuel would make a commercial out of, and Ray's money will go directly into paying off his father's medical bills back home. While this crazy summer will continue for Cory, a summer of bouncing from one party to another — in just days Cory will be getting on a plane to South Beach to attend a DraftKings party — Ray will be going back home to his reality. As he looks across the Strip and sees the sprawling Bellagio grounds glimmering below, Cory thinks about the scene in *Ocean's Eleven* with the guys standing in front of the fountains after pulling off their heist, and his thought is not about the $1 million he and Ray were walking away with, or the fact that they are now kings of the fantasy world, but instead his thought is simply how thankful he is to have his friend standing here with him. And so when he puts his arm around Ray's shoulder, he is telling Ray, but also himself:

"Enjoy this."

Back in college, Cory had become weirdly addicted to jumping out of airplanes. He did it once his freshman year at Ball State, almost as a dare, then did it again, then some one hundred times over his first two semesters alone. The sensation of hurtling through the air at 120 miles per hour had unlocked something inside him, having grown up sheltered in a small town in southeastern Indiana, the son of devout Christians, an introvert in high school who belonged to the crowd that was best described as "the virgin crowd." The thing about jumping out of airplanes is that, as death-defying as it seems, if you're careful, it's just about as safe as crossing a street on a green light in Manhattan. Cory found himself being drawn to activities that were thought of as extreme and risky but in which one can manage the risk. Which may be why, during college, jumping out of airplanes turned into playing poker.

So here is how Cory lost $500,000 on a hand at the World Series of Poker. It was 2008, day 6 of the tournament, the ESPN cameras rolling, and Cory, who was dressed in the de rigueur poker getup of sunglasses, track jacket, and a black hat that he was being paid some high four-figure amount to wear, was sitting on an ace and jack with a jack-high board. The man sitting across from him wearing the Lakers jersey had king-jack; he was toast. The ESPN viewers later would see that Cory Albertson of Warsaw, Indiana, had a 93-to-7 percent chance of having 1.1 million chips, which meant that with roughly 150 contestants left in the field, Cory would be one of the favorites to take the $1 million prize. Cory called; the Laker stayed in the hand. The card came up king — a card that Cory correctly estimated in that moment had cost him $500,000. Afterward, in an empty parking lot outside the casino, he stood by his car, alone, and sobbed.

Cory had done well for himself in that world, but he began to walk away from poker when he saw that it was dominated by players who grew up in former Soviet provinces and played nineteen hours a day, and decided that his edge was disappearing. Then Black Friday happened, and he could abandon it for good after he found his next death-defying activity. An acquaintance in the poker world said that he'd started playing some new kind of fantasy games, games that Cory might be interested in.

It was obvious why any successful poker player might be interested in daily fantasy games. Like poker, daily fantasy is a game of high variance. Anyone can go on a hot streak and go head-to-head with a shark, and anyone may very well win. But a difference in skill emerges over time. As in poker, a player's expected value will be actualized in the long run, after hundreds and thousands of lineups. On any given day there were thousands of contests going on in daily fantasy on the different sites; unlike online poker, you could play in an unlimited number of these contests at once. Wondering what to make of these games, any poker player, naturally, would ask: What would happen if one player walked into the lobby and took a seat at every table in the house — the high-stakes $5,000 buy-ins *and* all the $5 heads-up games? What if he took on every kind of player, not just the ex–poker players who brought their analytical strategies to these contests but also every novice who'd come across a daily fantasy ad listening to a podcast on the way to work and decided on a whim to enter a random lineup and had no idea that he'd just innocently plopped down at a table with a blood-smelling shark? The answer was that if that player knew what he was doing, then, well, he could become tremendously wealthy.

What made daily fantasy games particularly interesting to Cory was that there was actually more money involved than in poker. What made it even more interesting was the ecosystem, which he immediately found similar to poker's in the early 2000s: when it had been mainstreamed at that time, there were suddenly enough terrible poker players out there to make it worthwhile to invest your time and money. And, with daily fantasy, there was no doubt that, if you knew what you were doing, these games were worth your time.

But there was a reason why they called it a grind — the days, truth to tell, were a slog for anyone who played these games professionally. A word had become ubiquitous within the industry to describe the professionals who'd left their day jobs to play fantasy sports full-time: *grinders*. The term described the workmanlike, labor-intensive process of creating lineups on a daily basis. It wasn't just the manual labor of entering hundreds of lineups. In those ads that were now everywhere, pros were portrayed as dudes who put in a $10 lineup with the ease of putting in a pizza order on their phone, and the next moment were holding a million-dollar check standing under a blizzard of confetti standing next to someone who looked like Ariana Grande. That was, of course, the fairy-tale-rinsed version of what this was all about. No one talked about staring at rows of spreadsheets on an iridescent screen with bloodshot eyes, mindlessly entering data at your desk until you had carpal tunnel.

Which is what Cory's life was like before hitting his first big cash. At Notre Dame, while working toward his MBA, while everyone else was at class or at the bars getting sloshed and making connections, Cory was in his room entering fantasy football contests. His grades weren't hot, especially during the NFL season, but that didn't matter at the time to Cory because, well, as it was known within his circle of friends, from these games he was making more money than the dean of the business school.

In his wildest imagination Cory could not have foreseen the massive prize pools that were being handed out by the two companies, DraftKings and FanDuel, night after night. On any given day during baseball season, Cory and Ray had easily five figures on the line. It was clear what was going on: the two companies, in a war over customers, were each trying to beat out the other with prize pools, because anyone who simply had both sites up on their browsers could see how, in the hours and minutes leading up to the start of tournaments, the prize pools would keep escalating. It was clear that the two companies had people sitting around the office late at night monitoring the tournament-entry action, raising the amount of the prize pools simply in reaction to what the pools were at the rival company. The prize pools on any given day were fluid, with an indeterminate amount of money at stake; new tournaments appeared within minutes of the start of games, so long as there were fish ready to flow into the ecosystem. It was clear to Cory that the operators viewed the insane prize pools as a marketing expense to attract the fish — "casual" players — and, well, it was a strategy that was certainly working. Because on any given night during major league baseball season, the "MLB Mega Perfect Game" ($100,000 to first, with $400,000 in guaranteed prizes!), the "MLB Monster" ($50,000 to first, with $150,000 in guaranteed prizes!), and the "MLB All-Star" ($10,000 to first, with $200,000 in guaranteed prizes!), and those massive tournaments were in addition to the countless number of head-to-head games that they could challenge other players to thousands of dollars on any given night. For sharks who measured success in the long run and whose goal was to control the lobby, the strategy on most nights was simply to put as much money as they could on the line.

And that made for a very stressful life for someone like Cory.

But these games had also given someone like Cory a life in which having an MBA was meaningless. It allowed Cory to reinvent himself entirely. After college, he went from being a poker player and shaggy-haired beach bum living in Mexico to a bachelor living in San Francisco in a downtown apartment, one with a killer view of a ballpark and the Pacific Ocean. The pimpled, overweight, painfully shy and awkward kid in high school was now a triathlon runner who did Bikram Yoga before going out to dinner at the three-star Michelin restaurant wearing the blue blazer over the gingham shirt with the absurdly expensive eyewear, and who over dinner noted that the $20 tartare didn't have enough brioche and who could offer tasting notes on the $110 bottle of cab that he'd ordered.

The games gave him a life that was one party after another. From his three-day rager in Vegas, thrown by FanDuel, he flew back to San Francisco, still hungover and still high from winning the $1 million, and then days later got back on a plane and flew to South Beach for another three-day rager, thrown by DraftKings. The two main daily fantasy operators were also in a clash to throw the biggest, baddest parties, and if you were a high-stakes player in the summer of 2015, you essentially bounced from one party to another — from the Playboy Mansion to the Cosmo on the Strip to the Fontainebleau in Miami — with the prize pool escalating at each stop, culminating with the $2 million top prize on the line for DraftKings' NFL opening weekend bonanza, which far dwarfed FanDuel's opening week prizes. The massive prize pool was, to many, confirmation that DraftKings, after a 2014 season in which FanDuel seemed as though it was pulling away, was still on its rival's heels. Not that most of the sharks were keeping tabs on the company horse race — for the most part they had no dog in the fight and had no preference for one over the other; as long as they kept offering the million-dollar prize pools, they were happy.

But when the top players weren't taken care of, there could be trouble, and Cory knew there was trouble the moment he stepped into the hotel lobby in Miami and saw a daily fantasy pro, cocktail in hand, saying, "What the fuck?" as he stood there with a group of sharks who had just stumbled in from Vegas. The big news of the day among the players was that FanDuel was capping the number of entries for the upcoming Week 1 of the 2015 NFL season and telling players that they'd get kicked off the site if they played more than the limit. Some attributed this to FanDuel's lack of confidence in their product, questions about whether they could withstand the massive uptick of entries they expected for Week 1; others thought it was just the latest example of FanDuel's conservative tendencies, a reflection of their more cautious management style. Cory, as he heard the news, saw it as a poor decision by a company that was threatening all their best customers over a ban that, if it was a product issue, was not the players' problem but the company's problem. Yet it was the players who were getting screwed. With the ban, Cory estimated that their earnings potential was being cut by a third.

The pros were livid, but most kept silent, as they often did when it came to decisions made by the operators; it was rare that players openly criticized the companies. But Cory wasn't the type to keep silent — he was one of the most outspoken and critical sharks, one who never had qualms about going after the operators. Cory furiously tweeted from Miami, ripping FanDuel for capping entries. Soon he was getting calls and texts from FanDuel executives asking, *What are you doing?* That same day in Miami, Cory was approached by a DraftKings employee who'd seen Cory's tweets. Cory knew many of the executives from the two companies and had friendly relationships with them, so it was not so strange when the employee asked Cory what else he wanted, on top of the $400-a-night hotel room and all his meals and drinks being comped for the weekend. It was not so strange when the employee threw in a cabana to watch the Sunday games, and it was not so strange that when Cory asked how much the tab would be, the employee asked, *How much do you want it to be?*

But things did get a little strange when the employee offered Cory benefits to unregister from the FanDuel contests, take his money off the site and move it to DraftKings', and, while he was at it, continue to shit on FanDuel during the weekend. It was a brazen proposal, but, Cory gathered, not uncommon. When it came to the relationship between the companies and the VIP players, there was a strange gray area. There was full transparency when it came to some players, like Pete Jennings, who were billed as company "pros" and who went on ESPN and openly shilled for the companies, but there were others who were not outright spokesmen but were given benefits for promoting the games and the companies on Twitter and other social media. Cory was so unhappy about FanDuel's decision that he considered the offer from the DraftKings employee — taking his bankroll and going exclusively to DraftKings. He left it open-ended just to make sure the $1,000 tab at the cabana was really going to be a $1,000 tab. It was Ray — level-headed, conscientious Ray — who told him that it just didn't feel right.

"I'm not comfortable doing this. They'll fix it," he said, referring to FanDuel. "Just calm down." Grudgingly, Cory listened and turned the offer down.

The whole exchange did leave him feeling a little dirty, but before he knew it, before he could get even more pissed off about the FanDuel ban, he found himself on his second or third or fourth drink, on the dance floor at the Fontainebleau club, swallowed whole by purple strobe lights, standing next to other DFS dorks bopping their heads to the music, and then he was being led into a VIP area behind a rope, where he talked up millennial DraftKings employees soaking up the nightclubas-part-of their job experience, and suddenly Cory felt old. And then he had another drink and watched a DraftKings employee get up onstage and announce a *$5 million* NFL final to be broadcast live on ESPN in January 2016, and he listened to the roar of the crowd and watched as a hip-hop star got onstage when the club opened to the public, and he spotted members of the Miami Heat hanging out by the bar — and then, as DraftKings employees and NBA stars and fantasy dorks and the most beautiful women in the world all somehow ran into one giant swirl and he began to pour another drink out of the $300 bottle of champagne, Cory thought to himself:

Where are all the grown-ups?

At a table inside one of the glittery restaurants at the Fountainebleau, Cory was having dinner with a group of acquaintances in the fantasy industry and their friends. The popular topic of conversation in Miami was, of course, the crazy speed at which the industry was growing — the daily fantasy universe, so obscure for so long, had expanded far beyond what any of them had imagined. All you needed for confirmation was to turn on the TV and see the ads, which over the summer were running seemingly in an endless loop. At dinner Cory happened to be sitting next to a friend of a friend who had, until recently, been an employee of DraftKings and was now out of the industry. Cory peppered him with questions, genuinely curious about why he'd left the company — it wasn't often that you met someone who was getting off the rocket ship, and it seemed like an especially odd time to walk away, just as the industry was exploding.

"If you want to know the truth," he said to Cory, "it's because I'm not sure those stock options are worth anything."

Now Cory was hanging on his every word. The man — Cory would later call him his Deep Throat, a trusted industry source who knew the world inside and out — had previously worked for a poker company, and now he saw troubling parallels between the two industries. His thesis: the future of daily fantasy sports, circa Week 1 of the 2015 NFL season, was completely unclear from a regulatory standpoint. Because no one really knew what this industry was, and because of the resulting regulatory uncertainty, it was incredibly shortsighted of the companies to do these massive advertising campaigns costing hundreds of millions of dollars and drawing attention to themselves.

While he could imagine daily fantasy as a multibillion-dollar industry and the future of sports consumption, Cory also understood that there could be some issues making things, well, complicated. He could see the issues primarily because he'd seen this movie once before, with the poker industry. For years the specter of the federal government crushing online poker had always loomed, and then the feds finally did it: the government went after online poker in America and took it down. April 15, 2011, was a day that Cory would long remember. Thousands had their livelihood pulled out from under them. Within days of Black Friday, Cory was playing poker out of an apartment in a sketchy neighborhood in a small Mexican coastal town.

Cory did have some concerns about the daily fantasy game industry, and he didn't want to have to move to Mexico to play. The first time he visited DraftKings' offices was as a VIP player who was willing to offer a brain dump about the product to not only the product team but also Jason Robins himself. Cory spent the afternoon talking to Jason and giving his two cents on the games, and then he was hooked up with sweet Red Sox tickets for that night's game at Fenway Park. A year later, during one of his East Coast trips, he returned to DraftKings' offices, and much had changed, from the waiting area where he now had to sit before entering, to the CEO, who was, Cory suspected, too busy to meet with him because he was now head of a company that was hurtling toward a billion-dollar valuation. Meeting instead with DraftKings' executive on the product team, Cory was concerned enough to raise a number of issues. Cory had felt that the sites were so obsessed with growth that they had missed the finer points of execution, such as allowing software that would enable players to enter any number of games they wanted instead of the software which gave players the option of imposing a self-ban if they felt as if they had a gambling problem, or software that limited a shark from playing a $25,000 buy-in *and* a $1 buy-in on the same day. He voiced his opinion on the negative optics of people developing gambling problems by playing on the sites, believing that the issue was that it was too simple for a player to max out his credit cards and put in $10,000 and lose it all in one night.

The larger message that Cory wanted to convey to the companies was that they needed to get on the ball. The response was more or less a polite thank-you. As he walked out the door at DraftKings, he could see that now that the companies were already on the rocket ship, no one was going to come in and slow them down, because once the companies IPO'd, they were all going to be filthy rich. Cory thought that they failed to understand that they were running a *gaming* business — not a tech company, not a sports media company, but a gaming outfit. Gaming businesses were regulated everywhere in the world, and to think that they could get away with running without regulation was shortsighted.

Cory had always seen parallels to the poker industry. Black Friday had scarred him — he had been sitting at his computer, in the middle of a hand, with a six-figure bankroll deposited, when he heard that the feds were shutting down online poker. That bankroll vanished. The online poker companies were operating outside the law, and for years the government hadn't done anything. Then one day it came crashing down.

Cory, of course, had benefitted as much as anyone from the companies and their approach, making money on the games. And he could certainly have been more vocal, if he really did think that sweeping changes needed to be made at the companies. While he did have concerns, he didn't think that the industry was in any imminent danger — not until his conversation with Deep Throat.

"Look, DraftKings is a gaming company that is not behaving like a gaming company," Deep Throat said. "Just look around. How much is this weekend costing them? Does this seem like real life to you?"

Deep Throat had predicted how it was all going to play out: The escalating advertising campaign was going to attract the attention of people who were going to start asking pointed questions about this industry. Legislators would ask why they weren't getting a cut of the companies' revenues, and casinos would decide that daily fantasy was a form of gaming and that the industry needed to be crushed. Racetracks would believe that daily fantasy games were a threat to their product, and the news organizations would begin to wonder how this story about a gambling outfit operating in plain sight had slipped through the cracks.

Cory sat at the dinner table listening to how all the pieces fit, and suddenly he was on the other side of the window, peering in on a world carrying on in its own reality. Suddenly he was noticing the legal scaffolding that held it all together and seeing that it was made of cheap metal and thin plastic. He walked away from dinner needing another drink.

That night he couldn't sleep. He didn't want to sleep. He felt like he was going to wake up the next morning and the world was going to come crashing down. He called Ray up and told him everything that Deep Throat was telling him, peeling back the layers. He turned on the TV and within minutes couldn't avoid what was flickering on the screen:

"There's a game within the game that requires a different set of skills," said the voice of a famous actor. Images of a man giving his dog a bath, a dork with a woman dancing next to him at an office party, a dad getting sprayed by a water gun — all of them hyperfocused on their smartphones . . .

"There's no off-season. This is a play-as-much-as-you-want, whenever-you-want fantasy league. And we don't just play — we are players. We train. And we win . . ."

A beat, and they were all screaming and cheering, celebrating a seven-figure jackpot.

"This is DraftKings. Welcome to the big time."

Now Cory was thinking of a lawmaker, a casino operator, a racetrack owner, watching this and asking: *What is this DraftKings shit?*

Then — it seemed like just a blink later — a commercial for FanDuel.

The following morning seemed to dawn brighter than any other: it was the first Sunday of NFL games. Cory, hungover, managed to get himself out of his room and to the pool, where he settled inside his cabana. It was, in some ways, like any other NFL weekend: Cory and Ray had hundreds of lineups going in DraftKings' $5 million tournament alone. The day quickly began to get surreal: within minutes of kickoff, one of their lineups was already going off. But as he watched the games, Cory found himself thinking less about their underperforming tight end and more about the insane frequency of that DraftKings commercial and the FanDuel ads that were popping up in tandem. Cory began following the reaction on Twitter, searching for "daily fantasy commercials," and saw the companies being compared to ISIS.

He sank into his seat. He had a long way to go on that $1,000 tab that he'd promised the DraftKings employee he would blow up. He ordered another drink. Monday had the potential to be another fever dream, because now he was looking at his phone and through the afternoon slate of games. He and Ray had a lineup that was in the top ten of DraftKings' $2 million tournament, and now all they needed was for Adrian Peterson, the best running back in the universe, to have an Adrian Peterson–type game and the $2 million would be theirs by the next morning, on top of the $1 million that they had won just two weeks earlier in Vegas.

There was a bad hangover coming, he knew, so he wanted to cling to this moment, make it stretch out forever — it was as if rather than the $2 million itself, Cory needed the possibility of it, dangling in front of him. He couldn't shake it off, what Deep Throat had said to him — he'd seen, clearly, how this was going to play out, and deep down he knew that this was not going to end well.

He looked around now at everything swirling around him: the pool that glittered in the afternoon sun, the fantasy dorks in their pale dad-bods awkwardly circling the bikini-clad ladies, the half-empty bottles of champagne, the TV screens hanging from the bar, flickering between a football game and a DraftKings ad. And then a FanDuel ad.

And he thought:

How could I have not seen it? How could I have not seen that we are all doomed?

5

THE OUTPUT IS INSANITY

Orlando, Spring–Fall 2015

The fire-breathing dragon perched high above, the floating wizard posing for selfies, the two screaming boys waving glowing wands as they disappeared into the bright mass of humanity stretched out in front of her: Lesley tuned out all of it as she held the phone to her ear and tried to make sense of the words coming from the other end of the line. She looked up at the sky, which was painted precisely the shade of powder blue she'd imagined when she agreed to this getaway, believing that three days of Florida sunshine might save her. Instead, as she stood in the middle of a congested street, listening to what sounded like a hostage demand, she could sense that she was losing control of this game that she and her cofounders now found themselves in.

This was only three months removed from the 2014 NFL season, during which FanDuel brought in a staggering nine hundred thousand new users from the triumphant $70 million ad spend, but with another NFL season approaching, it was becoming abundantly clear that Draft-Kings was refusing to surrender — not after a barrage of advertising that had begun earlier in the year, during the NBA season and leading up to the start of baseball, as Lesley's machine was quiet, idling until the start of football. With DraftKings' onslaught — signage in NBA arenas, logos on the jerseys of WNBA players, even signs on New York City hot dog carts! — Lesley suddenly felt set back on her heels, because now she was on a conference call with a media company that, through the omnibus amusement park noise, had told her that DraftKings was *offering four times what you're offering . . . for a deal that is an exclusive . . . for a deal that, if you don't top it, will effectively end our relationship . . .*

"Do we have a deal?" those on the other end of the line were now asking, and perhaps detecting the hesitation on her part, they told her she had until the end of business that day: two hours to make a $20 million decision. Dressed in a white Mickey Mouse T-shirt, blue jeans, and sneakers, she looked like any other mother chasing her kids around in this tourist-overrun rendering of a London alley. But whether it was because of the way DraftKings was now closing in on them; or because of the way the board was breathing down her neck, looking for a return on her ad spend over the next six months; or because of the pressure she had been feeling in the last few days and weeks as she'd begun her descent into a dizzying rabbit hole of negotiations with the biggest media companies in the world — ESPN, NBC, CBS, FOX Sports — she was beginning to feel the pressure. And now, to add to her pile of problems of the moment, her phone was dying.

When the networks had allowed daily fantasy advertising for the first time, in week 1 of the 2014 NFL season, an all-out war between the start-ups to sign media players began to erupt. Rumors of a deal just weeks earlier, in early 2015 between DraftKings and ESPN, had sent shock waves through the industry. FanDuel had also been involved in negotiations with the biggest media player in the sports world, though with no intention of signing away their company to ESPN but only to drive up the cost of the deal to preposterous levels. To their shock, DraftKings, even after the escalation, was considering an exclusive deal, rumored to be worth $250 million; in return, DraftKings would get exclusive advertising rights and tie-ins to ESPN's fantasy content. Seeing this, other media giants wanted their own piece of the growing fantasy sports pie, and smelling a young company with a seemingly limitless war chest of cash, they were now circling FanDuel like vultures. Every major network outside of ESPN suddenly sought to anoint — while extracting the largest amount of money — the next king in the industry. They had the power to decide who would win the war: DraftKings or FanDuel.

The offers from the networks would appear in Lesley's inbox, an email with an attachment that included two pages of PDFs. There were the terms of one offer on one sheet. Then the terms of another — often longer — option on another sheet, worth more. Lesley had a choice between the two proposals. They were, for the most part, non-negotiable. All or nothing. First come, first served. The company that blinked would be shut out.

And here on this chilly spring morning was a radio deal being presented to Lesley, a renewal of one that had been a key part of her machine, just south of a million dollars the previous year, and had benefited both parties. Now that deal was exploding, in real time, into a three-year ad buy worth close to $20 million. If they were going to spend $20 million on radio, then what was the size of the buys going to be for TV? She did the math in her head and began to add up all the numbers, and they were astronomical. They were also her new reality.

She looked up and spotted Nigel in the distance — huddled in the corner, on his own call, with the board. *Some vacation,* she thought. She had a knack for seeing — many moves ahead — the best but also the very worst possible outcomes. She gamed out her current predicament: if the phone died, then the deal could die, and if *this* deal died, on top of the other deals that were being blown up, then . . . well, everything that she and the cofounders had built could turn to ashes.

She found herself asking, once again:

How, exactly, did we all get here?

Only three weeks earlier there had seemed to be a moment of clarity when the two adversaries, the two CEOs, were poised to call a truce to put an end to this battle — by doing the unthinkable.

The CEOs of FanDuel and DraftKings were an odd pair — not just because one was a Florida kid who grew up reading box scores and the other was an Irish farm boy. It wasn't just that they represented and embodied two companies with clashing cultures, temperaments, and ideologies: Edinburgh versus Boston, caution versus hyperaggressiveness, private equity versus venture capitalist, Hugo Boss versus New England gingham, single malt versus IPA. The two CEOs were an odd pair for all those reasons but also because, while they were bitter competitors and fierce rivals, they could understand each other as no one else could, and because they were the CEOs of two companies that were in many ways, despite all their surface differences, carbon copies of each other. Occasionally, the two found themselves in the same room, at trade conferences and various events, exchanging texts, griping about a trade organization's arcane rules. In January 2015, they were both at the Fantasy Sports Trade Association conference in Las Vegas, and when Nigel's phone lit up with a text from Jason inviting him for a drink, it was not entirely surprising. But the invitation did come at an interesting, charged time in the history of the companies, a time when a ceasefire did not seem possible, not after Lesley's promise had been realized and Jason and DraftKings, in the deadest time in the sports calendar, were on the retreat and regrouping for another NFL season.

In this moment, the conversation between the two was like one between rival coaches swapping tales at the end of a brutal season, in a setting that helped lubricate the discussion: a bar at the Bellagio. In the end they were both first-time CEOs learning the ropes of this jack-of-all-trades role; there were times when both felt utterly unprepared for the position. They could at the very least sympathize with each other's plight in dealing with the various eccentric partners and sponsors they shared — and they shared many, from the obscure fantasy sports blogs to the professional league commissioners whom they were both getting to know. And they could talk about the complicated dynamic between the CEO and the board, as well as the harsh realities of having their authority and control diluted by rounds and rounds of raising money.

"We both know how this is going to play out," Jason was saying, over the cacophony of the bar. "It sucks. We keep doing what we're doing —

killing ourselves to raise, raise, raise — and what do we have left? We can both see what's going on with the markets. We can both keep raising as much money as we want."

Nigel suspected that Jason had an agenda — he felt that Jason *always* had an agenda. Their interactions could have the feel of a bad date. They were cordial, but they always knew that the other had some ulterior motive, which made each interaction an odd dance, even before the food was ordered. Nigel, for instance, would keep watch on what Jason would order, aware of a practice in business negotiations of someone intentionally ordering the same thing as the person across the table. It was a power move straight out of a CEO handbook that advised one to order the same dish as your dinner guest to gain his trust.

Once, when the two had dinner in Boston, Nigel tried an experiment. After feigning deliberation, holding the menu up to his nose, Nigel ordered a steak.

"I'll have the steak," Jason said.

As the waiter collected the menus, Nigel said to the server, "Actually, I changed my mind. I'll have the salad," and waited for Jason's countermove.

Then, Nigel watched as, coincidence or not, Jason ordered a salad.

But now, after a few drinks at the Bellagio, they were loose and maybe even enjoying each other's company. Nigel could acknowledge that what Jason was saying was true: once, they were both conductors of their orchestras; now they were more like first-chair violinists. They were the leaders of a group but had no control over the larger tempo. Conventional wisdom is that startups that have raised a significant amount of money signal the success of their founders, but with each funding round they've ceded some power by inviting a new partner into the company.

"Here's the thing," Jason continued. "If we're looking to create more value for us and for our shareholders — well, we know there's a better way to do it . . ."

Now they were on their second or third drink. The bar was getting more raucous. Things hadn't gotten sloppy, but the guys were feeling good and generous. Nigel could begin to see where Jason was going with this.

"You're talking about a merger," he said.

Nigel was right. It might have felt spontaneous and rash — this suggestion from one CEO to another. In reality, Jason had scripted this meet-up with as much care as he put into a pitch to investors. It was a conversation he'd planned on having the moment he landed in Vegas. The idea of these two rival businesses coming together at this particular moment had never been seriously discussed, even within the industry. Although FanDuel and DraftKings may have been indistinguishable to the wider public, there was such a culture clash between them that anyone who was familiar with the two companies had a hard time envisioning them working together.

But Jason wanted to lay it out for Nigel: a merger made absolute sense for both companies, which would be able to share costs, combine user bases — and ensure dominance over the market. It also made sense because they both saw as inevitable a moment when a media behemoth like ESPN or NBC or Yahoo! would enter the space and wipe both of them out with their resources.

"It makes sense, doesn't it?" Jason said.

"I won't lie and say that I haven't thought about it," Nigel said. "It's an interesting idea."

The one thing that Nigel did respect about Jason was his ability to see the whole chessboard. Nigel's board members had always howled at DraftKings' approach, with its massive spending for such a fledgling company. *How reckless! How irresponsible!* Nigel could see the thinking behind it. He had an expression for Jason's behavior: "rational irrationality." He knew that Jason and DraftKings could have been just another one of those startups on their list, here today, gone tomorrow, and that any shrewd, cutthroat entrepreneur who wanted to actually make a mark on this industry would have certainly considered the scorched-earth approach that Jason embraced in his effort to win the market.

As he walked away from the bar, Nigel had countless questions racing through his head. Because FanDuel was twice the size of Draft-Kings, the merger would have to be on FanDuel's terms. His questions were all about how a merger would work in the DraftKings reality: What platform would be used? What would the name of the company be? And of course, who would be the CEO? Nigel could look at Jason's proposal in two ways. One was to see it as an olive branch — an offer from a bitter rival to find common ground. But he could also see it in another way: as a backdoor power grab. To anyone looking at the scenario Jason presented it was clear that one person was going to have to let go of his vision; one of them was going to have to take hold of the story, and the other would have to let go. Given FanDuel's lead over DraftKings, Nigel thought it was obvious whose vision would have to take hold — who would be CEO.

Wasn't it?

When the idea of a merger was tossed around within the FanDuel board, questions followed:

Can't we simply let this play out and win the market?

Can't we just crush them?

Within both the management team and the board, though, there was some pushback to this way of thinking. Mike LaSalle, for example, didn't believe that the daily fantasy market was necessarily winner-take-all. He believed that a broader fantasy market was in play. "We're kidding ourselves if we think that all of the sudden we're going to wake up and go, '*We won!*' It's not going to happen that way," he would tell others.

The board was more or less split on whether they *could* simply crush DraftKings and that a merger that ended with anything short of Fan-Duel's taking control over the other company made no sense.

In the days and weeks after their drinks in Las Vegas, Nigel and Jason, as well as members of the two boards, held a series of conversations about a possible merger. Once the alcohol and dim lights of Vegas were removed from the process, the discussion between the two rival CEOs became less cordial. In what reality would FanDuel consider a deal? For starters, the FanDuel board would control all the decisions — on platform, brand, personnel. The DraftKings' response: that sounds much more like an acquisition than a merger. Couldn't both sides, they asked, just agree that this was something worth pursuing — and they'd iron out the details later? Among those details: the question of who would be CEO.

In later years, the key players in the game would look back to this series of events as what set everything in motion, on an irreversible course. Nigel was as competitive as the next entrepreneur. And so, to DraftKings' proposal, and to every other scenario in which he and Fan-Duel would have anything less than the upper hand, Nigel had the same response in the end.

No fucking way.

But was the growth in fantasy sports sustainable? Had the fantasy sports war spun out of control? Was the race toward a billion-dollar valuation a race off a cliff? Onlookers, even some within the companies, saw the dynamics at play in this billion-dollar battle between FanDuel and Draft-Kings and saw not a winner-take-all game but a classic case of game theory.

One of the best-known examples of game theory, the Prisoner's Dilemma, provides a framework for people to understand the balance between competition and cooperation in cases of economics, politics, international relations, human behavior, and business.

In the Prisoner's Dilemma, there are two players. Each has a choice to make: cooperate or defect. Each player makes the choice without knowing what the other player is about to do. Defecting yields a bigger payoff than working together. The dilemma is that, if both defect, they are both worse off than if they'd cooperated.

By 2015, the two daily fantasy companies had grown so large that it was very difficult for another business to replicate the success of the two leaders; the amount a new company would have to raise and spend was astronomical. It was therefore essentially a two-horse race.

The companies had a choice to make: whether to cooperate — to get on the same page with their regulatory messaging, to not push the legal envelope with the games they were offering, to control their spending on tournament sizes and marketing — or to remain two competitors hell-bent on doing whatever it took to kill the other. Like Craigslist, daily fantasy was a marketplace business of liquidity — it was not a sports betting business where everyone could set up the house. You needed a liquid market, and most of those businesses were winner-take-all businesses.

And so the theoretical daily fantasy payout box, in early 2015, looked something like this:

DraftKings

		EFFICIENT	AGGRESSIVE
FanDuel	EFFICIENT	Safe growth for both companies *Little risk* [10/10]*	DraftKings takes major market share lead *Some risk* [2/12]
	AGGRESSIVE	FanDuel takes major market lead *Some risk* [12/2]	Hypergrowth for both companies *High risk* [5/5]

* The first number represents the FD payout, the second is DK's. The numbers are payouts used for this example and are proportional estimates.

It was always optimal for each company to be aggressive since its payout would be improved that way, and so neither company had an incentive to cooperate.* But the hyperaggressive approach was always

---

* Market factors (the size of contests and advertising spend) and the inability to collaborate (because of the rivalry between the two companies) created a dilemma for FanDuel and DraftKings. The two entities could simultaneously pursue an efficient approach to achieve an outcome that was positive but not the best outcome for each of them (a payout of 10 each). If one company chose to be aggressive while the other took a more efficient route, the aggressive company would take the dominant market share (with a payout of 12). If, however, both companies were aggressive, the two could be far worse off (5 for both) than if they had cooperated. The

at odds with the safest way for the industry to move forward: both companies spending efficiently on all fronts, coordinating messaging on the regulatory front, developing relationships with attorney generals across the country, and focusing on sustainable growth while taking the time to institute controls to protect the industry and ensure that the legal scaffolding was solid. An aggressive strategy yielded a higher short-term payoff than cooperation, but if both companies chose to be aggressive, then both could fare worse in the end than if they had cooperated. The complication was that if one company took the more conservative route while the other was aggressive, the aggressive company would start to take more and more market share until eventually it was the only dominant player in the space. Neither company was willing to take that chance.

Nigel would look back at the events of early 2015 and say that FanDuel, the executive team and the board, had made two serious miscalculations. The first was concerning just how much the capital markets would open up and pay for unadulterated growth at any cost; they didn't anticipate the cheap money flowing into the industry like a tidal wave and raising the stakes of the game.

The other miscalculation: how much Jason Robins would be willing to raise *and* spend in trying to win the war. No one could anticipate that he would be willing to strike a deal with ESPN worth $250 million.

"We'd been sucked into a force that was bigger than us," Nigel would say. "Playing out in a much broader dynamic, we created a dynamic such that no one could independently say *Stop*."

Stop? *Ha!* The mere thought of slamming the brakes on an industry that was growing at such an unprecedented rate was as preposterous as someone trying to stop a three-hundred-pound rhino barreling down a

---

downside of the aggressive approach was the financial risk (requiring hundreds of millions of dollars of investment money) and industry risk (garnering attention while operating in a legal gray area). These were the dynamics in play that created the hypergrowth of spending on advertising — in 2015, nearly $750 million in total between the two companies.

hill. Who would say *Stop?* Certainly not Jason Robins and DraftKings, who had made it clear from the start that they viewed the daily fantasy war as a winner-take-all game. Certainly not Nigel and FanDuel. How could Nigel match DraftKings' spending dollar for dollar? How could he *not?* Stop and cede the market to these guys who'd come in and taken *their* idea? Stop and walk away from everything they'd been working for?

And certainly, the investors and the board were not going to say *Stop* — they were as deep into the vortex as anyone. "Pot committed" was the term Nigel used. Indeed: the investors had invested so much that they had no choice but to see it through. "When you're $500 million in," Nigel reasoned to his cofounders, in explaining that this could be just the beginning of the madness as DraftKings continued to raise money, "you can always get the next $150 million."

"What no one understands is that you can't suddenly make rational decisions," Nigel would say, looking back. "The thinking of everyone inside this world is, *Given what I can control, this is the best decision for us.* Everyone's making rational decisions. That may be the case. But what is the output?

"The output is insanity."

The companies' internal numbers were as closely guarded as CIA secrets from the public, but both companies knew the other inside out: as different as their approaches were, their unit economics and business model were identical, so to know their rival's numbers, either company need only look at its own. To anticipate the other company's next move, they simply asked themselves what they would do next if they were in the same situation. And so when Nigel considered what it would take for DraftKings to catch up to them, he found it hard to believe that it could happen. He could do back-of-the-envelope math to calculate what it would take for FanDuel to relinquish its lead in the market; it was just a question of how much Jason would have to spend, a simple math problem.

At the start of 2015, Nigel knew that Jason was planning on raising and then spending more money to close the gap between the companies.

The number that had been rumored was staggering: $100 million. But that wouldn't have made a dent in FanDuel's lead. Nigel and some board members did the math on how much Jason would have to raise and spend to catch them. The number was preposterous: north of $400 million.

Then, one night at an industry event in Manhattan where a number of industry bigwigs had gathered for drinks, Nigel ran into a partner at one of DraftKings' investors.

"They have something big planned," that partner said.

"Yeah?" Nigel said. "How big?"

"Big."

Nigel took a sip of his drink.

"Five hundred million big."

Nigel felt the blood drain from his face. The number was preposterous, but it didn't make him laugh. He had just one thought:

Oh, fuck.

As the daily fantasy war erupted, it became different things to different people, from a case study in game theory to a cautionary tale of excessive growth in the age of casino capitalism and venture capital. But to Lesley Eccles, as she stood in the middle of a crowd at Harry Potter World, it was, as she would describe it, "hand-to-hand combat." It had quickly become a winner-take-all fight between two sides, with both refusing to leave the cage until the other was on the floor and dead.

Tapping out texts and emails on her dying phone to her marketing teams in the Edinburgh and New York offices, she asked, *Just how bad is this?* She'd sent them a copy of the proposed deals in an email, attaching a PDF that laid out all the terms in one simple sheet: non-negotiable. Would she blink?

Value-destructive: this was the term Lesley heard again and again in these emails and texts from her marketing team back home in Edinburgh and in New York. *This is value-destructive. It's going to set a dangerous precedent.* The offers were flooding in: DraftKings was closing in on a deal with CBS. FanDuel was close to a deal with NBC. Virtually every professional sports team was now calling, wanting a piece. They began to sign deals not only with media companies but also with teams, to advertise in their stadiums and arenas. By early 2015, sixteen of the NFL's thirty-two teams had formal partnerships with either FanDuel or DraftKings. That off-season some NFL stadiums were beginning to construct fantasy sports lounges, where fantasy players could come for advice, to set their lineups, and potentially to win cash while at an actual NFL game. There was FanDuelVille at the Jacksonville Jaguars' stadium — a three-thousand-person-capacity section. There was the DraftKings Fantasy Sports Zone at the New England Patriots' Gillette Stadium. Just a year earlier NFL teams wouldn't return their calls; now, they were lining up to do monster, and both companies felt they had no choice but to say yes to all of them.

"This is not going to end well, is it?"

Lesley looked up and saw Nigel's face. His call with the board was over, and he had seen the terms of the latest media buy.

Nigel was the CEO, but at the end of the day he left it to the head of marketing to make the call on what the marketing spend would be — it was Lesley who, in the end, would say yes or no to each deal. Yes, the deals were value-destructive, but no one quite understood what Lesley had gone through to get to this moment — what all the founders, in fact, had sacrificed to get to this moment, and everything they would be giving up if they now conceded.

Now Lesley's phone was on its last dying wheezes. She had to make the call now, here.

"Yes. Okay. We'll do it," she said.

The day had dimmed, and now the lights of the park were illuminating her surroundings in an almost dreamy glow. The two boys were in front of her now waving their glowing wands, deliriously happy, and this made Lesley smile. They were together now as a family, and this was a rare thing. This stretch of watching Nigel bounce between the UK and their New York office, and to wherever a partner needed tending to, seemed to be endless, and Lesley had been hoping for a break from the insanity before the start of summer.

But now that hope was long gone. Today she'd landed a blow, but in doing so she had also raised the stakes even higher. What she didn't know was how high the stakes could get. She said yes having little idea what, precisely, she was about to unleash.

In Boston, at their new offices inside the downtown skyscraper that sat like a spaceship ready to take flight, they were ready. The employees of DraftKings were ex–poker sharks, fresh-out-of-school Ivy Leaguers, fans, frat boys, oddball quants, jocks, and computer science nerds, and above all, believers in their story.

It was the story of an upstart company coming back to catch the leader in the market. It was Facebook versus Myspace, Apple versus IBM, and other great enterprises that followed in another company's footsteps and only got stronger in the face of adversity.

It was the story of three nerds who were upending an industry. "We've been talking all week about the biggest disrupters in America," shouted the famous TV personality into the camera, on the CNBC set outfitted with a basketball hoop and sports paraphernalia. Jim Cramer, sleeves rolled up, rocking back and forth on his feet on the brightly lit set as he spoke, continued: "Which brings me to the one I hear about more than any other . . . one that is revolutionizing one of my favorite pastimes, fantasy sports . . . The company just got a huge stamp of approval last month — reportedly in the form of a $250 million investment from Disney, which, remember, owns ESPN, but the deal is not closed yet." Cramer introduced Jason Robins and Matt Kalish. "I want to ask you two a question many are asking," Cramer said, and then he screamed, "You thought of it, and we didn't! Tell me: HOW DID *YOU* KNOW?!?"

The DraftKings story was the story of Jason Robins. "How Jason Robins of DraftKings Is Blowing Up the $15 Billion Dollar World of Fantasy Sports" read the cover of the *Fortune* magazine coming out at the start of the 2015 NFL season.

When Nigel had told Jason thanks but no thanks to the idea of a merger, Jason had no choice, really. New media channels were opening up. Investors were ready to pounce. The world was changing. Not long after talks with FanDuel fell apart, Jason picked up the phone and called around to the biggest media players in the world.

He had a new plan and had a rallying cry to go with it.

DKE.

DraftKings.

Everywhere.

PART II
THE FALL
2015-2016

I TRIED DAILY FANTASY SPORTS AND IT IS EVIL . . . Daily fantasy sports — the most addictive thing you can do on your phone, except maybe cocaine . . . *These days, it feels like you can't turn on the TV without seeing one of three things: a zombie, a Kardashian, or a fantasy football ad* . . . Online fantasy sports betting is an unregulated marketplace that seems to be screwing everyday Americans out of their hard-earned money . . . **YOU AREN'T GOOD ENOUGH TO WIN MONEY PLAYING DAILY FANTASY SPORTS . . .** What we have here are a couple of companies that are stealing money from the people who play, running horribly misleading and untrue advertising, and actually taking bets in the state, which is a felony every time they do it . . . **TODAY WE HAVE SENT A CLEAR MESSAGE: NOT IN NEW YORK, AND NOT ON MY WATCH . . .** *It is clear that DraftKings and FanDuel are the leaders of a massive, multibillion-dollar scheme intended to evade the law and fleece sports fans across the country* . . . This is no different than El Chapo down in Mexico advertising heroin or methamphetamine on our airways a thousand times a day to get kids to try it . . . **THE DEATH OF DAILY FANTASY: WELCOME TO THE BEGINNING OF THE END.**

6

FRIENDS AND FOES

New York, Fall 2015

The headline appears one afternoon in the form of one of those news alerts reserved for terrorist attacks and natural disasters and celebrity deaths, the notification popping up on devices and websites with the same urgency: "Insider Trading Scandal Rocks Fantasy Sports Industry."

Within moments it is breaking news on cable TV news outlets and then part of the lead-in to the *NBC Nightly News* on a day when there's been deadly flooding in the South and major developments in the war in Afghanistan. The words FANTASY SCANDAL swoop in front of the in-studio anchor, who looks into the camera and, to the militaristic thrums of the broadcast music, says, "The hugely popular world of online fantasy sports rocked by accusations that big paydays may be going to insiders rigging the game . . ."

A slickly produced package of images flicks by: stills of shadowy figures in darkened rooms hunched over laptops, screenshots of spreadsheets on computer interfaces that resemble those of a day trader. Then a clip from a television ad promoting this hugely popular world of online fantasy. The words $1 MILLION WINNINGS EVERY DAY flash by, and then an image of fans, watching a game in a living room, suddenly erupting into cheers as they celebrate an event from a Sunday-afternoon football game as if it's a moon landing. The clip is instantly familiar to many TV viewers because they have been bombarded by these ads during telecasts of sporting events, to the point where the fantasy sports ads are universally reviled and ridiculed for their frequency and their messaging. "The ads you see during pro football games promise big prize money, and millions have signed up to play," the anchor intones, "but tonight there's a major controversy after an employee of one of these sites cashed in big himself."

The anchor, Lester Holt, throws it to the man on the scene, who has more details. The reporter lays out the facts, citing the *New York Times* article with the initial headline that broke the story open as he reports that a "midlevel content manager" at a fantasy sports company called DraftKings admitted to unintentionally releasing confidential data before the start of games on an NFL Sunday. That employee, named Ethan Haskell, later won $350,000 at the site of another fantasy sports company, FanDuel. The reporter explains that the incident has raised serious questions about who at fantasy sports companies has access to this data and how it is that a casual player wasn't aware that he was facing the company employees, who were privy to confidential information in what was sure beginning to look like a rigged game.

"Are the contests fair? It's a question dominating the sports world," says the reporter, who is speaking from a glittering seafront in Boston, on a sun-splashed October afternoon. "New York City–based FanDuel and DraftKings, headquartered here in Boston, issued a joint statement saying, 'Nothing is more important than the integrity of the games we offer and we have since barred employees from entering fantasy sports contests for money.'" The reporter sends it back to the anchor in the studio, saying, "The controversy is poised to linger, with billions of dollars and now credibility at risk," leaving everyone watching the Tuesday evening telecast of *Nightly News,* and everyone who clicked on the initial headline, with one question.

Who's going to jail for this?

When the *New York Times* story broke and the storm was first gathering strength, Jason Robins was somewhere over the Atlantic Ocean flying back to Boston from London after a week of meetings and media en-

gagements to talk about new ventures in the UK. He and his communications director, Sabrina Macias, had boarded the plane knowing that
the *New York Times* was working on a story, but with the Wi-Fi down on
the flight, they were unable to read the story when it posted. They had so
many emails and texts when the plane touched down at Logan Airport
that it would take them some time to fully comprehend the magnitude
of the storm. They stepped out of the airport gate and into the terminal,
just feet from the newsstands that sold the issue of *Fortune* with Jason's
face splashed on the cover. It wasn't until they looked up at the hanging
screens in the terminal that they began to fully grasp the scope of what
was happening. They couldn't hear what they were saying on CNN, but
the ticker told them everything they needed to know: DAILY FANTASY
SITES EMBROILED IN AN INSIDER TRADING SCANDAL.

Now, days after the headline, Jason Robins has become the face not
of a young rebel reshaping business, but of a national scandal. Two days
after the *New York Times* alert, he finds himself on an afternoon news
show that is covering the daily fantasy scandal for the entirety of its half
hour, an attempt to peel back more layers on the story.

"We welcome chief executive officer Jason Robins, who joins us . . ."
the host of the show is saying from his seat in a studio with an elec-
tric-blue lighting scheme, shown on-screen above a chyron that reads
DAILY FANTASY SPORTS ISSUES: ALLEGATIONS OF INSIDER TRAD-
ING HIT DAILY FANTASY SITES.

"What has it been like for you, not just for your company but the daily
fantasy sports industry?" the host asks. Wearing a plain white shirt that
is nearly as pale as his complexion, Jason says, with an air of impatience,
"The two most important things here are that this is a real and important issue. And secondly, this particular incident was based on complete
misrepresentation, and bad reporting frankly, and we have finished our
internal investigation and hired an independent law firm to conduct
their own investigation, and what we found is that there is absolutely no
evidence of ethical wrongdoing."

"I'd like to say hello and bring in a sports gambling attorney who was
with us yesterday," says the broadcaster as the screen turns into a split

screen between Jason and the new guest. "We say hello to Daniel Wallach, to this now three-way conversation. Dan, I'd like you to comment on what you've been hearing."

In front of a backdrop that is a body of water with large boats milling around, attorney Daniel Wallach appears on the split screen from Fort Lauderdale, Florida, with a furrowed brow and look of concern that makes it clear that he's here for a fight. "We're already hearing Jason admit that as many as fifty people within the company are playing on FanDuel," says Wallach, who is on this show for the second day in a row and has become the go-to expert for media outlets on this hot topic, as a "sports gambling attorney" he has become, overnight, the most in-demand legal expert in America.

"Let's do the math: 0.03 percent of the total FanDuel prizes equals close to $10 million, according to a report today. Ten million divided by fifty people means we're having employees winning in excess of, or close to, $200,000 per employee, and we have an executive at DraftKings openly admit that employees are earning more money playing at FanDuel than they earn at DraftKings. That is a very telling statement. Is this the equivalent of an employee compensation scheme off the books?"

Jason, expressionless, says, "Any request that's made of us, certainly by the government, we'll provide any data that they want — as I've said we do have good monitoring in place. Daniel is right, the goal is complete transparency."

"Dan, I've got a minute," the host interrupts. "Your final thought *right now*."

"Two quick questions for Jason: Are you in favor of regulation, and if not, why not? And more importantly, *is daily fantasy sports gambling?*"

Inside a room enclosed in glass, with floor-to-ceiling windows overlooking yellow-and-orange-rinsed Manhattan in autumn, a dozen men and women sit around a long table, watching Jason Robins on ESPN and the rest of the news coverage: here is the ex-McKinsey man who is the company CEO; the chief financial officer, a former director at private equity firm KKR; the chief legal officer who was once a Department of

Justice prosecutor; the PR director who once ran New York City mayor Mike Bloomberg's campaign; the crisis manager who advised President Obama during the battle for health care legislation; and the two in-house media managers. Some here are sports fans, many are not; most, until this week, had never met. Those gathered in this room of laptops, lukewarm coffee, bland sandwiches, and fluorescent-light-washed complexions and bloodshot eyes have just one thing in common: they, the leadership and crisis management team at FanDuel, are trying to figure out how this media tsunami gathered and began to move with such speed and force, and what to do now in the face of the flood of negative headlines. Some are overcome with emotion; one has to leave the room to cry. Others see the situation as an absurdist play.

"I mean, it's just fantasy sports!" screams the young media manager, who had boarded the rocket ship just two months earlier, thinking that she was joining the new Facebook of sports but was now being told that she has, in fact, been working for a potentially criminal operation.

Another woman, standing in front of a whiteboard, scribbles two words on it: "Friends" and "Foes." She begins writing, under the second heading, a list of newspapers, websites, bloggers, attorneys general, retired state legislators, casinos, any of the many individuals and entities who have begun to line up against the industry. She turns to the other heading, "Friends," and pauses.

"We don't have any fucking friends!" she says.

The woman at the whiteboard feels a familiar knot in her stomach, something that tells her that there is nothing that she — that they — can do. Because better than just about anyone, Justine Sacco, the communications director at FanDuel, knows what it's like to face the mobs. "Sometimes you can't do a thing about it," she will later say. "You want to fight back, to try to save yourself, but you can't. You can only hope to survive."

Colin Drew had no intention of starting this tsunami. The thirty-year-old daily fantasy player and sales director at an online company in Washington, DC, was the first person to call attention to Ethan Haskell's post. At around 2 p.m. EST on the afternoon of September 27, 2015, Drew was at home scrolling through Twitter when he clicked on a link he saw in a DraftKings tweet, thinking that it was the ownership figures for players on teams whose games had kicked off roughly an hour earlier.

What he found was ownership data for players involved in the upcoming afternoon games. Drew thought this was odd, since the games had not yet started, and anyone who could see ownership data of other daily fantasy players would, in theory, have an edge.* If employees and other players could view that information ahead of time, Drew wondered, what else could they see? Drew posted his discovery on a thread on the player forum website RotoGrinders — "IMO this is a big leak and should never happen," he wrote — and the thread was almost immediately locked by a site manager to give Haskell, the employee who wrote the original post, time to explain himself. He did:

> Hi All,
>   As Cal mentioned — this was published in error originally by myself. I've fixed the error and we'll be putting checks in place to make sure it doesn't happen again. As Cal mentioned, I was the only person with this data and as a DK employee, am not allowed to play on site. 100 % my fault and I apologize for any issues.
>   Ethan

What Colin Drew and the rest of the RotoGrinders community didn't know was that Haskell was entered in a contest on DraftKings' rival site, FanDuel. What they didn't know was that, a day after his post, Ethan would place second among 229,885 players in FanDuel's tournament, and that he would win $350,000.

As players began to take note of the curious series of events — em-

---

* In a large tournament like the one in which Haskell won $350,000, the advantage in knowing ownership trends is being able to bet *against* the field. A daily fantasy pro's strategy is not so different from that of a stock trader who wants to find undervalued stocks. You want to find undervalued players to slot in your lineups. Low-owned players allow you to separate your lineup from the rest of the field.

ployee accidentally reveals that he potentially has ownership data before games lock . . . employee goes on to win $350,000 in a tournament — those who knew Haskell quickly came to his defense. Those defenders were in the minority. Over at another site, DFS Report, the comments board went mad:

> Complete scam sites. All these top players are just getting inside information from people like Ethan the cheater. That's why they make last minute swaps after the information is passed to them.

and:

> Glad one of the scumbags made a huge mistake that exposed them for what they are. This just confirms what we already knew.

and:

> Expect the CEO of DraftKings to step down this week. Too much money from ESPN, Disney, FOX, Cowboys, NFL, MLB, for these groups to be involved with insider trading scandals regarding gambling.

and:

> Ethan will also be forever known as the greedy criminal who brought down DraftKings and FanDuel. RIP DFS.

and:

> If you don't think this has been rigged from the start, you are living in a vacuum. Of course they have information they leak over to other parties. This is just the tip of the iceberg.

• • •

The internet is an insatiable machine fueled by shock, insult, and out-rage and smoke-and-mirrors diversions, a machine that gives us a new hero or villain every moment. By the fall of 2015, thanks to hundreds of millions of dollars spent on advertising, the public had already begun to cling to a picture of daily fantasy sports: the bro standing on a stage with a check. But now there was an even better poster boy for the industry: an insufferable Patriots fan who cheated others on his way to winning hundreds of thousands of dollars.

The initial breaking-news headline had evoked images of a rogue em-ployee with sophisticated hacker skills sitting at his laptop in a dark-ened room surreptitiously redirecting, with a few keystrokes, hundreds of thousands of dollars, but anyone who had this idea that the employee in question was some MIT-level mastermind had second thoughts once they spent a moment Googling the person at the center of the scandal. An internet search of the name "Ethan Haskell" resulted in head shots of a dude staring back with crossed arms, baseball cap worn backward, a smirk, and a wink. They could also search and find that he was an ear-ly-twenties "Content Manager" at DraftKings; that he recently scored pimp seats at the Patriots' season opener at Foxborough; that industry acquaintances had nice things to say about him ("We did some incredi-ble work hosting shows at the Playboy Mansion").

Justine Sacco's first thought, when the *New York Times* reporter reached out to tell her they were digging around about this thread on RotoGrinders, was that Ethan Haskell was not FanDuel's problem. A part of her always believed that the Haskell story was going to die on a thread seen only by a few hundred members of an obscure fantasy sports site. Haskell was an employee of DraftKings, after all, and if he was go-ing to take down her company's rival, then, well, *c'est la vie*. Employees playing on other sites was one of those things that was brought up oc-casionally within the leadership of the companies but never seriously considered. Though it was a small number who played at Haskell's level, more employees played daily fantasy, most at small stakes, than didn't. There was still no evidence that any FanDuel employee playing on Draft-Kings had ever done anything wrong. She did not talk to her counterpart at DraftKings because, as far as having a communications strategy — well, it was just odd to have a strategy with the company whose endgame was to obliterate you.

But when her phone pinged with the *New York Times* alert, she knew, immediately, that this *was* a problem. Then she read the opening sentence of the *Times* story — splashed on the front page of its print edition, in the coveted "A1" spot — which read like a grocery store paperback: "A major scandal is erupting in the multibillion-dollar industry of fantasy sports, the online and unregulated business in which players assemble their fantasy teams with real athletes."

She called Nigel, who was at home in Edinburgh having dinner with Lesley and the boys.

"You need to come to New York," she said. "This is bad."

It was part of her job to imagine the worst headlines in a potential brewing story, and Justine had ten versions of this story written in her head, but this one —"Fantasy Sports Employees Bet at Rival Sites Using Inside Information"— was way worse than any of her hypotheticals. What she immediately noted was that DraftKings was not in the headline — the entire industry, not just daily fantasy but the entire fantasy sports industry, was being implicated. The first rule in Justine's communications management handbook was that first impressions die hard, that the initial headline, even with the short shelf life of the internet, was as permanent as if written in stone, because even though the *New York Times* would drop the words "inside information" from its headline, it was too late: now every media outlet jumping on the story included the words "insider trading" in their own headlines.

And the story was not going away. It was getting bigger.

The talking heads on the networks and various media outlets — from NBC to CBS to CNN to FOX News to NPR — continue to give updates on the developing story.

On a network morning show, a man in a magnificent blue suit appears on the TV screen — trim, with a tuft of graying hair and big, piercing eyes lined by thin dark rings — and talks about these online games in grave, very measured tones. "We're looking at either illegality or fraud," says Eric Schneiderman, the New York attorney general. "If they make representations to people that you've got as much of a chance to win a bet, which essentially they do, and that's not true because there's a whole group of people who have access to information that enables them to pick football players every week that are more likely to result in a big win, then it's a rigged casino."

A rigged casino: the words hang in the air. The man who has stood up to evil conglomerates, big banks, and Donald Trump has now found his next villain to take down.

On a Sunday night a British comedian with the expressive face of a cartoon character sits behind a desk looking into the camera. He solemnly acknowledges the deadly Paris terror attacks from the day before, then segues into the main topic of his show, a twenty-minute screed on online fantasy sports: "The most addictive thing you can do on your phone, except maybe cocaine," as John Oliver describes it.

"DraftKings advertises on its website that it is 100 percent legal," he continues, "which is immediately suspicious. If the guy at TCBY said this frozen yogurt was 100 percent legal, you would know that somehow it was a product of the illegal sex trade."

Now fantasy sports games have become fodder for late-night comedians, a punch line on monologues. On *The Daily Show*, Trevor Noah quips, "These days, it feels like you can't turn on the TV without seeing one of three things: a zombie, a Kardashian, or a fantasy football ad."

Then he adds, "Online fantasy sports betting is an unregulated marketplace that seems to be screwing everyday Americans out of their hard-earned money."

Now twelve candidates for the presidency of the United States stand on a stage, including a former governor with a famous last name, a current governor shaped like Humpty-Dumpty, and a TV reality show star. They talk about ISIS, they talk about health care, they talk about immigration policy, and then, after a brief discussion of student loans, they turn to the topic of fantasy sports.

> MODERATOR: Daily fantasy sports has become a phenomenon in this country, will award billions of dollars in prize money this year. But to play you have to assess your odds, put money at risk, wait for an outcome that's out of your control. Isn't that the definition of gambling, and should the federal government treat it as such?

> CANDIDATE BUSH: Well, first of all, I'm 7-and-0 in my fantasy league.

> MODERATOR: I had a feeling you were going to brag about that.

> CANDIDATE BUSH: Gronkowski is still going strong. I have Ryan Tannehill, Marco, as my quarterback, he was 18-for-19 last week. So I'm doing great. But we're not gambling. And I think this has become something that needs to be looked at in terms of regulation. Effectively it is day trading without any regulation at all. And when you have insider information, which apparently has been the case, where people use that information and use big data to try to take advantage of it, there has to be some regulation. If they can't regulate themselves, then the NFL needs to look at just, you know, moving away from them a little bit. And there should be some regulation.

> CANDIDATE CHRISTIE: Are we really talking about getting government involved in fantasy football? We have $19 trillion in debt. We have people out of work. We have ISIS and Al Qaeda attacking us. And we're talking about fantasy football? Can we stop?

There are some attempts at coordination between the companies; a summit is held in a midtown Manhattan office between a group of executives, each with their own thoughts on the best approach to combat all the negative press. But as the two companies attempt to work together, what becomes apparent is the enormous differences between their executive teams and their cultures.*

At FanDuel the conversation becomes focused on how the companies have to work together in light of Eric Schneiderman's latest move: he has sent a cease-and-desist letter to the companies telling them to stop operations immediately in New York. Both companies must get on the same page in terms of messaging and strategy — it is the only way they can overcome the growing mob. Meanwhile, lawyers representing both companies are taking multiple calls a day from members of both executive teams. Fifteen to twenty people sit in on calls, making each one disorganized and ultimately useless. "We just need order, fast," says one lawyer. "We are a nation's punching bag."

The story has shifted from Ethan Haskell to other employees at the operators who are playing these games and making big money on the competing sites. These employees are named in the articles and, suddenly under fire, being accused of insider trading and profiting from what is being described as some lucrative off-the-books employee compensation scheme.

No bystander to this viral story — no reporter even — seems particularly interested in the actual guilt or innocence of Ethan Haskell. An independent investigation led by a former US attorney concludes that Haskell did not receive the ownership percentage information until forty minutes after his winning lineup had locked. These details are completely lost in the more sensational news items, because it is, of course, too late for thoroughness or for nuance.

Because, amid all the chaos, another salacious story has emerged.

---

* Inside the offices where the summit was held, when Jason Robins appeared on the TV screen for another interview, boos filled the room. People balled up paper and threw it at the TV set. One FanDuel employee in the room, believing that the only thing that could save them now was working together, shook his head and, with a very popular HBO show never far from his mind, thought, *Forget Jason Robins. Don't you guys see it? The White Walkers who are going to come and kill us all?*

"Uh, why is Sac trending on Twitter?" someone asked in FanDuel's war room.

It had all begun with a headline. Justine Sacco, of all people, knew how one headline could lead to an unraveling. She had seen a world obliterated once before by that mad, amorphous mob — in fact, that obliteration had led her to the world of daily fantasy. She was looking for a job in the fall of 2014 when a headhunter cold-called her to ask if she'd have any interest in working with a company looking for a communications officer, a company, the headhunter said, that was in the business of something called daily fantasy games. Justine said, "Before we get too far, you probably want to Google me."

Anyone who'd Googled her would learn that Justine Sacco was *that* Justine Sacco — the PR chief at the media conglomerate IAC who was walking through Heathrow Airport in 2013 and sent out a tweet about AIDS in Africa and who boarded her plane to South Africa not knowing that by the time she landed the mob would have turned her life upside down. The Justine Sacco about whom tens of thousands of vicious tweets had been sent in response to her joke. Who had her own trending hashtag: #HasJustineLandedYet. Who was thrown into a modern media nightmare hell as she lost her job, was ridiculed and harassed, and became, as the *Daily Mail* in London would put it, "a global hate figure," a Twitter villain to end all Twitter villains. She became a chapter in a *New York Times* bestseller, the subject of think pieces. And then she disappeared. The story of Justine Sacco ended there. But a new story began. Justine disconnected from the world, traveled for a month in Africa, spent time with her mother in Los Angeles, and then returned to New York City.

She was still sifting through the wreckage when Nigel Eccles, after receiving Justine's name from the headhunter, pulled her from the wilderness to run FanDuel's communications team. At the time, if you were a reporter looking to do a story on FanDuel, you went to their website and entered a query, and a few days later you would get a reply from someone named Lesley Eccles. Communications officers were gatekeepers — they held the keys and ultimately were the ones who granted the reporters access to the executives — and they also played a crucial role in molding the image of the companies.

Not only did Justine have a vast amount of experience working at a media conglomerate, but at IAC she'd worked closely with a group of brash pretty boys who were one of the first entrants into the daily fantasy industry and who badly needed some publicity. At the time of her ignominious firing, Justine juggled a number of tasks at IAC, and among them was working with Brian Schwartz and Mark Nerenberg and the DraftStreet bros to get the word out on daily fantasy. It turns out that of the people who were possibly qualified for a job in public relations for a daily fantasy sports company, Justine Sacco was at the top of the list.

She interviewed for the job at FanDuel's shoebox offices in Manhattan, and Nigel, based on her résumé and his interview with her and nothing else, offered her the job on the spot. There were more than a few people, from other executives to board members, who, when Nigel told them who they were hiring, said, "Are you insane? Have you even Googled her?" Nigel had, and didn't care. Justine took the job — her first since her public execution. She'd joined as part of a wave of hires by the company as FanDuel was finalizing its Series D financing, and she had arrived at a time when the mainstream still needed plenty of educating. And so Justine played an important role in the meteoric rise of the company's brand, shaping the media's coverage of *The leading daily fantasy operator in the world . . . A new media company in the age of mobile to change the sports landscape . . . Run by a group of brilliant young, fresh-faced entrepreneur/disrupters . . . The Facebook of sports . . . And look at these boys winning six figures playing fantasy sports!*

The coverage was glowing. All of the reasons why she was a good communications director at IAC before her life collapsed — she was fearless, a straight shooter with reporters who genuinely liked working with them — were the reasons why she was a perfect fit for a young startup in a nascent industry. "As far as lemons and lemonade?" she told her friends. "The job is perfect."

And now, a year after her life unraveled with one tweet, she is watching one headline obliterate another world. The daily fantasy sports narrative had careened off the cliff, and once again she is finding herself facing the mad mob armed with pitchforks and hazy facts. She is leading the way in helping the companies save their image and their brand, and the task is considerable. And to make matters worse, just a few days into the scandal Justine gets an email asking for comment: the *New York Post* is planning an article whose headline will read, "PR Guru Who Posted Racist Tweet Surfaces in Fantasy Sports Scandal."

The article will begin: "The most controversial woman in public relations is under the klieg lights again . . ."

A year after he turned Justine Sacco into a global hate figure by posting her tweet on the blog Valleywag — the headline was "And Now, a Funny Holiday Joke from IAC's PR Boss" — the site's editor, Sam Biddle, posted another story on the site, this one with the headline "Justine Sacco Is Good at Her Job, and How I Came to Peace with Her." Justine and Biddle had met up for drinks, and Biddle wrote a piece saying: "Justine Sacco has a PR job she enjoys now, but she deserves the best and biggest PR job, whatever that may be. Give it all to her."*

But this was already a few months after Nigel had taken a chance on her. Having a part in growing FanDuel and the industry: that was something she was proud of. The Ethan Haskell stretch — she was not even sure that she and her team were doing a particularly good job. She did her best. And she did understand how it happened.

"A good story is a good story — no matter what the facts are," she would later say. "There was just so much for reporters to grab on to, and you had attorney general opinions and FBI probes and crazy people on forums, so reporters don't have good resources so they start going to . . .

---

* It always irked Justine that people thought she'd been destroyed by her tweet. The narrative that her life was ruined — it pissed her off that people thought that she was so fragile. She didn't want to downplay what had happened to her — it was real, it was terrifying, and she would not wish it on anyone, ever — but the thought that she would just be a castaway, or lost, or never work again never crossed her mind.

it just spirals. The wave, it comes and goes, and there is something to riding the storm as best you can."

This storm was relentless. In the days and weeks afterward, she was on the phone constantly: seven o'clock in the morning with ESPN, 11 p.m. with the *New York Times,* and the avalanche in between. Did those conversations make a difference? Perhaps, perhaps not.

"Someday you'll Google me and my LinkedIn will be the first thing that pops up," she had told Biddle in her interview with him one year earlier. She believed it then. She had believed that one day she would be able to walk into a room and not feel the baggage of that one tweet. But these last few days had been confirmation that, after all this time, she was still *that* Justine Sacco. And something about that fact told her that, when it came to the mob that was now at the gates of her company, the stain would likely be indelible, the damage perhaps even everlasting. These last few days were also confirmation that the machine remained as relentless and vicious as ever.

During the worst stretch that October, she received a message. It was a surprising note from FanDuel's rival company, an unexpected moment of solidarity: a DraftKings employee telling Justine he was sorry to see her name dragged into this.

I know what it feels like for you, too, Justine replied to Ethan Haskell. *And it just sucks.*

7

OPEN AND NOTORIOUS

Edinburgh, Fall 2015

It's less than a decade since Edinburgh businessman David Car-ruthers, then chief executive of online gambling group Beton-Sports, was arrested after his flight from the UK touched down in the US. BetonSports was one of the biggest players in what was then a rapidly expanding US online gaming market. Follow-ing Carruthers' arrest investors took flight and wiped more than $1 billion from the sector. Carruthers ended up in a Dallas court-room wearing a prison-regulation orange jump suit and shackled to a chain gang of other inmates. He was eventually convicted of racketeering conspiracy and sentenced to 33 months in prison. The clampdown on online gambling was as sudden and unseen as the maelstrom that threatens to envelope FanDuel.

— London *Times*, November 15, 2015

E*veryone is looking at me.*
     She knew it was preposterous, this thought she had as she walked through her neighborhood on this late November morning. Yet despite that realization, Lesley still felt the paranoia closing in on her like a fog through the grime-covered stone houses that lined the street. The arti-cle had dropped the day before: splashed over the pages of the London *Times* was a photo of the husband-wife founders of FanDuel smiling

brightly in the Edinburgh offices back in the company's halcyon days earlier in 2015, but the image might as well have been one of the two of them in handcuffs because of the alarming nature of the story under the headline: "Fantasy Turns into Hard Facts for FanDuel."

All of it was taking its toll: the declarations from the attorneys general, one after another, that the startup that she'd cofounded and helped grow was, in fact, an illegal gambling operation;* the fact that her role at FanDuel was shrinking as the company slashed the ad spend in the aftermath of the *New York Times* story and directed resources instead toward the company's escalating legal costs; and the negative headlines that characterized their game as a crooked one, won by employees who used insider information to turn casual fans into suckers. And now this London *Times* piece, which recalled the notorious British businessman David Carruthers, who in 2006 had famously gone to jail for enabling illegal gambling in the United States. The implication was clear: the Eccleses — the cofounders of a company being accused of false advertising, defrauding customers, and operating an illegal gambling ring — could be on the front pages of the tabloids any day now as a husband-and-wife pair in orange jumpsuits.

Of course, Lesley's anxieties had been building long before the fall. In the summer of 2015, DraftKings, with its $300 million funding round in 2015 and its ad spend through basketball and baseball season of that year, stunningly closed the gap in market share entering the 2015 NFL season. While overseeing a marketing campaign that, in response, had ballooned from $50 million to $250 million over the course of the summer, Lesley had sat down for an interview in the FanDuel offices with a UK website to talk about FanDuel's future as a billion-dollar company; she had felt so weak and frail that when the spotlights flashed on, she was overwhelmed, almost blinded, by the lights and answered questions in a haze. She'd lost significant weight because of the stress of overseeing such a huge ad spend — over the next year she would lose more than ten

---

* By December 2015, DraftKings and FanDuel were banned in New York, Illinois, and Nevada.

pounds from what was already a slight frame — and now the stress had turned into fear that the company was going to be shut down. Or worse.

Lesley was receiving texts from relatives and friends who'd clearly read the *Times* story and were asking, *Everything okay?* Her two boys were now seven and nine, old enough to have a sense of what it was that their parents did for a living and old enough to have friends who asked questions that confused them, questions like, *Are your parents going to jail?* Because those friends had heard from their own parents that there might be trouble in the Eccles household. The gated school the boys attended, a twenty-minute walk from their house, was one of the most prestigious private schools in Scotland, and the Eccleses were known, from the occasional splashy profiles of the company in the *Scotsman* or the *Daily Mail* or the *Guardian* or the *Times,* as the husband-and-wife entrepreneurs making waves in the tech world in America. The UK press had covered the rise of FanDuel even more thoroughly than the tech and sports media in the United States: with a sense of pride, it hailed FanDuel as the rare success story in the barren UK tech world, a trailblazer that was also turning the sports landscape upside down in the US. The coverage was fawning: just months earlier one of the papers reported that FanDuel, after a recent round of financing, was now one of just two billion-dollar unicorn companies in all of Scotland, and one of just over a dozen in all of Britain.

Nigel's name had appeared in one of those papers, the *Irish Times,* on "The Rich List," a ranking that most certainly grabbed the attention of anyone inside the couple's circle of friends, since their acquaintance's name appeared next to a rather eye-popping number — £350 million — that was meant to be an approximation of his net worth. That number, and his ranking as the forty-first richest man from Ireland, just below U2 and, to his amusement, ahead of a who's who of famous natives — Liam Neeson, Conor McGregor, even *Enya* — had led to questions: questions from the boys, who still had fresh memories of their mother scrounging for coupons and shopping for toys at the local thrift store.

"So are we . . . rich?" one of the boys asked, to which Nigel and Lesley — without going into the fact that the number in the newspaper was a preposterous imaginary number based on other imaginary numbers — answered, "No, we are not . . . *rich*."

After the *New York Times* story, in October, Nigel and Lesley had hired their own lawyer for the legal problems that could come.

"Here's the thing: you guys are open and notorious," that lawyer had told them, soon after the cease-and-desist letters had arrived and Nigel was facing the real possibility of a US federal indictment.

"Open and notorious?" Nigel asked.

"If you see white-collar crime, there's criminal intent. Someone's done something, and they've clearly known it was illegal, or suspected it was so, because it was hidden. It would be unusual — *very unusual!* — to claim that you were doing something illegal when you were doing it so openly — *so, so openly* — for five or six years."

"Open and notorious," Nigel said. "Can we use that as a defense? Sounds more like a rap song!"

Even though she took the law seriously, Lesley viewed the question of whether daily fantasy was gambling or not gambling, and thus legal or illegal — whether or not it was or was not a game of skill — as a silly question. Daily fantasy, like poker or blackjack, resided in a gray area on a spectrum: they were games of skill with an element of luck involved. She saw the gambling laws as emblematic of the inexplicable American mind-set: asked about the ban on gambling in the United States by her friends in Scotland, where gambling was legal, she'd reply, referring to Scotland's national dish of sheep intestines, "I mean, *haggis* is illegal in the US. Give me a break!" Still, there was no way she could rule out a grandstanding attorney general or district attorney deciding to take up the cause and crack down on the operations as illicit gambling and throw the operators into prison. So now she was sitting in her living room, telling her boys that people weren't going to show up at the door and take Mum and Dad away in handcuffs.

For years she and Nigel had felt as though they had succeeded in shielding their boys from the day-to-day stress of their manic jobs, maintaining a sense of normalcy in the house, with the rule that always one parent would be home with the boys while the other was abroad. While there were clear disadvantages to remaining in Scotland as their company was exploding in the United States, there was one major benefit: the ocean was a buffer against the war. But now things were changing as their boys were being asked questions about what it was that their parents really did for a living — now they, like the others who were following this sordid saga of daily fantasy sports, could have that image of their parents in the orange jumpsuits. Now they, like everyone else, could read online others casting their parents as drug kingpins — like the state representative in Washington State who stood in a statehouse chamber in front of a microphone and blustered:

"What we have here are a couple of companies that are stealing money from the people who play, running horribly misleading and untrue advertising . . .

"This is no different than El Chapo down in Mexico advertising heroin or methamphetamine on our airways a thousand times a day to get kids to try it!"

Lesley had sat the boys down in the living room after they returned from school. Her children weren't growing up in a household full of worry and fear about money, as she had, but as she looked at their faces, she saw that they were now, as she once was, living in fear of the knock on the front door. She tried to explain to her young boys that despite everything they were hearing and reading, despite what their friends were saying, the FBI wasn't going to show up at their house and lead their parents away in handcuffs.

"Mum and Dad are not going to jail," she insisted to them, in that strong, unyielding manner that she used in conference and board rooms and in interviews, the side of her that exuded strength and confidence, regardless of whatever uncertainty she felt below the surface.

"Mum and Dad are not going to jail," she repeated, and then thought to herself:

But are *Mum and Dad going to jail?*

A week later, she was still making sense of the madness around her when she arrived in the heart of London on a train that had taken her from

Edinburgh. Outside, she hurried through a fierce rainstorm and dashed past the towering columns to the entrance of the imposing limestone building that looked out onto Trafalgar Square, where a yellow glow illuminated the square's fountains and the falling sheets of rain. She had been invited to this building called Canada House many months earlier, as a founder and the chief marketing officer of one of the half-dozen billion-dollar unicorns in the United Kingdom, a successful entrepreneur, and a leading female in the dog-eat-dog, male-dominated tech world. For all those reasons, she had been asked to speak to an audience of UK entrepreneurs, business leaders, and members of the media who had closely covered the tale of the embattled startup with the fervor of the latest tabloid scandal. "Unicorn to Unicorpse?" read one headline in the London *Times*. Through these last weeks and months, Nigel had remained a ghost outside the walls of the FanDuel offices, leaving Jason Robins, who sat through a series of interviews on the cable networks in the days after the *New York Times* headline, to become the face of the industry. No one from FanDuel had spoken to the media or appeared in any public forum, and certainly no one expected Lesley to show up for a conference in Trafalgar Square, not in the middle of the storm. Some at the company, in fact, had advised her not to go: there was nothing to gain from speaking now, they argued, nothing to be gained from becoming the face of the scandal.

In the days leading up to her trip to London, the negative headlines had continued, announcing news of the California attorney general's launch of an investigation into fantasy operations, which were not clearly defined by law in her state; of the Georgia legislature's also beginning an investigation into the legality of daily fantasy; of the NCAA's asking FanDuel to stop offering college contests because daily fantasy was wagering and in violation of NCAA bylaws.

Faced with the decision of whether to board that train for the four-hour ride from Edinburgh to London, Lesley at the last minute had felt that compulsion that she had often felt, going back to her high school days when she said yes to going out for the school play, yes to going out for the student council, yes to taking on every challenge that was a part of starting a company from the ground up, yes to whatever it was that would take her out of her comfort zone.

"I have nothing to hide from," she said. "I'm going."

She was defiant. She'd always been defiant, even as it became clear to others in the company — soon after the start of the NFL season and before the *Times* story — that they were beginning to lose control over their machine. They continued to relentlessly test customers, and the numbers coming in had begun to spell trouble. First, numbers in the early fall showed that 10 percent of the people loved the ads — and 90 percent hated them, a sign that the brain-assaulting repetitiveness of the ads made it impossible for millions of Americans to feel anything but hatred toward the companies. Cracks in the machine appeared as the ads came under sudden and intense legal fire, first with a lawsuit from former NCAA football players regarding ads that had aired an image of a collegiate player, a screwup by an outside ad agency. There were countless eleventh-hour tweaks and edits they had to make so that they could not be sued into oblivion — the voice on the ads could no longer say the company was "giving away $75,000 every week"; it now had to say it was "giving away $75,000 a week" because saying *every* week meant that in any week in which they weren't giving away precisely $75,000, the ad was deceiving the customers. Suddenly, marketing was essentially being run by the legal team.

Commercials that were once running every ninety seconds were now nowhere to be seen. Suddenly, the companies, a constant presence in virtually every home in America in the early fall of 2015, had become ghosts. And in the public eye, so had the people behind them, including Lesley — until the moment she emerged at the Canada House, in a room full of entrepreneurs and startup investors and also journalists there to cover the event. She strode to the stage, wearing a black skirt and cream shoes. She noticed a man sitting alone in the front row, and guessed, correctly, that he was there as a backup speaker to take her place at a moment's notice, in case she didn't show.

As she approached the lectern she was so nervous that her knees were literally knocking. Now it was true: everyone *was* looking at her.

She leaned into the microphone. "I heard it was even odds that I wouldn't be here," she said.

The room erupted in laughter, and Lesley exhaled. 'To those who bet I wouldn't be here, sorry. But it's good to be here."

Six years earlier, she'd been in this very room, at this very conference, sitting in the front row of the audience next to her cofounders. She'd had a notebook in her lap as she listened to tech leaders like Guy Kawasaki, marketing maestro at Apple; she hung on each word, scribbled notes down in a notebook like a diligent student in a lecture class. It was 2009, the founders were about to launch FanDuel, and Lesley was learning about the business and marketing world through Google and the stack of books on her bedside table. Now she was the one on the podium telling the story of her company — of the ups and downs of a startup, of waking up each morning and going to work in the room with the vomit-colored walls at the University of Edinburgh, wondering what the day would bring. She talked about the five founders hitting a dead end with their initial idea for a news prediction game and then, out of ideas for how to save their company, meeting up at South by Southwest in Austin, Texas, for a week of desperate brainstorming. She explained that as they sat around in the backyard of a house they were renting and stared at note cards pasted on the side of a shed, feeling as if they had hit rock bottom. She talked about the countless moments over the years when the threats had felt just as existential as they felt that day, and about how any truly disruptive company — Airbnb, Facebook, Uber — always found itself in a period of regulatory upheaval, but that such a period was an important step in its evolution and the company would be stronger when it emerged on the other side, despite what the world around her was saying.

"We're going to come out the other end," she said. "And we'll be stronger."

Through these last few weeks and months, she had formed a new theory on life: there was no such thing as sustained happiness. She came to believe that happiness was little, sporadic, isolated moments, and that the only thing one could do was to hold those moments close, in order to not be swept away by the inevitable tsunamis. Moments like those Friday curry nights out with the other cofounders, the five of them flashing their University of Edinburgh IDs to get the restaurant discount even though all of them had long since graduated. Like the rare weekends with her parents and her kids, the family all together — the time, in particular, when they were in a hotel room and her father turned on the TV and the first thing he saw was one of Lesley's ads. Moments like the weekend in 2014, sitting on the floor in an empty NBA arena with twenty-four thousand seats, there in Orlando with her four other cofounders, gazing at the name of the company that they'd created together, the name emblazoned on the scoreboard and on the court floor, the word FANDUEL, glistening like a newly shined jewel.

Every one of those moments was inevitably offset by a moment of disappointment, anguish, fear, sometimes even sorrow. To add to the immense challenges of getting this startup off the ground, the maddening puzzle-fitting in the early days, Lesley dealt with a series of personal and unexpected devastations that rearranged her world. They included not only her mother's sudden death in the summer of 2014 but also the fall evening, a year earlier, when she was in a cab with Tom Griffiths in Manhattan, on their way to a company event, and suddenly she felt faint, light-headed. Lesley looked down at her seat and saw a pool of blood. She'd always been a worrier, adept at envisioning the worst-case scenarios, and at this moment, as Tom ordered the cab to go to the nearest hospital, she couldn't help but think that she was dying. She was pregnant with their third child, and when it was confirmed at the hospital that she'd had a miscarriage, she had the thought, again, of how fragile and fleeting everything was.

There was yet another moment that had shaken her and changed her in ways that she would never be able to fully explain. One night she was with Nigel and the kids in an apartment in New York where they were staying, having a quiet dinner with a small group that included Tom and a few other executives. Lesley suddenly couldn't breathe as she chewed on a piece of chicken — she quickly realized that a piece was lodged in her throat. Everything that happened next happened over the course of only a minute, maybe ninety seconds — Lesley staggering to the kitchen, her face turning purple, Nigel grabbing the kids and ordering them to go to the bedroom, someone calling 911, Tom racing over to Lesley, hunched over the sink, and, after an attempt at the Heimlich maneuver, putting his thumb and finger in her mouth and attempting to pull the piece out himself and eventually nudging the piece just enough to create a small hole for air to pass, and then Tom shouting to Lesley, "Cough!"

The early days had been a difficult stretch in the company, a time when the founders wondered if they'd all made a terrible miscalculation with this pursuit. Nigel and Lesley had given their life savings to this company, but there was also plenty on the line for the others: Tom had left his PhD program, and Rob, recently married, was starting a family. These founders had become close friends, but as the pressure increased the internal disagreements grew about every little detail in everything from product to marketing, and a particular tension grew between the heads of those two areas, Tom and Lesley. But the moment in the kitchen had brought her closer to Tom, whom she would always view, after the incident, as someone who had saved her life; now all their disagreements seemed to fade away. More than anything, perhaps, those life-and-death incidents were merely confirmation to Lesley that there were no guarantees in life, no safety net, a way of thinking that translated to how she approached her work.

And now she felt as if she — and her company — were in a complete free fall. Under the suddenly overpowering lights of scrutiny, everyone seemed to be examining every potential crack in the company. The events of the fall of 2015 were laying bare the missteps made by the leaders at both FanDuel and DraftKings. *How on earth could the employees at the companies be permitted to play and win money from the games? Why were these contests skewed so heavily toward the professionals? Why were there so many damn ads, and if these weren't gambling operations, why was the messaging all about winning money?*

The second-guessing was also occurring internally. Investors and board members who a year earlier had dreamed about buying castles on islands were now wondering if they were ever going to get their money back and if this whole enterprise was about to be deemed illegal and fraudulent. They'd all made mistakes — that was clear now.

FanDuel board members began to sense trouble when, as early as opening weekend in the NFL, old college buddies began texting them, saying, *Dude, what's up with the ads? Please stop.* Two weeks into the season, they gathered for a board meeting, back in Edinburgh. The meeting opened with an executive saying, "Guys, do you all realize that last week DraftKings was the biggest TV advertiser in America — outspending Geico?" There was silence, and a look on everyone's faces: *Can that possibly be true?* Even *they* couldn't believe it. But it was true, according to the rankings at iSpot.com: DraftKings, followed by AT&T, Warner Bros., Geico. The looks on everyone's faces said something else: *Okay, so now what do we do?*

The game was on. Many of the deals that Lesley had agreed to were prepaid deals that they couldn't back out of; they were actually ten percent under budget because of a lack of inventory. DraftKings had bought up *everything*. At the height of their war with DraftKings, Nigel insisted that they go all in and increase their ad spend even more. One board member recalled walking out of the room thinking: *Did we just say yes to that?* They did. And three weeks later, the final week of September, there was a new top advertiser in the country: FanDuel, which spent $17 million with 2,536 airings of their TV ads over seven days.

When the board met again, in October, the company was under siege. This time, Mike LaSalle asked: "Is there nothing we can do? Turn the ads off? Can we do an alternative creative, at least?" The answer was no — there was no alternative. Alternative creative was in the works, but the new ads — focused on the brand, not the money — wouldn't be ready until November. They were all in.

The ads: yes, Lesley would defend them to the end. She would cite the number of users they'd acquired in the weeks leading up to October — and they were still blowing the doors off, acquiring new customers at an impressive clip. But those results were long forgotten. And by November, Lesley could feel things slipping away — her voice, her responsibilities, her power in the company, which was diminishing as the ad spend was slashed and the board seized more control.

She was being backed into a corner; really, she'd felt this way from the start. Always in this world, in every room she stepped into, she was aware, at every turn, that she was a woman. When they first started in the office at the University of Edinburgh, Lesley decided she would never clean up after the other cofounders, because once she did, as the only woman in the room she'd be expected to always clean up after the slobs at the end of each workday. She just had to live with the mold in the coffee maker.

Once, the marketing team flew to Los Angeles to meet with a contingent of San Diego Chargers executives who were interested in partnering up with her. As they were meeting at the stadium, Lesley introduced herself as the head of marketing and a cofounder. Still, throughout the meeting, one executive's attention seemed fixed on the two junior males in the group, brushing her off. The slight was so egregious that a FanDuel executive pulled him aside and said, "Hey, Lesley is the marketing director — *and cofounder of FanDuel*" — a comment that always got a strange look: a woman is the cofounder of FanDuel?

That additional complication: her last name. In a room full of investors, after Nigel was introduced, someone would introduce Lesley as "Nigel's wife." Nigel would snap back: "No, this is the chief marketing officer and cofounder of the company. We just happen to be married."

She had described the last year to others as like trying to push back an ocean. As the astronomical deals from advertisers were coming in, each one even more value-destructive than the last, she felt as though she was standing alone in front of the water, and the big waves and the water were rushing in, and she was doing everything in her power to push back the ocean, and all the force behind it.

Now she felt the ocean swallowing her whole.

In early December, as the storm around them became a Category 5, the FanDuel executive team gathered for a weekend of football in the Florida sun. During Week 14 of the NFL season, the executive team, whose members were scattered among Edinburgh, New York, and Los Angeles, descended upon Jacksonville to watch the home Jaguars play the Indiana-polis Colts from the area in the stadium concourse called FanDuelVille. This virtual-reality playground, one of a handful at NFL stadiums across the country, was a cross between a Florida beach club, with its bikini-clad women and deejay and flowing cocktails, and a sports arcade featuring multiple screens flickering with live football games from other cities and tablets propped on tables for fans to log on to their virtual teams.

FanDuelVille had opened that football season, and it was the first time that all the executives were seeing this shrine to fantasy sports and FanDuel, with the company logo plastered on chairs and tables and on the makeshift turf football field. As fans and the executives mingled, the atmosphere should have been celebratory, since FanDuelVille embodied the rise of the startup that was now a partner with a handful of NFL teams, including the Jaguars. Because of the grim developments of the past few weeks, however, the afternoon felt funereal.

After the game, the executives huddled together for an official meeting, in a room behind a door with a black sign that said FANDUEL WAR ROOM. A dozen men sat in rectangle formation, facing one another across a table with a conference phone system in the middle. It was rare for the executive team to be together in the same room, and because many of them had joined the company within only the last few months, a number of them were meeting for the first time, under strange and difficult circumstances. Nigel began the meeting as he typically did, with a temperature check — it was a common CEO exercise to go around a table and ask each employee to comment briefly on how they were feeling: *Exhilarated, blocked, or exhausted? Green, yellow, or red?*

In Nigel's version, team members were asked to give a number between zero and ten — zero being, *Get me out of here.*

"Four."

"Five."

"Three."

When it was the turn of one of the new executives, a veteran of the gaming industry, he offered what he believed were needed words of reassurance.

"Stuff like this happens all the time for a startup in a nascent industry," he said. "Don't let this bother you. Don't worry about it."

Of course, many within the company were shaken. Paul Martino, a FanDuel board member at the time, had been asleep when he received a call at two in the morning from an investor, distraught over what was happening. "I'm going to lose my job. My wife is going to leave me. How can you be so calm?" They were on the phone for an hour.

In Jacksonville, there was one notable absence from the meeting: a key board member, a founder. She was back in Edinburgh because it was her turn to be with the boys, and she had dialed in from home. As she listened to the words of the executive, meant to comfort the room, something in Lesley snapped. The comment felt flip, even disrespectful, given the dire circumstances. Still numb from the London *Times* article, still shaken from having to tell her boys that the FBI wasn't going to lock them away, still feeling crushed and defeated that the bitter rivals had caught them in the war, Lesley had long been feeling a sense of defeat. But it wasn't until that moment, as she began to fight back tears, that she realized that she'd hit her breaking point.

She shouted back, her voice piercing the air in that room in Jacksonville: "It really doesn't feel okay when your kids are asking if you're going to jail!"

The words hung in the air. Lesley stammered: "I just . . ." she said, unable to get the words out. Even those who'd been in the company from the start had never seen this side of Lesley Eccles — the side that let her emotions get the better of her. Yes, to investors and outside partners, she was the unflappable fighter, but even within the company she was the most feared executive — impenetrable to those who found themselves intimidated by her calm, her simmering poise.

She had never allowed her mask to fall away. The room was quiet, cloaked in a mostly stunned silence, because almost everyone in the room could feel that Lesley was unraveling, because now she was permitting herself to do something she had never done before in front of the others.

She began to cry.

8

NIGHTMARE AT 35,000 FEET

San Francisco, Fall 2015

Cory Albertson? *Am I speaking to Cory Albertson?"*

Trying his best to mask his excitement over hearing the instantly recognizable voice on the other line, Cory replied, in as muted a tone as possible, "Yes, this is . . . him."

All week long he had been expecting his phone to light up with a call from this famous sports analyst, a former NFL player who was now a talking-head fixture on NFL Sundays, but even still, as he sat on his living room couch, he had to pinch himself as he listened to the unmistakable voice.

"Cory Albertson!" the famous broadcaster, the Legend on the other end of the call, said. "I hear that you, Cory Albertson, are the wizard — the brains behind it all! — the guy behind DraftKings and FanDuel!"

Cory was alone in his downtown San Francisco apartment, trying his best to process the moment. Around him was a space outfitted for the life of a professional fantasy games player: a plasma-screen TV set hung from the wall, a standing-desk workstation with dual monitors sat in one corner of the room, a treadmill and yoga ball rested in another, and windows with a sick view of the oceanfront and downtown baseball stadium, which now sat empty, like an unopened present, with its glistening corners. It was September, that beautiful stretch during which the NFL and baseball regular seasons overlapped and as the daily grind of baseball collided with the intense crescendo of an NFL Sunday, Cory spent full days staring at a screen, toggling from spreadsheet to spreadsheet while sifting through injury reports on Twitter and messaging with his partner, Ray, the hourlong stretches at his desk broken up only by occasional walks to his refrigerator filled with kombucha drinks. Cory's head had been drowning in stacks and fades and overlay numbers, EVs and ROIs, when his phone lit up.

The man behind FanDuel and DraftKings? Yes, that was an odd, and inaccurate, way to describe Cory, and perhaps it showed the Legend's lack of understanding of the industry, which was not a surprise, even though the Legend was employed by a network that had a stake in a daily fantasy company. If you were a prominent figure in the sports world, and especially if you were a former star like the Legend and hadn't had meetings with representatives at either FanDuel or DraftKings about a potential partnership or ownership stake in a company, then, well, you either needed a new agent or you weren't nearly as famous as you thought. By now, the four professional sports leagues that had wanted no part of fantasy sports for decades were entering this world through the oddly shaped and narrow side door of daily fantasy sports. Suddenly, just about every media conglomerate — CBS, ESPN, FOX, NBC — had partnerships with a daily fantasy operator, and Jason Robins's vision of the industry as a virtuous circle was becoming a reality. A dozen teams from the NFL, the very league that had been most resistant to sidling up to something that smelled even remotely like gambling, had struck partnerships with either FanDuel or DraftKings, those companies' names plastered all over stadiums. Two of the most prominent team owners in the NFL, Jerry Jones of the Dallas Cowboys and Robert Kraft of the New England Patriots, were investors in the space, with an equity stake in DraftKings. A number of prominent athletes held equity stakes in the companies, including a Hall of Fame NFL quarterback whose early investment was one of the worst-kept secrets in the industry.

The Legend was just the latest sports celebrity to want a piece of the pie. He wasn't interested in a stake in a company; he wanted to launch his own. The Legend had been given Cory's name by a mutual acquaintance and was calling Cory because he needed help getting his venture off the ground.

"I need your help, Cory!" the Legend was saying. *Is this real life?* Cory thought to himself.

Cory had expected the call to be a job interview of sorts; instead, it was a brief conversation that ended with an invite. In a few days, the Legend explained, he would be in New York City to meet with with the president of a major cable network. They were all going to get together to discuss a potential fantasy games business. What that business was, exactly — well, the Legend needed the wizard behind FanDuel and DraftKings to come up with some ideas and make a play at some of this fantasy sports money being thrown around.

There was a time when Cory could imagine daily fantasy as a multibillion-dollar industry and, yes, the future of sports media, and you could still persuade Cory that there was a massive upside to fantasy sports — but his perception of daily fantasy as an industry that was here to stay had changed during that dinner in Miami when he listened to Deep Throat paint a picture of doom as he pointed out how short-sighted it was to unleash a massive advertising campaign for an industry with such uncertainty around it from a legal standpoint. A reckoning, Cory thought, was coming, one spurred by the negative optics that could have been avoided but were being created by that massive advertising campaign pointing to an industry that had been completely unregulated.

Just one week after that weekend in Miami, one week after Cory watched the ads from his cabana and imagined the world seeing the commercials and asking, *What is this?*, a US congressman who'd undoubtedly seen the commercials was doing precisely that. Cory was familiar with Frank Pallone, the congressman from New Jersey, because Pallone had led the crackdown on online poker just six years earlier and had pulled the rug from under Cory and thousands of professional poker players. Representing the interests of a state that had been mired, since the passage of the Professional and Amateur Sports Protection Act in 1992, in a seemingly interminable if not Sisyphean battle to offer legal sports betting of the traditional variety, Pallone called for a congressional hearing into daily fantasy. Why, Pallone asked, was daily fantasy being treated differently from traditional sports betting? Why were regulators allowing gamblers to be deceived into thinking they could easily win million-dollar prize pools? Why were daily fantasy advertisements playing so frequently on television that his office was actually fielding complaints?

"Anyone who watched a game this weekend was inundated by commercials for fantasy sports websites — and it's only the first week of the NFL season," Pallone said in his statement.

Within days the attorney general in Massachusetts announced that her office was looking into the legality of these games. The vision that Deep Throat had presented to Cory just days earlier in Miami was already becoming a reality.

Yes, a reckoning was coming, Cory thought — but first he had a plane to New York to catch.

When Cory was young, his father was laid off from Caterpillar, the company he'd worked at for nearly two decades, and Cory, who was born into a trailer park in a small town in southwest Indiana, into a family that was always one missed paycheck away from dire poverty, learned something about how hard it was to draw a regular paycheck in this world. Through the constant current of uncertainty and fear they lived with, his parents held on to religion, and for most of his formative years Cory was such a devout Christian that during high school he led Bible study classes and even converted a handful of his friends. Cory grew up without the internet in his home and ignored his parents' wishes to stay away from the evils of the online world only when he snuck off to the library, found a computer, and logged on to check his fantasy football team. He played trombone, had acne, was overweight, got the varsity letter for keeping stats for the high school baseball team, and then enrolled in the nearest major university, Ball State. His worldview began to change there; after growing up in a household in which connection to the outside world was prohibited, Cory, at Ball State, suddenly had access to everything, because as far as he was concerned, having the world of information at your fingertips was like an epiphany; the world just seemed so big. It was during his freshman year of college that he began following the story of an accountant from Nashville named Chris Moneymaker, an unknown in the poker world who went on to win $2.5 million at the World Series of Poker. Like countless college students in the early 2000s, Cory, inspired by Moneymaker's story, began playing poker online. Cory was one of the very few who was immediately good at it. He was even better at daily fantasy.

The fact that he'd earned a living doing both: what did that make him? A "gambler"? He'd always disliked the term because of all its negative connotations. In fact, he hated most varieties of gambling; he had last stepped foot in a casino in 2007, and he hoped that he never stepped foot in one again. He'd become estranged from his parents in recent years. He was still self-conscious about what his parents thought of a moneymaking pursuit in a world that could not be further removed from theirs. And yet, it was becoming clear to him that he had to find a way to accept that a gambler was precisely what he now was. Some — and certainly anyone in his parents' circle back in Indiana — might go so far as to call him a "scoundrel" because of his line of work, which was fine, Cory thought, just as long as those very same people recognized that what he did was ethically no different from what, say, a trader on Wall Street did. Or what a media conglomerate did when it swallowed other businesses whole in acquisitions, putting at risk thousands of employees whose pensions and 401(k)s hung in the balance. Or what venture capitalists — playing with not their own money but with the money of university endowments, pension funds, and insurance funds — did every time they made a new bet on a group of pimple-faced millennials with a story to tell. Every business was an exercise in managing risk, and making money off calculated risks — wasn't that what the *entire* business world did essentially? The only difference at the end of the day was the size of the bets. The only difference was that a day trader or a CEO put on a suit every morning and went to an office, while Cory rolled out of bed, got on his treadmill desk, and could go to work in his underwear.

If anyone had any ideas about a job that he could do, and do well, he was all ears! The money allowed him to live a life away from the trailer park and not fret about the consequences of a missed paycheck. It allowed him to have a comfortable apartment in downtown San Francisco, and now that nerd from Warsaw was being flown out to New York City and was hanging out with some of the most powerful people in the sports and media industry. In New York, the plans for his visit were vague, other than that he was to show up for a dinner in a Manhattan restaurant at an appointed time.

"Cory Albertson!" the Legend said, spotting him at the dimly lit restaurant. Cory sat down at a table with the Legend, a handful of the Legend's business associates, and a man in a suit — the network president. Cory understood why the TV executive, whose network made gobs of money airing live sporting events, was here and would be interested in talking about fantasy sports. He understood why TV networks, whose business model relied on the ratings and advertising dollars of sporting events, were exploring options for new money streams. Fans were beginning to cut the cord on cable packages, and overall viewership, which had been decreasing for years — ratings in the NFL and NBA were all trending downward — was now dropping at an alarming rate. It was a harsh reality for networks and leagues, but one they had no choice but to face: eventually all TV would be streaming TV, and soon the billions made from TV live-sports-rights deals would dwindle. All the media players who were looking for an answer to this problem watched as two little startups raised hundreds of millions of dollars, virtually overnight, with a game that engaged with fans in a new kind of way. Couldn't you just replicate what those companies did?

That was the question those at the table were presumably all here to answer. That is, once the Legend was done regaling everyone with stories from his years in the NFL and decades as a famous analyst, bouncing from one tale to another. With each one, laughter from the table filled the room around them. Cory had to admit that it was thrilling to be here with the famous and the powerful, knowing these people had the power to actually turn a half-baked idea — one of *his* half-baked ideas maybe — into a loft space occupied by an army of coders. Cory did have some ideas that he believed could change the world around him, or at least help a network stuck in a rut.

He had been thinking about a number of variations of next-level, in-game fantasy products that centered on allowing players to simultaneously follow their lineups and games in real time. Cory envisioned a second-screen experience tailored to your own fantasy lineup, a product that could automatically go to a game in which player's team was at the goal line, about to score the points that would put your lineup over the top. The idea was a no-brainer: it was clear that features like those were the future of the industry, but it was always hard to simply explain an idea like that to a room full of rich people who'd never played fantasy games before.

At the steakhouse, they had their own private room. The Legend regaled the room with stories, and the network president talked about his vague visions for the future. Cory waited and waited and waited to be called upon so that he could present his thoughts and offer a picture of how they could offer new kinds of fantasy games. But as the dinner wore on, he started to think that no one was really interested in what he had to say.

Not until the network president turned to Cory and said, with a straight face, "You're a degenerate gambler, aren't you?"

Cory was taken aback. "Excuse me?" he said.

"You're a degenerate gambler. Really, at the end of the day this is what you do, right? What you all are? Degenerate gamblers."

Cory didn't know what to say. "I'm sorry, I respectfully disagree," Cory said, "with that term."

To be called out as a kind of problem actor just because he played fantasy sports, and made a living off of it, seemed . . . odd. Perhaps it said something about how the rest of the world viewed daily fantasy sports.

He spent the rest of the dinner mostly silent. Maybe it was best for everyone if the fantasy player nerds just stayed in their little corner of the world of degenerate gamblers.

That's more or less what Cory would do. Because after that weekend, he never heard from the Legend again.

He was in his hotel room, in Manhattan, getting ready to fly back home to San Francisco, when his phone lit up with the *New York Times* news alert: "Insider Trading Scandal Rocks Fantasy Sports Industry." The nuke had gone off, just as Deep Throat had presaged, only a month earlier. Deep Throat had nailed it. Cory had imagined a number of doomsday scenarios, but an employee using internal data to win money wasn't one of them. He, like many others, were caught off guard and didn't see it coming — in retrospect it was obvious that employees shouldn't play. The story did sound alarming to him, and his anger was immediately directed at the companies, which he felt had dropped the ball on protecting the industry. Cory felt no allegiances or loyalty to DraftKings or FanDuel. He viewed daily fantasy as a utility, like the water that comes out of the faucet. There was some management of what went into the water — you needed it to not have lead in it — but if the companies ceased to exist, there would be another company the next day to provide that utility. Cory's immediate reaction was unlike that of most of his peers, who were attacking the *Times* for their reporting. Cory thought that maybe it wasn't the worst thing for reporters to look into what was happening if there was, in fact, genuine fraud going on at the companies.

After the *Times* story broke, his phone began buzzing nonstop. A year earlier, while he was a student at Notre Dame's business school, Cory had been the subject of a profile in the *Wall Street Journal* headlined "A Fantasy Sports Wizard's Winning Formula." ("He considers it hard to believe, though more plausible by the day, that the side business he started last year with $200 could actually make him rich.") It was a splashy profile that was one of the first stories in a national publication about a daily fantasy player; as a result, Cory found himself becoming a go-to source for reporters in search of quotes, from the player's perspective, on the fantasy sports industry. Now his phone was lighting up with calls from the *New York Times* and ESPN and *NBC News,* who wanted him to appear on a segment with Lester Holt. He said yes to a *Wall Street Journal* request to pen a first-person op-ed. Within hours of sending it out, it was posted online. It began:

> Let's cut to the chase here: Playing daily-fantasy sports games for money is gambling. And it should be regulated. I should know. Over the past few years, I've made millions of dollars playing these games on sites like DraftKings and FanDuel — the sites now at the center of a scandal.

Cory found himself virtually alone among the top sharks as someone who would speak critically of the companies. For starters, he thought it odd that there was no communication between the sites and the players — that the obvious expectation in the industry was that everyone needed to hush up and support the sites. All the players, it seemed, had lined up against Eric Schneiderman and the *New York Times;* everyone was attacking the *Times* for what the industry viewed as a hit piece on the daily fantasy sports industry instead of looking at the facts that it was reporting. Cory thought it odd that players were so eager to defend the sites without even knowing the total scope of what was going on in these companies. It felt to him almost like a smoke-filled-room type of conspiracy between players and sites, where it was in players' best interests to protect the sites at all costs and, as a result, no other players were asking tough, probing questions.

After he wrote the op ed, he got an email from one of the executives at a daily fantasy site, asking whether it was appropriate to be bringing up certain issues. The executive's complaint was that Cory had mentioned pros taking on newer players — Cory had pointed out that that was a problem that needed to be addressed. "For starters," he wrote, "no professional winning six figures at daily fantasy should be flooding $1 and $2 one-on-one contests against novices. Accordingly, Ray and I have opted out of playing daily fantasy contests that are below a $25 entry fee and with five or fewer participants on DraftKings and FanDuel. We have encouraged other high-stakes players to do the same. A fairer playing field should be the cornerstone of the industry. At minimum, the sites need to empower independent auditing and oversight of their operations — unless they want US congressmen to do it for them."

Beyond the Ethan Haskell issue, which Cory agreed seemed flimsy at best, there were some truly troubling bits of information buried deeper in the stories. Cory had reached out to a casual daily fantasy player who was quoted in a *New York Times* story as having been challenged in head-to-head contests on FanDuel by a DraftKings executive. The player had believed that the executive was challenging him because he felt he wasn't a very good player and thus would be easy to repeatedly win money from. Now, fresh off the Haskell headlines, the player also believed that the executive could have had access to inside information. Cory began to believe that this employee was looking up the losers on DraftKings and taking the email addresses from their account and challenging those email addresses to play them in games on FanDuel. He had no further info, but it was entirely possible to him that employees were using insider info regarding the relative ability of daily fantasy users and using that data to try to exploit them on DraftKings or FanDuel — attempting to prey on unsuspecting players while playing on the rival site. Suddenly Cory had a pile of questions: Was there a wider scope of players being defrauded in this sort of way? How did he know that an employee wasn't just looking at his lineup every day a few minutes before the games locked and using those picks on FanDuel to play against these other people who were losing on DraftKings?

Cory was taken aback by the lack of outcry on the players' parts — or at least, their lack of questions. Why did it seem like he was the only player asking them?

After those few days in New York City, Cory had been looking forward to going home and returning to his life as a daily fantasy player, though something was telling him that things would never be the same. Then, as he was walking through a cavernous, fluorescent-lit terminal at JFK Airport to catch his flight back to San Francisco, his phone rang.

Nigel Eccles, Rob Jones, and Lesley Eccles at the first FanDuel office at the University of Edinburgh in 2011.

Daily fantasy founders meet in 2013 at the Fantasy Sports Trade Association in Las Vegas: Jason Robins (DraftKings), Brian Schwartz (DraftStreet), and Tom Griffiths (FanDuel).

Cory Albertson and Ray Coburn — rayofhope — at the 2013 DraftStreet Fantasy Football Championships in Las Vegas.

Mark Nerenberg celebrates after IAC's investment in DraftStreet in 2013.

DraftKings cofounders Matt Kalish, Paul Liberman, and Jason Robins in Boston in 2012.

Cory Albertson and Ray Coburn, with Bo Jackson, at the 2015 FanDuel Fantasy Baseball World Championship in Las Vegas.

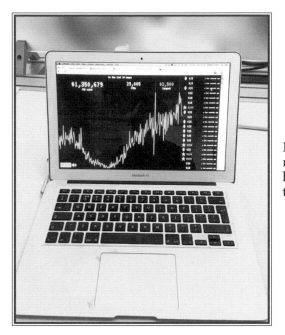

FanDuel's entry fees surpass $1 million in less than twenty-four hours during opening week of the 2015 NFL season.

Jason Robins and Matt Kalish appear with Jim Cramer on *Mad Money* in 2015.

Nigel Eccles appears on CNBC to discuss FanDuel's $1 billion valuation.

The five FanDuel cofounders at the Amway Center, home of the Orlando Magic. FanDuel partnered with over a dozen NBA teams in 2015.

Lesley Eccles speaking at the 2015 EIE conference in Edinburgh.

DraftKings employees in their Boston offices.

FanDuel employees in New York gather around to watch news coverage of the allegations of "insider trading" at DraftKings.

Protestors outside of New York Attorney General Eric Schneiderman's Manhattan office, in the aftermath of the AG's decision to shut down daily fantasy operations in New York.

Fantasy Sports Trade Association chairman Peter Schoenke addresses the media after a hearing at the Massachusetts State House on January 12, 2016.

Nigel Eccles, Lesley Eccles, and Jason Robins, with Virginia governor Terry McAuliffe, at the 2016 signing of a fantasy sports bill that made Virginia the first state to regulate the daily fantasy sports industry.

Cory Albertson in the California Redwood Forest, in the winter of 2017.

American Wagering CEO Vic Salerno in Las Vegas in 2017.

Nigel and Lesley Eccles at Super Bowl 50 in Santa Clara, California.

Jason Robins at the opening of the DraftKings Sportsbook in Scarlet Pearl, Mississippi, in 2018.

FanDuel and DraftKings ad blitz.

"Cory Albertson? *Is this Cory Albertson?*"

"Yes?" Cory replied.

"This is Agent A—— with the FBI. The Federal Bureau of Investigation in Tampa, Florida."

Cory stopped cold, in the middle of the terminal, surrounded by a mob of luggage-pulling travelers and screaming babies.

"I'm sitting here with screenshots of you sitting in $10,000 buy-in fantasy sports contests. *Rayofhope*. That is you, correct?"

"Yes . . . ?" Cory said.

"I'm here with my colleagues, four fellow FBI agents; we are here in the office. And we are interested — very interested! — in having a conversation with you. A conversation on record. Cory, I'm sure you've been following the news. And perhaps you are aware, we are investigating daily fantasy companies DraftKings and FanDuel. And we need your help."

There was a pause.

"Cory? Cory — I don't want to make you do this."

Cory was clear-headed enough to know that what Agent A—— was saying was that while he didn't want to make Cory do this, he *could* make him do it. The rest of the conversation was a blur. He would later only remember hanging up with a clear read on the conversation he'd just had. The FBI in Tampa, Florida, wanted him to come in as an informant and go before a grand jury. They wanted him to go under oath and help bring down the two daily fantasy companies.

But first, he had to go home. This whole week had felt like the longest trip he'd ever taken. In a daze, he boarded his flight, and settled into his seat. It was here, Cory would later say, that he let the moment get the best of him, when his fantasy life became a nightmare. Because now he was in front of those touch screens that let you order a drink, or as many drinks as you wanted, with three taps of your finger and a swipe of your credit card, a convenience that was dangerous if you were someone in Cory's state of mind. The thing was, he knew that the scenarios running through his head were all almost certainly overreactions, but recent events had proven that anything was possible in a world that no longer seemed rational. He'd already wondered what town in Mexico he was going to have to move to in order to keep playing daily fantasy games on offshore sites. Now he was wondering if he was going to get a call from FBI agents in California.

The first red wine seemed like a not terrible idea to take the edge off, but then, as his head spun with these dizzying thoughts, one became two and two became three, and after the fifth or sixth he began to realize he was getting strange looks from the other passengers on the plane. After the seventh or eighth, those strange looks dissolved into a thicker fog. When he stepped out into the gate, he stumbled around like a zombie into the overpowering lights of the airport. No one was there waiting for him, and the only thing he wanted to do was get back on a plane and disappear to somewhere far away.

9

CROWNING THE KING

Boston, Fall 2015–Early 2016

O nce upon a time, there was a man who crisscrossed the country in a powder-blue Chevy Bel Air with a trunk stuffed with milkshake mixers. The salesman had survived the Great Depression working an assortment of odd jobs — shuffling door-to-door peddling paper cups; making cut-rate real estate deals; playing the piano in makeshift bands in dingy lounges. He was in his early fifties, not rich, stuck in a rut, unsuccessfully selling multi-spindle mixers for an equipment manufacturer. One day a restaurant in San Bernardino, California, came calling, asking for a curiously large shipment. To learn why, the salesman traveled to the end of Route 66 to find a hamburger stand run by two brothers. It was a marvel of efficiency, with an assembly-line kitchen that dispensed menu items, cheaply and quickly, for a line of hungry customers snaking through a parking lot. Eventually, the salesman persuaded the brothers to franchise their operation — to let him run national outfits of their company; not long after, that door-to-door salesman was CEO of a chain of two thousand restaurants. "I was 52 years old. I had diabetes and incipient arthritis. I had lost my gall bladder and most of my thyroid gland in earlier campaigns," Ray Kroc, the founder of McDonald's, wrote in his autobiography, *Grinding It Out.* "But I was convinced that the best was ahead of me."

Origin stories in the business world have a way of becoming outsized legends. There's the legend of a hippie who, out of his parents' garage, conjured the idea of a personal computer. The tale of the Harvard nerd who began writing code in his dorm room and tinkered the notion of a boundless online social network into existence. The story of the college dropout who spent $800 on a private driver one night on New Year's Eve and came up with the idea of a shared car service. Jason Robins was drawn to all of those renowned genesis stories, but something in particular stuck with him when it came to the tale of the outsider who paved the way for fast food in America. Something about how a man who'd been told *no* at every turn, a man at the end of his rope, would never quit — something about a man who seemingly willed his way to his own success. "I've always wondered: What was going on in that guy's head?" Jason would ask.

The story of three coworkers hatching an idea for a fantasy sports game in the spare room of a town house: that was not a bad start to a story either. Because within only two years that operation would be a company valued at over $1 billion. But just as the story of Ray Kroc was no accidental folktale — before he could become CEO of McDonald's, the traveling salesman had to wrestle control of the company from those two brothers at the San Bernardino hamburger stand — the DraftKings story also had a much more complicated past with some unknown truths. One was that Jason Robins was not the CEO of the company at the start.

The truth was that the first CEO was Matt Kalish. It was Matt's idea from the beginning. It was Matt who one day was having dinner with one of his colleagues at Vistaprint with whom he occasionally played poker and talked sports and had beers.

"I'm miserable," Jason had said across the table from Matt. "I want to start something. And if I don't do it now, I don't think I ever will."

"Well, there's this idea I've had . . . " Matt replied.

It was Matt who was the hard-core gamer, the poker player who saw fantasy games as the next cash cow in the gaming space, Matt who looked at the other fantasy sites and said, "They're doing it wrong — we can do it better." It was Matt who attempted to lead the initial pitches in investor meetings, arguing how three coworkers from Boston who'd never run a business were going to overtake FanDuel and DraftStreet.

"None of us even made director in corporate America," he says. "We were very much midlevel guys at the company, and while we were delivering really, really well in our jobs, it was just the frustration of corporate America: it can feel like you're a little lost sometimes. We wanted to take ownership of something. Things that attracted us were things with a lot of white space. We were just trying to find the right idea. For a while Jason wanted to do this so bad: a fast-food chicken restaurant chain in Boston. I can't tell you how badly he wanted to do that. *Everything* was on the table."

Instead, they stepped into rooms pitching Matt's idea for a new fantasy sports game; the two of them would stand in front of prospective investors and Matt would introduce himself as the CEO and Jason as the chief operating officer. But as they faced more investors, Jason would dominate the pitches. "At that time I felt that I had emerged more as a leader in general in the group," Jason recalls. "To me, it felt natural." And so it became Jason who laid out the vision, Jason who told the story of how DraftKings was going to be a successful company — a story that, at the start, was one investors couldn't persuade themselves to get behind. After one rejection by a venture capitalist, Jason reached out to him just days after the pitch, wanting to know why. If there was nothing else that Jason had learned, it was this: investors bought into the founders, not the idea, and Jason wanted to know what it was about them, exactly, that could give others pause. There was a confused message in the room, the VC told Jason: Matt was the CEO, but Jason seemed to be the one steering the larger vision. "If you guys don't have the roles right now — it means, well, you don't know what the hell you're doing," the VC had said.

A few days later, in Paul's town house, Jason told Matt that they needed to make a change. Matt was caught off guard. What was he talking about? What kind of change?

Jason laid it all out there: if they were going to get any sort of real funding, there needed to be an official change in roles. He'd taken the

VC's words to mean one thing: it would be best for the company if he led it. He should be CEO.

To Matt, this was coming out of nowhere. "It just felt completely arbitrary," he later recalled. Jason, in that moment, explained to him that he'd spoken to others, and they'd agreed. Jason retrieved an email from an investor, saying that yes, maybe it did make sense for Jason to be the CEO. Then he got a consultant on the phone to tell Matt that Jason should be leading their company because of the way he led the presentations and set the vision. Hearing all of this, Matt walked out the door, and it was unclear if he would come back.

They were dead: Jason was sure of it. Because it was Matt's idea from the start, they were dead, and he would be left on the outside looking into this world that seemed as though it had been created for him, this world that had occupied its own strange corner but was on the verge of exploding into something much larger. Jason was convinced that he was going back to being a mid-level analyst answering to someone else — that this startup would just be the latest to crumble before it even took off because of early cofounder disagreements. But then something unexpected happened. Two days after walking out, Matt showed up at the town house. He was back in. There would be lasting distrust, not just from Matt but also from Paul, who would challenge Jason on strategy at every turn, and Jason in those first few months would feel a need to prove himself not only to prospective investors but also to his two cofounders. "Just because you're CEO doesn't mean shit to me," was a frequent way arguments between Paul and Jason would end.

Jason began to prove himself, in his own eyes, at least, by going out west in the fall of 2013 and coming back with four term sheets. He'd raised $24 million.

By the summer of 2015, the daily fantasy race was a dead heat, and the stakes of the race rose when, in July, FanDuel announced a Series E financing round of $275 million, from the private equity group KKR, at a $1.2 billion valuation. Two weeks later, DraftKings announced a $300 million round with a $1.2 billion valuation and a raft of investors, led by Twenty-First Century Fox. Just one year after Jason told Brian

Schwartz that DraftKings was going to become a billion-dollar company, DraftKings had become a billion-dollar company. With a hellfire marketing campaign, they had closed the gap in market share and were in a position in September 2015 to take the overall lead in the market. FanDuel's 65–35 lead was gone. "After week one of that season, people at FanDuel were saying, 'Please put in a good word with Jason,'" says one DraftKings employee. "'Do you think Jason will hire me?' They thought it was over. That DK had won and would just take them over. It was just astonishing."

The story that Jason Robins had been crafting was becoming reality. DraftKings' new downtown offices were a realization of his vision, an office that included many employees who had a door swing open in front of them, and found a miracle on the other side: a world that seemed to have been made for them. In the summer of 2015, their days thrummed with anticipation as they looked forward to the opening lines in the mornings, the happy hour in the afternoons, and, of course, the slate of games at night. Workers sat inside their offices, side by side, like seamstresses in a factory — with headphones on, bouncing on yoga balls in front of laptops, rising suddenly to dash off to a meeting with their open laptops on their palms, like waiters holding plates of food. In rooms enclosed in glass, they listened to others standing at whiteboards, blueprinting plans for an impossibly hopeful future. They had one eye on the dashboard on the wall; it flickered every few minutes, the changing numbers telling them how quickly pages were loading, how many users were logging on to the site, how many contestants were entering each tournament.

They arrived early to the office and stayed late. They played beer pong with their bosses, were comped sick seats at Fenway, spent weekends on Cape Cod, and were flown out to boondoggles at the Bellagio. "It's a room full of dudes," one investor of a rival company would later note, "who were like, *Holy shit, can you believe we do this for a living? This is a fucking dream come true — let's crush it!* Walking around, you felt the passion for what they did oozing off the walls."

In the early years they listened for the chime off their laptops that signaled the acquisition of each new user after a promotion promising "A Free Deposit" and "100 Free Dollars" popped up on RotoGrinders, or a personality like Matthew Berry dropped their name on a podcast. When one of their advertorials exploded, the computers chimed collectively because the deposits were coming in all at once and it was like they were in a room full of slot machines that had all hit the jackpot simultaneously. By 2014 they were adding thousands of users a day; then, by the next football season, in 2015, *tens* of thousands a day; and then *two hundred thousand* new users on just one NFL Sunday.

And then the storm hit.

Through the years, up until the moment of the *New York Times* story, Jason had read countless business books, some that even purported to offer advice to young entrepreneurs, to describe what the ups and downs of building a startup were like. But in his first three years of running DraftKings, Jason learned that anything that presented itself as a guide for a first-time entrepreneur was, to a CEO of a fantasy sports company, as useful as a guide through the Amazon for someone wandering the Sahara. Nothing, Jason suspected, could properly prepare one for running a company; like childbirth or pitching the ninth inning in front of forty thousand at Fenway, being a startup CEO was something you just had to experience yourself. But the events of the fall of 2015 were turning his experience into an even more extreme version of a typical founder's. The very same questions that raced through his head raced through Nigel Eccles's. How do you navigate through a media storm the size of the one beating down on them in the fall of 2015? How do you tell your family members that there is a possibility of the FBI knocking on the front door? You're a billion-dollar company one moment, a company whose very existence is threatened the next.

The weeks following the *Times* headline were harrowing, with Jason waking up for calls at six in the morning, standing in front of his employees taking questions for as many all-hands meetings as he could, trying to manage the feeling of paranoia rippling through the offices, particularly among the employees who were being named in news reports and the employees who wondered if they would be the next to get dragged into the stories. A handful of employees, told that they could no longer play daily fantasy games after the employee ban, walked away from their DraftKings jobs, which didn't always pay more than playing daily fantasy games. Some employees were shaken. "It was terrifying. You did wonder how this was going to spin out of control," said one employee who spent his nights in the aftermath of the *New York Times* scandal watching documentaries on the wrongfully accused.

Jason could only do so much, however, to clamp down on the paranoia that permeated the office, with all the conspiracy theories that were floated about by the media, by players, by employees, and even, in some cases, by DraftKings lawyers. In Concord, New Hampshire, for example, a group of media members and industry experts got together for a panel discussion at a University of New Hampshire law symposium, one of countless panel discussions taking place at renowned universities up and down the East Coast. Most of these discussions devolved into legal experts going around in circles asking a question: *Is daily fantasy skill-based or chance-based?* During the UNH panel discussion, a man named Paul Kelly — a former assistant US attorney for Massachusetts, counsel for the NHL Players' Association, introduced as "a DraftKings lawyer" — leaned into his microphone. Among Kelly's assertions was explicit confirmation of what had been suspected: that no fewer than three federal investigations were under way in Florida, New York, and Massachusetts. Subpoenas, he said, had already been issued in the Florida investigation. Kelly postulated that these grand jury investigations, kept heavily under wraps, were either focused on whether DraftKings and FanDuel executives violated any federal laws, or whether managers or employees engaged in fraud, racketeering, mail fraud, or money laundering. He also described the extent to which zealous investigators would go to find fault: they had the capacity, he noted, to infiltrate either company with people posing as employees and wearing wires to record conversations.* Among Kelly's remarks, according to a transcript, were the following:

---

* According to one panelist's account, Kelly "derangedly, albeit in the calmest and most normal of tones, meandered through a 30-minute complete gift of confes-

At any time, unannounced, the FBI could show up at DraftKings or FanDuel and literally take everything that's not nailed down —every piece of paper, every computer, every telephone, cell phone, everything they want, they do it all the time . . .

And you have no ability to refuse to testify . . . It's a very powerful tool, we used it very effectively, particularly in organized crime, getting mafia figures to testify, under threat of sending them to prison . . .

They have undercover operations. And this is a significant concern for those of us in daily fantasy sports. Have they put agents among the employee ranks of our companies? Do we have agents currently working within the company, gathering documents, gathering evidence, snooping around, talking to people? Probably they do . . .

They have electronic surveillance. They can tap telephones, they can tap cell phones, computers, paging devices. You name it, we can tap it. And they do . . .

They can pressure companies to waive their attorney-client privilege. DraftKings just did an elaborate internal investigation about some of the matters . . .

In short, when the federal government decides to dig in and investigate, it has a formidable arsenal of weapons at its disposal."

It was a bizarre moment during a winter that was getting more bizarre by the day. Meanwhile Jason and DraftKings weren't going to comment to anyone about the investigations; it was reasonable to think that once they'd survived the initial barrage of negative headlines, the worst would

---

sionary divulgence, detonating a series of small informational bombs in the process, a lobotomized knight slowly impaling himself on his sword." *Legal Sports Report* published a full transcript of Kelly's comments. In a statement to *LSR*, Kelly said that his "comments on March 17, 2016 were taken out of context and, as presented, do not accurately reflect reality."

be behind them — that in the end the damage was optics. Brand perception, which had taken an undeniable hit, was one thing, but the business itself was still strong; in fact, three weeks after the *Times* story, DraftKings saw the most entries in the company's history and an all-time-high entry fees total. Perhaps all this would pass quickly.

That hope vanished on November 10. That afternoon Jason was sitting in the office of a California state representative who had introduced a bill legalizing daily fantasy sports in the most populous state in the country. Despite all the negative headlines, the lawmaker was still serious about a law that clarified the legality of daily fantasy games. Jason was in his element as he connected with the representative, talking sports, telling the story of the founders, of the industry, of the rise of DraftKings, and explaining why this piece of legislation meant so much to the California constituents who played fantasy sports. Jason kept his composure, even as he knew that news was about to break that Eric Schneiderman was shutting down the daily fantasy operators in New York. Things were about to hit a new low point.

But Jason was not alone in the fight. For starters, seated next to him was a man who was ready to help Jason and the industry fight back: Jeremy Kudon, the fantasy sports industry's secret weapon.

Like everyone else who found themselves in this strange world of daily fantasy, Jeremy Kudon had arrived in it in a roundabout way. For the first decade of his legal career, Kudon was a litigator at a New York corporate law firm, where he specialized in mergers and acquisitions of billion-dollar companies. He left New York to work in Washington, DC, for a lobbyist, and in his first big case he represented two media companies, Dish Network and DirectTV, that were fighting discriminatory taxes that state legislators were passing at the behest of global telecommunications behemoths like Comcast Ventures. For Kudon — who grew up in the DC area and followed Beltway politics as passionately as his Redskins — brokering deals in back rooms on Capitol Hill and going toe-to-toe with lawmakers was exactly the kind of work that quickened his pulse.

Soon after he helped DirectTV beat Comcast Ventures, he got a call from a curious little startup that was in the business of disrupting the car service industry and just getting off the ground; they needed someone to start laying the groundwork on the legislative side. Kudon was ready to get to work for this company, called Uber, but a conflict of interest forced him to turn down the job. He looked on as Uber became *the* case study in how a disruptive startup navigates the regulatory world — by toppling mighty incumbents outside the reach of regulators, while rattling a cage of concern around taxation, licensing, consumer protection, and a host of other issues. "I don't get depressed," says Kudon, a force of nature who, with an undersized frame, a youthful face, and a high-pitched voice that runs at 100 miles per hour, calls to mind Jimmy Neutron and the Energizer Bunny, "but I got depressed after that. Lawyers *die for this*. You want the chance to test yourself on something *big*."

Kudon couldn't know then that his next case would be one with even bigger headlines than the Uber case and would present a legal battlefield loaded with just as many mines and explosions. Kudon had received a call from a friend saying that he had a venture client who was interested in investing in a daily fantasy sports company. They wanted to move into the space quickly. A sports nut who'd been a serious season-long fantasy player since his college days at Miami of Ohio — he was still bitter about the season decades ago when he was saddled, because of arcane league rules, with an injured Darryl Strawberry on the roster of *two* of his teams — Kudon was intrigued. He didn't, however, know the first thing about what fantasy sports of the *daily* variety entailed. He was driving in his car, listening to sports talk radio, when a man's voice came over his car speakers: *"One-day games so you're not locked in. It's like a new season every time you play. And best of all: you can win a shipload of money on DraftKings!"*

This sounds like gambling! Kudon thought to himself, understanding immediately why an investor wouldn't want to touch the space. Before he could even say yes or no to working with his venture client, his phone rang again. *Never mind,* his friend said. *These venture guys asked around and want nothing to do with this space. It's gambling!*

Kudon wasn't so sure that was true — in the legal sense, that is. For starters, after he tried playing the games, he thought there was a simple reason why they *could* be deemed games of skill: If they were purely games of chance, he would win a fair share of times. Instead, every time he played he lost, consistently, to others. He tapped out an email to the CEO of the leading company in the industry, cold-pitching the idea that someone needed to lead the inevitable legal battle to come. A fight in that battle would be won or lost in statehouses across the country.

To his surprise, the CEO quickly responded.

Great timing. We have a problem. We need you to help us kill a bill in Washington State, Nigel Eccles replied.

And so, like a nor'easter blowing in from the east, Kudon, after responding to Nigel's email, arrived in Spokane, Washington, eager to help. He met with legislators and furiously explained to them why their bill was unfair, why these games were games of skill and not illegal gambling operations, and why a movement to crush these operations was simply screwing their constituents who played fantasy sports — and there were many more than they imagined. "Under fire, Jeremy is like a mad genius," says one lobbyist who saw Kudon in action. "He's not super-organized, to put it nicely, but you get into these hearings and it's like, *boom,* he's putting all the issues together in a brilliant presentation, and it's like, *Where did this come from?* He's like the guy in college who was out all night, doesn't seem to have it together, and he shows up to the test and aces it." The bill in Washington was killed before it reached a vote. Kudon was hired.

Kudon would join FanDuel chief legal officer Christian Genetski in the regulatory effort. Later, he would meet with Jason Robins, and began finding lobbyists in states where there were bills defining the legality of daily fantasy games. Despite all the thorny legal issues surrounding their unregulated, untaxed operation, the regulatory piece had clearly not been a high priority for the two top daily fantasy companies: their combined initial budget at that time for regulation-related services was less than $500,000 — for Kudon, the Fantasy Sports Trade Association, and all the lobbyists. Given that the two companies had sneezed out $50 million worth of advertising during the last NFL season, the laughably small figure exposed just how serious the companies were about regulating their industry. That is to say, not serious at all. Kudon's challenges were considerable. He represented the entire industry but also found himself in the middle of all the squabbles between DraftKings and FanDuel. "I'm the guy between two warring couples," he says.

Soon after Nigel Eccles, then an FSTA board member, threatened to kick Jason Robins and DraftKings out of the FSTA for insisting on providing NASCAR and golf games, despite their questionable legality, Kudon's job in the early part of 2015 was to simply keep them together in the FSTA. He helped create Fantasy Sports For All, a grassroots umbrella organization formed just in case there was a divorce and the companies' collective lobbying efforts needed to continue.

Kudon was also dealing with lawmakers who struggled to understand fantasy sports, let alone the daily variety, and who also didn't understand why this topic was worth caring about. That began to change when the great ad war erupted into hundreds of millions of dollars of spending during the summer and early fall of 2015, shining a light on two companies that were raising gobs of money at a breakneck speed. Outside interests were suddenly taking notice, and there were signs that the companies were going to run into some opposition. Kudon began to sense trouble when the MGM Grand and Wynn casinos in Las Vegas came out with aggressive statements against daily fantasy — not coincidentally, around the time that signs for DraftKings began appearing all over Las Vegas.

In 2015, Kudon went to Vegas for the Global Gaming Expo, a conference that attracted thousands of heavyweights in the gaming industry from across the world. Walking around the convention with other executives from the daily fantasy sports industry "was like Travis Kalanick walking into a taxi convention," Kudon says, referring to Uber's lightning-rod CEO. "You could feel the hatred. You got a sense that the ads that were ramping up were like a big middle finger to these guys." A big middle finger that might be interpreted as: *Here we are, gambling companies that circumvented the regulatory process, and we're going to take your business!*

When the billion-dollar valuations were beginning to make headlines in 2015, there was talk of IPOs on the horizon. FanDuel was just getting the ball rolling with the process, interviewing banks, eyeing an IPO as early as the first quarter of 2017. With that possibility on the horizon, investors began to tell their executives: *Don't get caught up in this like Uber did: regulatory is your number-one priority.* That $400,000 budget, in a matter of months, had become over $7 million. The increase had come too late. Because soon came the *Times* story, followed three days later by an announcement from the attorney general in Nevada. After a long day at the office, Kudon was on his way home to help his young daughter with her science project, and just as he emerged from the subway, he saw the news alert: citing a study that had deemed daily fantasy to be gambling, the Nevada attorney general's office was shutting down FanDuel and DraftKings in his state. "That," Kudon says of the Nevada decision, "was an absolute low point. It hit hard. We didn't see it coming."

Just a few weeks later, another low point came as Kudon sat with Jason in the California representative's office. Kudon did his best not to glance at his phone as Jason spoke. But after one alert, he couldn't help it. When he caught Jason's eye, he flashed him a look. Jason knew. They had both been tipped off earlier in the morning that Eric Schneiderman was considering shutting down DraftKings and FanDuel in the state of New York, and Kudon's look was confirmation. The news was devastating: the shutdown would wipe out nearly 10 percent of the DraftKings user base. The insider trading allegations were going nowhere, but the issues the daily fantasy operators faced kept changing and expanding, and now there *were* direct threats to the business: attorneys general in states across the country who were going to shut down these companies that had been deemed illegal gambling operations.

As Jason Robins walked out of the lawmaker's office, Kudon at his side, he now sensed that a real existential crisis was looming. A new battle was upon him, one in which he would have new enemies — and new allies.

10

THE CIRCUS

Dallas, Spring–Fall 2016

The billionaire in the fitted hoodie and white sneakers, clutching a bottle of water as if on his way to a morning workout, arrives at the podium to a blast of applause. Mark Cuban looks out into a crowded hotel ballroom, at the rows of men dressed in the muted colors of business casual, sitting at long tables that extend wall to wall, and says:

"Now you know what the war is."

The Fantasy Sports Trade Association conference is an event held in hotels and conference centers across the country, bringing together those who make a living, or seek to make a living, from fantasy sports. In attendance is every industry big cheese and every wannabe entrepreneur from a basement operation looking for an investor. The vast majority of them are white guys, in pressed khakis and tucked-in polos emblazoned with the logos of various fly-by-night startups, each of them wearing a laminated name tag, all of them massed within a confined carpeted space where small packs huddle in booths talking loudly, trading favors, and swapping business cards and start-'em-sit-'em strategies. They have always been a unique breed, the type whose pulse quickens to the panel discussions with titles like "Comparing the Profiles of the Season-Long Player and the Daily Player" and "Climbing the Hill: An Update to the Legislative and Regulatory Process." These events have a comforting familiarity to them, from the old faces to the impossibly ugly free T-shirts, but the vibe of this year's conference, in Dallas, is different. "Together Toward Tomorrow" is the theme — a motto for a band of brothers digging into the trenches, rather than an industry hurtling toward a shiny future.

Earlier in the morning the breakfast buffet had been abuzz over the latest doomsday headline: news was trickling in that the Texas attorney general was shutting down daily fantasy games in the state, the very state where anyone who is anyone has convened for what is supposed to be a commemoration of the industry's achievements. For industry members — particularly the professional players who have planned on having some action on games during the convention — it is an unfortunately timed development. For the Texas AG who is the subject of a developing story regarding securities fraud, the timing of the splashy headlines in local newspapers and on websites that morning — "Fantasy Sports Convention Gets Cold Welcome in Texas" — is perhaps an impeccably timed diversion.

The latest news makes things all the more awkward for the famous keynote speaker; suddenly Mark Cuban finds himself, unexpectedly, stepping onto a battlefield. The face of the Dallas Mavericks is known as the antiestablishment NBA team owner, but to many within the industry he in fact has long been aligned with the establishment, the teams and the leagues that want nothing to do with fantasy sports. His presence at the 2016 conference — a commitment locked in many months before the fall of 2015 — was to signal a tipping point.* Mark Cuban at the conference should have been the latest proud moment commemorating the arrival of the industry in mainstream sports. But more than anything else,

---

* "A few years earlier, I'd run into Cuban at a conference, and he couldn't have been more dismissive of fantasy sports," says one VC. "We started talking, and I told him I was interested in some kind of social gaming infrastructure. 'I'm not interested in fantasy sports,' was the reply. 'I'm just not interested in that industry.' Even with his perception of the market, as a team owner, he didn't want to hear the pitch. A few years later, he was the FSTA keynote speaker." And also an investor in a daily fantasy site, FantasyLabs.com.

Cuban, at the podium, is playing the role of a general rallying the troops — his troops. Now he is on their side of the fight. He is bullish: "There's a whole lot of upside for the industry; this is a stepping-stone we'll have to step across, and it's going to make a foundation that will make things much, much stronger," he says. Then he cuts to the chase: "There's going to have to be some regulation, this will lead to specific rules that you'll have to follow," he says. "This will lead to some taxes. Why? Because everything gets taxed. And that is the endgame."

It isn't exactly Churchill at the House of Commons, but to convention regulars this is still a moment — to the old-timers most of all. Like Peter Schoenke, who stood offstage as Cuban spoke; Schoenke, the FSTA chairman, was attending these events back in the days when the convention was a gathering of a few dozen guys meeting up on a break during a card-trading conference at the O'Hare Airport hotel in Chicago. Over recent years, the FSTA old-timers like Schoenke looked on in astonishment at the money being showered upon daily fantasy. The theme of the previous year's conference: "A tsunami is coming."

But when the industry veterans were asked about the daily fantasy war erupting between the two companies, some liked to tell a cautionary tale. The tale was about an industry that boomed many decades before daily fantasy existed: the baseball card industry. Baseball cards were such a profitable business in the 1970s and 1980s that cards were hailed as an alternative to stocks for potential investors. By the late 1980s, sales had risen to $1 billion a year. The industry responded by kicking production into high gear, with a number of new companies, smelling a fortune, entering the space and, in a race to win the space, saturating the market: one company alone sold *four billion* cards within a few years. By the mid-1990s, however, the industry was one-seventh the size of what it had been in its heyday, owing in large part to the companies' inability to cooperate for the good of the industry. To the longtime industry members, it wasn't a perfect analogy to what was going on in the fantasy sports business, but it showed how greed could dwarf the need for companies to spend efficiently on all fronts and focus on sustainable growth.

The tsunami that did arrive in 2015 was different from what the old-timers like Peter Schoenke expected — they certainly didn't expect one that threatened to wipe out their own industry.

Long before Nigel Eccles and Jason Robins stumbled onto this new fantasy game, countless wannabe entrepreneurs were already attempting to make a fortune out of fantasy sports. The movement began to take on a life of its own in the late 1990s, when the internet boom gave rise to a group of individuals who believed that huge sums of money were to be made from ushering fantasy games into the internet age. The vast majority of those prospectors quickly arrived at the land grab to make their fortune and just as quickly left, dejected, empty-handed, and a bit poorer. A select few, though, managed to strike gold. Peter Schoenke was one of them.

Schoenke had a permanently cheerful mien to match his boyish looks; his floppy brown hair always looked as if it had gotten a good brush by his mother before he left the house. In fantasy games he seemed to have found a kind of fountain of youth. Even in this room of fantasy geeks at the FSTA conference, he was a geek of the highest order: growing up in a suburb of Minneapolis, he recorded by hand all the stats for his neighborhood Wiffle ball games in a notebook — a ritual he continued into his early twenties, when he began juggling dozens of Rotisserie baseball leagues. Schoenke was a journalism major at Northwestern in the early 1990s; after graduating, he moved to New York to cover financial news on Wall Street. As he covered the financial world from the New York Stock Exchange trading floor, Schoenke was struck by the power of a new computer software system that was revolutionizing the way stocks were traded. The Bloomberg Terminal enabled traders to access a service through which they could monitor real-time market data and even make trades, but it had many other uses as well. What Schoenke was fascinated by was the news arm of the service — traders no longer had to wait for industry journals for the latest news on IPOs but could instead receive the information immediately. The terminal also did something that few other services did at the time: it aggregated news updates from a multitude of websites and wires. In a volatile market, that real-time news was becoming essential to gaining an edge.

Schoenke being Schoenke, his mind wandered to a peculiar idea: what if fantasy sports players had access to a service like this? This was the early 1990s, when longtime players like Lex Nerenberg still used legal pads and fax machines to manage their leagues and players scoured the tiny print on the "Transactions" page in the sports section of a newspaper to find out about injuries or demotions that had happened days earlier. When a group of his friends from Northwestern decided to start an internet site, Schoenke quit his job and joined them, with the idea that he could begin learning the web tools he'd need to build a new kind of service: a Bloomberg Terminal for fantasy fans. Within months Schoenke developed a commissioner service — a site where people could create a league and then return through the course of a season to track updates on the league — and soon after he developed a simple way to organize the news of the internet in a manner tailored to fantasy players.

With RotoWire, users had a place to go for the latest information every time a player was injured, dealt, or benched or there was a development that impacted his value in fantasy terms. The days of fantasy players destroying their team's chances by, say, starting a running back who, unbeknownst to them, had suffered an unfortunate case of food poisoning and was a last-minute scratch were over. Within two years RotoWire was being run out of an office a few blocks from Wrigley Field in Chicago by a staff of three and, remarkably, had become one of the ten most trafficked sports sites on the web — ranking higher than even the National Football League's official website, NFL.com. The concept was new and would be replicated by every major sports outlet within a few years, but it originated with Schoenke's site. The miracle of his creation wasn't that people came to the site; the miracle was that after Schoenke, confident in the quality of his service, began charging a monthly fee for it, people happily paid, just as traders happily paid for the Bloomberg Terminal. If it was going to end up winning a player back his money — or at least giving him some bragging rights — well, the investment was worth it. The company had defied the odds: you could, it turned out, make a little fortune off fantasy sports even if you weren't one of those media behemoths. In 1999, Schoenke sold RotoWire for a healthy sum.

Around this time the concept of games with shorter duration than season-long was already being kicked around inside offices — even inside the offices of RotoWire — but anyone hoping to monetize a daily game quickly realized that the undertaking was futile. There were salary-cap games in the late 1990s in which contestants drafted players who were assigned salaries, but the process of running a daily version of those games was riddled with challenges. For starters, getting money from customers in a time before payment processors like PayPal was nearly impossible. And the games themselves were horribly flawed. One company held a contest: a million dollars would go to the users who picked the best-performing NFL players that week in the Sunday slate of games. It sounded like a great game — until users discovered that since player performances fluctuated wildly, they could find better odds if they walked down to their local bodega for some lottery tickets rather than trying to pick the very best players on any given Sunday. As more sites offered massive prize pools, people saw the money the companies were giving away and began thinking, *This must be a way to make money*. Only it was a terrible way to make money. In 2007, a company called OneSeason.com, which offered paid contests that ran like season-long stock market games, raised $3.5 million from investors, a figure that sent shock waves across the industry. It felt like a watershed moment. But within a few years, that company had folded too.

There was another reason why this was risky business: the lack of legal clarity. There had always existed an uneasy tension between players' unions, which collectively owned the rights to players' names, and the fantasy operators, stemming from the leagues' unwillingness to regard fantasy games as anything more than shady operations. Talking about fantasy sports in the early days was akin to talking sports gambling, which was illegal in every state outside of Nevada. In 1989, after Kansas City Royals star third baseman George Brett appeared in a game in left field, he quipped to reporters, "Oh, that's for all the Rotisserie league guys," referring to his new position eligibility in the outfield, which allowed fantasy players to put the All-Star hitter in the outfield in their lineups for the rest of the season. Soon after, Brett received a call from the league office and was roundly chastised for merely mentioning fantasy sports. Major League Baseball, which was still emerging from the rubble of the Pete Rose betting scandal — a black mark on the sport in which one of the game's biggest stars was banned from baseball amid allegations that he wagered on baseball games while he played for and managed the Cincinnati Reds — reacted as if Brett were giving a wink to a criminal underworld.

"The reaction was like he was talking about drug dealers," recalls Schoenke. As late as the early 2000s, media companies, including ESPN, wanted nothing to do with the industry, even though it was apparent to anyone who'd ever played fantasy games that the invention was changing how fans consumed sports. No longer were the majority of viewers watching games merely to see how their home team was performing; fans had more at stake. Every FSTA conference in the 2000s invited a representative from ESPN, whose purpose there seemed to be to take a tongue-lashing from industry folk wondering why ESPN or another network would go to such great lengths to avoid talking about player performances in the fantasy context. "Who else is watching highlights of a lousy Royals-Tigers game in August but fantasy sports geeks who want to see how their players did?" they would cry.

The evidence became irrefutable. In 2002 the NFL conducted an official survey that found that fantasy sports consumers were like über-consumers of its product — they watched more games (the average fan watched some 4.0 games a month, while fantasy players averaged 8.4) and went to more games. The lightbulb finally went on in the executive offices. A commercial aired in 2003 in which Rams quarterback Kurt Warner sings the virtues of fantasy sports, and industry insiders viewed it as a seminal moment — the long-awaited acknowledgment by the league that fantasy sports players did in fact exist and perhaps weren't as corrupt as drug dealers. Individual player performance stats began appearing in the ticker with scores from other games during live broadcasts, a clear nod to the fantasy player on his couch who only had whatever game was on TV that afternoon as his way to follow his team. Who else but he and his ilk needed to know immediately that Kurt Warner's third receiver, Ricky Proehl, had two catches for twenty-three yards?

And yet, even as fantasy coverage became more mainstream, for Peter Schoenke at RotoWire, and for any other operator in the industry, it was always unclear if they owed the actual professional players money by profiting from the use of their names. If they wanted to use player names for marketing or an ad, they clearly had to pay the players' unions for the rights to the names. For fantasy games, however, it was less clear. For roughly a decade, between the mid-1990s and mid-2000s, the big media companies paid players' unions vast sums of money for the rights to use players' names — which is why, for much of the 2000s, there was no way for a startup to raise hundreds of millions of dollars: with the threat of unions suing you or denying you the rights to use player names, no one would invest in a company that would be required to pay a huge fee or be denied a license. In 2006, Major League Baseball purchased all the name rights from the Major League Baseball Players Association, effectively saying that it was going to own this fantasy baseball thing and no one else could have a piece of it. Taking away the player names from an operator like RotoWire was like taking away the beef from a hamburger stand. Suddenly Schoenke and much of the rest of the fantasy industry faced an existential threat — there was a good chance that the other leagues would follow suit. But shortly after MLB's deal, a man named Charlie Wiegert, one of the founders of one of the country's most popular fantasy sites, CDM Fantasy Sports, sued Major League Baseball; after a two-year legal battle, Wiegert and the industry won.

One cloud was gone, but one still remained: the issue of whether fantasy sports was gambling. Peter Schoenke had faced this perception issue from his early days at RotoWire. When he was attempting to start the company, he tried to hire an accountant in the Chicago area to manage its finances. "No, I can't do this," was the reply he got. "This is gambling — and I can't do gambling!" Poker sites constantly knocked at Schoenke's door looking for partnership opportunities, and Schoenke turned them all down, not wanting to be associated with anything gambling-related. He knew there was always a chance that he and the others in the industry would be viewed as aiding and abetting illegal gambling, and he always thought that the issue would come to a head. Through the years, Schoenke would read a story every so often about some guy who was fired because he was part of a fantasy football pool in his office, and he would think, *Oh, no. Here we go. Here comes the storm.* Four employees at a Texas investment firm were fired for playing fantasy football. Eleven cops showing up at the door of a fifty-eight-year-old schoolteacher, who was hit with felony counts and jail time because he ran an $837,000 office pool. The reason other games had been permitted to exist — why they could exist under the radar, unlike, say, online poker — was simple: at the end of the day the money in fantasy sports was peanuts, certainly not worth the attention of the feds.

All along, Peter Schoenke and others also knew the reason why the scaffolding that supported fantasy sports was shaky and thin: the language that gave rise to daily fantasy in the Unlawful Internet Gambling Enforcement Act wasn't actually in the legislation regarding gambling at all; instead, in the final hours of a congressional session, without a vote, it was tacked onto a bill that had nothing to do with gambling. After the passage of the UIGEA in 2006, operators no longer had to work in the shadows, and overnight the industry turned into the Wild Wild West, with fly-by-night websites experimenting with different models: salary-cap games, snake drafts, and daily games, offered at sites like Fan-Duel and DraftStreet and every other fledgling site on Tom Griffiths's spreadsheet. Players, curious about this new kind of game, visited sites, punched in their credit card information to deposit 40 bucks, lost a chunk of that on a few losing lineups, and then tried to get their remaining $20 back but couldn't when they attempted to cash out. On some sites, you had owners of the websites challenging their own customers. No one caused an uproar because it was a $20 loss here and $20 loss there. At the end of the day, daily fantasy games still occupied a small corner of the fantasy sports space — a novelty side game that, even as late as 2013, Schoenke viewed as simply the latest fantasy variation to come and go.

Schoenke shared the opinion of just about everyone else in the industry: daily games would have trouble passing legal muster if the time ever came that someone bothered to ask questions about their legality, but given the industry's size, that time might never come, even if it was blatantly clear that daily fantasy was created by opportunists who looked up the law, saw a loophole, and said, *Well, we can engineer this like poker.* When the founders of a daily fantasy startup approached NBC Sports with a marketing deal, the consensus among industry insiders was that the concept was great but it was never going to happen because it smelled too much like online poker — too much like gambling — for a large company like NBC to get involved. Schoenke assumed that the NBC lawyers wouldn't sign off on it. They did. The legal basis for the decision was that fantasy was specifically separated from sports betting by the UIGEA, and so the foundation existed for all the daily fantasy companies over the years to latch onto the exemption in question, through future scandals and controversies, as if it were a buoy in a swirling ocean, and everyone had lashed themselves to it in hopes that it would float them to dry land. The law was repeatedly cited by proponents for its "exemption" or its "safe harbor" for daily fantasy, but in truth, daily fantasy games were not explicitly named in the bill — they could not have been since, in 2006, daily fantasy existed only as a half-baked idea in the minds of people like Mark Nerenberg.

Gambling in the United States had always been a big turf war among billionaires, as Art Manteris, one of the most prominent bookmakers in Vegas, had seen decades earlier. In this turf war among the casinos and the Indian gaming industry and the racetracks and the politicians looking to get their piece of the pie, any shiny new thing that threatened to cut into their turf was a threat that had to be addressed. Fantasy sports presented no such threat, or opportunity, for a simple reason: the money just wasn't big enough.

Things began to shift in early 2015. Schoenke got a call from the office of Sheldon Adelson, the casino magnate billionaire from Vegas. "We're not against you, *yet*," Schoenke was told by one of Adelson's lackeys. Schoenke began to suspect the money was getting big enough. In January of 2015, a bill had been proposed in the Washington statehouse that was trouble for the daily fantasy companies. At the time Schoenke's goal had been merely to keep the status quo in terms of the legality of fantasy sports across the country. He had arrived in Washington State to meet in person someone he'd been talking to on legislation to pass a fantasy sports bill. "In the middle of the hearing, the legislator got up and said, 'I support fantasy games, yes,'" Schoenke says. "But then he continues: 'But — not daily fantasy sports.' We were getting stabbed in the back by one of the sponsors. I'm like, *Oh my God, what have I done?*"

Soon Jeremy Kudon and Schoenke, along with FanDuel chief legal officer Christian Genetski and the hired lobbyists in each state, would become part of a traveling band that met with legislators, readying themselves to fight for the legality of their games across different jurisdictions with widely different gambling statutes, one state capitol a time.

In late 2015, after the bottom fell out of the industry, it was becoming abundantly clear that UIGEA, that gift from the heavens for the FSTA and everyone else in the industry for nearly a decade, would no longer serve as a buoy: the way for the industry to get safely back to land would have to be a fifty-state approach to legislative lobbying. Instead of taking a federal, industrywide approach, it would be a long, hard road, and nothing was going to change overnight. There was no magic bullet, no new federal law in the works that would save them. The timetable they put on that process was two or three years, maybe more, before the majority of states would legalize daily fantasy games.

In Manhattan, on the morning of Nov. 25, at the New York Supreme Court, the public relations war began during a public examination. The line outside the courthouse snaked around the block. The companies rolled out high-priced lawyers for arguments: David Boies stood in front of the judge on behalf of DraftKings and began to frame the argument.

"Anyone who has ever played a daily fantasy sports contest knows that this is a contest of skill," Boies intoned.

In Albany, New York, in December, Schoenke and Kudon sat together in a New York chamber, taking questions during a hearing that lasted six hours. "It was the longest anyone remembered in ten years," says Kudon. "Prison reform apparently only lasted ninety minutes." One lawmaker said to Schoenke, after Schoenke had answered a question, "I've got twenty more questions for you." After Schoenke laughed out loud, thinking it was a joke, he proceeded to be asked twenty more questions.

In Springfield, Illinois, Schoenke sat in front of a legislator who compared daily fantasy to heroin. In Saint Paul, Minnesota, a state senator said that daily fantasy was as despicable as prostitution. In *four* different states, on one January afternoon, there were four different hearings on the legality of daily fantasy sports.

When the tsunami arrived, it landed with even more ferocity than Peter Schoenke could ever have imagined. The storm predicted for decades by Schoenke and the other longtime members of the FSTA — the nerds who had been in the industry longer than anyone else — was here, and they were utterly unprepared for it. Schoenke lived in a quiet neighborhood in the suburbs of Chicago; every night, after returning from his RotoWire offices in Chicago, he and his wife watched the evening news together while cooking dinner. Schoenke did not grasp the tsunami's reach until Lester Holt began talking about daily fantasy as a billion-dollar con. Schoenke's phone lit up; media requests for interviews were nonstop. Things had gotten truly bizarre when he started getting attacked on Twitter, from dubious accounts, for his defense of the companies and their operations; these attacks, he believed, came from accounts with roots in the casino industry, a sector that had always viewed daily fantasy as a competitor to their trade. The moment before the scandal, he was the leader of the all-fun-and-games Fantasy Sports Trade Association, and overnight he had become the head of the unregulated gambling society that preyed on youth.

Schoenke was on a golf course with three other FSTA executives for their weekly round when a phone rang. All of them were about to learn that the US attorney for the Middle District of Florida was convening a federal grand jury to examine whether the two biggest daily fantasy operators had violated the Illegal Gambling Business Act of 1970 as well as Florida law. They were about to learn that it was one of three federal investigations into the companies to open up in the fall of 2015, with Boston-area and New York–area federal probes joining soon after. They were all about to learn that the FSTA executives were being subpoenaed.

As he stood on the golf course, Schoenke was speechless. Because now the scenarios were endless. He asked himself, *Are they going to raid the offices tomorrow? Are we all going to walk into the office and be put in handcuffs, because all these years I've been enabling illegal gambling?*

Can I tell my wife anything?

Where does the conspiracy end?

Then, on May 11, 2016, Schoenke found himself in Rayburn House Office 2123, testifying in a congressional hearing before the House Energy and Commerce Committee on behalf of the companies. Schoenke, in a quiet moment before the hearing began, looked around the ornate gallery and asked himself: *How did I end up here?* Schoenke was there to represent FanDuel and DraftKings, and after giving his earnest testimony he spent most of the day listening to the lawmakers on the podium prove how clueless they were about the issue. At one point, a representative from Oklahoma asked the panel of witnesses if there was a regulatory body for the industry, apparently unaware that the lack of a regulatory body for the industry was the main reason why the hearing had been scheduled in the first place.

Elsewhere along the podium, one congressman was particularly prepared for his moment. "Both companies maintain that daily fantasy sports is not gambling," New Jersey representative Frank Pallone Jr., the ranking Democrat on the committee, began, practically shouting at Schoenke. "So what is DraftKings' rationale for getting a gambling license in the UK if they say that daily fantasy sports is not gambling? And what about FanDuel's?"

That Pallone would be the rep to go after the companies was not surprising. He was, after all, the one who had called for the hearings eight months earlier, having seen the barrage of ads. A month later the *New York Times* story broke, and they rescheduled the hearing. Now here was a moment that clarified where Pallone's interests lay, and perhaps the interests of some others in that room: not in daily fantasy but in something else entirely. This might be a prime opportunity for Pallone, who happened to be a staunch supporter of the legalization of sports wagering in his state, to walk into a crowded House chamber with the cameras on and turn the argument against daily fantasy into an argument *for* something else.

"In New Jersey, voters approved a two-to-one referendum in 2011 to allow sports betting at casinos and racetracks," Pallone said. "In response, every major professional sports league joined together and sued the state to stop the plan's implementation and stifle the will of the voters. How can the professional sports leagues oppose sports betting at casinos and racetracks but support and prosper from the betting that is taking place every day in daily fantasy sports?"

In the end one simple question cut through all the months of headlines and conspiracy theories and gesturing, one question that cut to the core of the intentions of those who truly had something at stake in the fantasy sports war that was about to become something bigger.

If this fantasy sports game was going to be allowed across the country, then why not sports wagering, and why not all over the United States?

11

THE MOST MISERABLE MAN
AT THE SUPER BOWL

San Francisco, Winter–Spring 2016

One afternoon, Nigel had an idea: to list, on paper, all the ways they could die.

He sat down and began:

- California AG next to come out negative

Then he continued:

- Payment processors pull plug
- Criminal — NY AG
- Boston FBI investigation
- Tampa FBI investigation
- Class action suit
- Pro leagues pull support
- IRS defines player winnings as gross revenue, not net
- Pulled from Apple app store
- Run out of cash

There, he stopped.

Nigel was not a self-help kind of guy, but he had been persuaded by acquaintances to try a popular meditation app; after a handful of sessions, however, his conclusion was that even a year in the Himalayas wasn't likely to give him balance in his life, let alone ten minutes in a dark closet with his earbuds in. He went on long runs, seeking to clear his head, but during his jogs through Edinburgh's Stockbridge neighborhood, when he reached the stretch of houses called "the colonies" — small two-bedroom houses, built in the 1880s as affordable housing for working-class families and struggling artisans — the man who months earlier was celebrated as the CEO of a unicorn and hailed as "Northern Ireland's Newest Billionaire" by one UK newspaper now found himself looking at the small row houses and thinking: *When we go broke, this would be a very fine place to live.*

The exercise of listing all the ways they could die was his latest attempt to regain a semblance of control over his life. The list he was now staring at was not having the intended effect.

Through all these last harrowing months for the daily fantasy sports industry, Nigel was among the ones who hadn't cracked. After the *New York Times* headline, he'd found those weeks last fall — with the hands-ons with fearful employees, the crisis strategy planning with the executive team, the meetings with investors wondering why they shouldn't kill their million-dollar partnerships — strangely energizing. He was, for starters, as focused as ever. Back when Nigel was a teenager in the army cadets in Northern Ireland, his troop had conducted a casualty simulation: a casualty, dressed in rags, would stumble straight to him, and he would, out of instinct, approach the casualty, calmly walk him to a bed, and patch him up with bandages. His captain would later tell him that to do so was a mistake; with his attention focused on this one casualty, others in his brigade, he was told, had died. Nigel thought of that simulation during those weeks in the fall of 2015 during the crisis: "What I realized is, one of the things that was going to kill us is that everyone was going to focus on the crisis — and people forget that they have a day job, we've got customers to serve, we've got products to develop, we've got a marketing plan. You can't just focus on the crisis in front of you."

A sense of purpose, a survival instinct, kicked in. He believed that no one in his company had done anything wrong or broken any law, but he also understood that while there had been no engagement from the FBI, there was no reason to hope that the crisis would just fade away; investigations like these had no finite end and were fishing expeditions that could lead in any direction. Nigel also had no idea what skeletons might be in the closets of rival fantasy sports companies; FanDuel's fate, however, was inextricably tied together with theirs. Within FanDuel's halls, he kept a calm face, a picture of cool rectitude. In the first all-hands meeting in the days after the *New York Times* story, Nigel stood in front of the company and took a moment to welcome a wave of new hires who were joining FanDuel as part of a massive expansion that had been set in motion before the company was under fire. "Well, I hope you like running into burning buildings," he quipped. The night before the New York State Supreme Court hearing over the request by Eric Schneiderman for an injunction to shut down FanDuel and DraftKings in New York, Nigel called up FanDuel's general counsel, Christian Genetski, who had spent a miserable, sleepless week preparing arguments for the hearing. "You know, I was just thinking," Nigel said. "I want you to know that I'm totally comfortable with whatever the outcome is. We believe in what we think is right, and we still believe it. We'll make our best arguments, but if it turns out we're wrong, we'll fold it down. I'm at peace with that. You should be too."

Christian was struck by Nigel's calm and thought, *He's the one with the family, the one who's spent the last six years of his life building this thing . . . but he's telling me to be calm!*

But now it was February, and the *drip drip drip* of states shutting down the company through a bitter winter — the count of attorneys general who had deemed them illegal gambling operations was now at seven — was wearing Nigel down. One night he lay in bed and experienced a vision. They had just moved to their sparkling new office in Manhattan's Flatiron neighborhood, a sprawling two-floor space that would accommodate the expansion that the company had experienced over the last six months and that, they once believed, they would see over the next six. In his dream, he was almost floating as he moved toward the center of a sparkling office atrium, to the railing at the top of an open space that was as tall as a cathedral, a perch from which he looked down at a grand, glittery space as vast as an ocean. Every wall was made of glass, every corner illuminated brightly by chandeliers. Looking down, he saw everyone's faces, all of them gazing up and staring at his, everything hushed in silence. He stepped up to a railing, knowing that they were all waiting for him to speak.

"We've gone bust," he said. "It's over. It's all over."

Nigel woke up. It wasn't over. They hadn't gone bust. Worse: they were stuck in purgatory.

"Can you believe we're . . . *here?*" Tom said to Nigel, as he took in the scene around him. They were squeezing through the crowd in a pedestrian arcade, closed-off street blocks where banners hung from the streetlamps, bright LED screens flashed and blinked all around them, mascots in larger-than-life costumes sashayed among the mass of fans decked out in sports jerseys in an assortment of radioactive colors, and music blared from the soundstage at the other end of the block. Tom turned to the sadsack bloke next to him, the man with the hollowed-out face that even in this California sunshine was somehow colorless and solemn as a headstone. This man who seemed oblivious to the party around him.

Through the years, as the two FanDuel cofounders had become darlings of the sports business world, they had lived the fantasy life of any fan: soaking in the World Series in seats behind third base; sitting courtside for NBA All-Star Games; and attending countless other events in the pampered comfort of VIP suites in venues across the country, the guests of CEOs from the media world, team owners, league honchos. Still, at least as far as Tom was concerned, this weekend in San Francisco, where they'd come as guests of an NFL team owner to the biggest sporting event of the year, was taking the cake as The Best Weekend Ever — even if their company was on the verge of going bust and any of its executives, at any moment, could be indicted by the FBI.

"This will be great — Peyton Manning, man!" Tom said, trying to get Nigel to forget the troubles of the moment.

Nigel looked blankly at Tom, a look that said only: Peyton . . . who?

Since moving to New York and adopting the Giants as his home sports team, Tom had become a true NFL fan. Nigel, who had been living inside a shell these last months and had yet to be converted into a fan of American sports, could barely keep up with the headlines in a world gone mad — rumblings of a Brexit back home in the United Kingdom, a preposterous presidential election playing out in the United States — let alone name the starting quarterbacks in the Super Bowl. He also wasn't exactly in the mood for a party. He and Lesley had planned to be here long before the *Times* story, for this weekend of Napa wine tastings and dinners in San Francisco, including one with the team owner of one of their NFL partners, the Cleveland Browns, at one of the most exclusive restaurants in the world; given the circumstances, Nigel and Lesley had lost their appetite for the $400-a-head dinner at French Laundry as Nigel began to schedule a series of meetings with investors and partners who held the fate of the company in their hands.

Nigel's head was still numb from an early morning meeting he and Christian Genetski had had in the offices of one of FanDuel's payment processors, in San Jose. PayPal, one of the services that FanDuel relied on to process the accounts that customers deposited online, was thinking of ending their relationship with FanDuel because, well, just about everyone was having second thoughts about their relationship with a company that was being compared to a Mexican drug cartel. It was simple: if the payment processors pulled the plug, they were dead in the water.

Stay with us, things will turn around, Nigel told them. *Things look bad, but there are too many people invested in this to let it fail.* The meeting with PayPal had gone better than expected, but now, as he walked with Tom through the Super Bowl circus, his attention turned to his next meeting, one in which he'd face some of the most influential figures in the sports universe, all in town for the Super Bowl but also possibly eager to hear why they shouldn't abandon what was sure looking like a sinking ship.

"What are we going to tell them?" Tom asked, referring to the partners in the upcoming meeting.

Nigel said: "How about that Peyton Manning!"

The evolution of the daily fantasy industry began with networks finally, in 2014, accepting advertising. Then it was getting the professional leagues on board. Jason Robins's 2013 marketing partnership with MLB was a watershed moment because it was the first daily fantasy partnership with a professional sports league, but it also was a ghost deal — at MLB's behest, there was no press release at the time, simply DraftKings signage popping up in major league ballparks and DraftKings banners on MLB.com sites, a professional sports league just dipping its toes, a way to gauge reaction to a sports league doing business with a gaming startup. When Jason signed away an equity stake in the company, some early employees who knew the details of the deal were taken aback by the size of it, but what it did accomplish was to give the industry legitimacy and also give DraftKings an inside track to a bigger deal, which was announced in the spring of 2015. DraftKings' MLB deal paved the way for an exclusive partnership between FanDuel and the NBA, and by mid-2015 both daily fantasy operators had partnerships with more than a dozen professional sports teams.

"Someday we were going to have to become legitimate," said Nigel. "There was going to be a day where this gets all called into question, and if the leagues are on our side, we're fine — and if they aren't, we're dead. Any time we had these league discussions, it was kind of an insurance policy — what kind of value would I put on a league supporting us? If shit hits the fan, well, a tremendous amount."

Shit had hit the fan, and as he arrived at a conference room at a San Francisco hotel, Nigel knew he needed the support of the owners and executives in the room. Nigel looked up and saw a propeller plane in the air, dark clouds surrounding it, rain coming down in sheets. The image was being projected onto a screen in the conference room. They were all looking up at the words on a slide that read A PERFECT STORM. WE WILL PERSEVERE. A perfect storm: yes, between the billion-dollar valuation and the $500 million carpet-bombing and the *Times* story and the media firestorm and the headline-hungry attorneys general and the lawmakers, that's what these last months had felt like — a perfect storm of elements that had caused those on the plane to wonder if there would be any survivors after they all went down, together.

Nigel knew why these men had not jumped out of the plane, parachutes at the ready, during the fall. He also knew that they were not there in the room simply to show their support to an embattled CEO out of the goodness of their hearts. These new online fantasy games that FanDuel and DraftKings had popularized had entered the sports landscape at a critical time — a time when, it could be argued, the leagues needed fantasy sports as much as the fantasy sports companies needed the leagues. As clueless as he was about quarterbacks in the NFL, Nigel by now had spent enough time in rooms with the most powerful people in American sports to understand the complicated dynamics in their industry and the immense challenges they faced. For the men in the room, their own reckoning was coming. Sports was still a booming business, and there was no better barometer of how big a business it was than the rights deals between the leagues and the networks. ESPN was months from striking a number of deals that signaled a booming business — they would pay nearly $2 billion a year for the NFL, nearly $1.5 billion for the NBA, and over $500 million for the College Football Playoff — but even as rights fees were exploding, as the leagues were stuffing their pockets with unprecedented money, something unexpected was happening: fans were beginning to cut the cord on cable packages and viewership was dropping, fast. Dropping TV ratings backed up this trend: the NFL's ratings were down 15 percent, and even the ratings in the NBA, a league exploding in popularity, were falling. Baseball's revenues had doubled since 2000, but part of that revenue was from massive deals that local and regional cable networks had struck with teams, and the value of those deals was tied to the very cable bundles that were about to see significant decreases in paying customers.

Nigel knew that all of it was part of a new reality for networks and leagues: sooner or later, just about all TV would be streaming TV. Soon, the billions made from the cable packages would run dry. The biggest bubble fueling sports was about to burst. The professional sports leagues were suddenly faced with a future of great uncertainty as they, along with the media companies, began to realize this truth: if any of the big shocks to the TV rights market fees came to pass, as many believed they would, if the bubble was indeed about to burst in the sports world, they needed something that would generate enough money to stop the hemorrhaging.

There were two things that were going to save the leagues. One was fantasy sports. The other was gambling, which was not legal — not yet at least.

At the Super Bowl, in a room full of investors and partners, Nigel found himself in a delicate position. He had to tell his investors, *Everything's good, we'll get through this!* while at the same time turning to the partners he owed money to — the NFL owners and network executives — and saying, *But not so great that I'll be able to pay you on time!*

"We're confident in fantasy sports as a future, for DFS as a future, we just don't know what 2016 will look like," Nigel told the room. He told them a plan was in motion, but there was a long road ahead for his small army of lobbyists and lawyers, the men on the front lines like Jeremy Kudon and Peter Schoenke, and the state-by-state route was long and full of mines. He told them that money hadn't necessarily been earmarked to go toward the fight on the regulatory side but that now they would have to view the extraordinary legal and lobbying costs as an investment in the long-term surety of the business. "We were a small unregulated market — we became a very large unregulated market in a very short period of time," he said. "Two or three years ago we said, 'We are going to become regulated.' We knew it was going to happen. We just didn't know how it was going to happen."

The men in the room asked questions: What was regulation going to look like? *A state-by-state process which, if I'm being honest, will be slow. It could take two years, and probably more.* What was the ad spend going to be? *Significantly lower than it was in 2015. Which, I'm sure, will be a relief to everyone.* The room laughed.

Nigel felt better after the response from the investors and partners in the room in San Francisco, which more or less was: *We're not going to throw you under the bus — yet.*

One afternoon he was home in Edinburgh, on the phone with Fan-Duel's chief legal officer, Christian Genetski, who was losing optimism after another attorney general seemed to be turning on them.

The bad news kept coming. Then, soon after he hung up with Genetski, Nigel's phone rang. "It's Adam," the voice said. It was the NBA commissioner, Adam Silver. Nigel held his breath. It had been less than a year since FanDuel had struck a four-year exclusive deal with Silver's league. The partnership was a turning point: it legitimized Nigel's still unknown business and a fledgling industry. The very next day, coincidentally or not, the *New York Times* published an op-ed written by Silver in which he argued that Congress should "adopt a federal framework that allows states to authorize betting on professional sports."

But that was a year ago, before the negative headlines, when it became an open question as to whether anyone would stand by the two embattled companies. It was great to have NFL partners behind them, but to have the NBA commissioner's support meant everything.

"I'll be honest. I don't know how this is going to end," Nigel said to Silver over the phone.

"I do," Silver replied. "With you and me testifying together in front of Congress."

The NBA, in other words, was still at his side. Nigel breathed a sigh of relief.

After those few days in San Francisco, Nigel knew that, no, the company wasn't going to go bust — not with all their team partners in the NFL and NBA *and* Adam Silver behind them. And yet the alternative — their new reality — somehow felt worse.

It was his biggest fear — the biggest fear of any entrepreneur, really: that his or her company will become a zombie company. Any entrepreneur will tell you that they will take the quick end over purgatory. With a quick death, an entrepreneur would lose some money and feel a bit of humiliation from losing other people's money but would move on. A good number of VC-financed entrepreneurs, particularly in Silicon Valley, which was good at ripping the bandage off — selling quickly when it was clear the vision fell short — bounced back from failed startups like basketball players bounced back from missed free throws. Much worse was hitting a series of endless bumps, with no end in sight. Purgatory was a company being funded to grow, but slowly, and so everyone, being in no position to sell, just hung around to create a lot of shareholder value. Purgatory was having a conservative burn rate to last many years and even (possibly) a positive cash flow. Purgatory was not going bankrupt but also having zero chance of ever becoming a high-growth company. Purgatory was a place where no one was happy: not the investors, not the shareholders, and not the founders, who saw no exit.

Purgatory was the New York FanDuel headquarters in early 2016, where it was business as usual but not business as usual. The bright, open space of staircases, large screens, brushed steel, and glass occupied two floors, and with its large windows that overlooked Park Avenue, the offices felt bigger and grander than the DraftKings' office in Boston. All over the offices were LET'S REINVENT THE WHEEL, PEOPLE posters, quotes from Derek Jeter and Wayne Gretzky. There were focus rooms encased in glass; inspirational quotes etched into the walls; a Ping-Pong table and Pop-A-Shot machine; pantries overflowing with rivers of organic energy bars; reminders of Thirsty Thursdays, the weekly 5 p.m. happy hour; and, plastered inside bathrooms, *The Half-Time Report*, the company newsletter (*Two Truths and a Lie: The founders were originally going to name the company Fanzilla . . . Tom Griffiths and Rob Jones have known each other since they were teenagers*). They'd moved here, five blocks north of their old space, in early 2016; months earlier, they had signed the lease soon after their unicorn designation. The company had already grown from fifty employees to four hundred between 2014 and early 2015, and the plan, after another anticipated hiring round of marketers, coders, and engineers, was for the company to have a space ready to accommodate the next wave. Every desk and cubicle would be occupied, every corner incubating a new idea.

But now the feeling inside was of a world frozen in time. After the

New York attorney general's office shut down operations in the state, things took a surreal turn: employees showed up to work every day at an office situated in a location where the games were deemed illegal. With the overall uncertainty, hiring was frozen; now, in the summer of 2016, swaths of the office, which was large enough for five hundred or more, sat unoccupied: rows and rows of empty desks and cubicles. Projects — new variations of daily fantasy games — were put on hold. Given the astronomical legal costs and the revenue lost from the states where their operations had been shut down, the scaling back had been anticipated for months.

First, they took away the weekly massages, then the breakfast spreads. More cutbacks on perks and benefits followed. And then the layoffs began — one morning in the winter of 2016 employees were ushered into a conference room, and an executive at the front of the room informed them that they were all being let go. Employees sitting outside glanced into the room, through the floor-to-ceiling glass, and tried their best not to stare. "It was like a public execution," said one of the sixty laid-off employees. Two months later, another fifty were let go.

Through that winter and spring, the days had a strange pace to them. There was still a company to keep operational, but nothing like the daily rush that had coursed through the office in late 2014 and early 2015. One morning that winter the team held a meeting in one of their big conference rooms. It was led by Zack Jenis, their young product manager who, with his hoodie and Michigan hat worn backward, had the appearance of a visiting high-schooler on spring break. "We have LA, we have Scotland, we have NY," someone said as video feeds blinked on the screens at the front of the room. Sitting around the table in front of their laptops was a mix of men and women, all young and of various races. It was a weekly meeting in which one of the leads of a department would answer questions for the entire staff. Zack's job was to size the tournaments; how big the prize pools were, and how many tournaments the company was providing, were determined each night, in real time. Filling a tournament was more of an art than anything, and it was Zack's job to stay up until the wee hours, sizing every tournament until the end.

His job had changed with the diminished prize pools and the five states out of operation — still including New York — but it was in some ways more important than ever to be as precise as possible. There may have been a time when overlay in a tournament could be viewed as a marketing expense, but those days were long gone.

"With all the regulation, how is that going to affect the size of contests one month in advance of MLB?" asked a staffer.

"They were 75 percent of the size of what they were on opening day a year ago," Zack replied.

"When, ideally, do you want a tournament to fill?" asked another employee.

"One minute before."

"And how much do you look at what DK is doing?"

"We usually post first — so we don't have that luxury. We see what happens, we post something, and DK comes out and posts a contest two times the size of ours. We haven't discussed the strategy of how we're going to change."

"Yes we have," a voice from the room said. Andy Giancamilli was FanDuel's vice president of revenue. "We *won't*."

"And what if a tournament doesn't fill?"

"It *has* to fill," Andy replied. "If we don't fill, we lose money. If we lose money, we're not here." Andy paused. "Not to be doomsday." Everyone laughed.

During spring and then summer, when baseball was the only game in town, the days could be a slog. One afternoon, on cue at five o'clock, a large flock of employees congregated in a conference room, where they sat down with their laptops at a table, grabbed a beer from the stash at the center of the table, and logged on to a Swedish online game site. As they kept one eye up on the screen that projected the real-time data from that night's tournaments, the eight employees, dressed in hoodies, caps, and long-sleeve T-shirts, clicked on their trackpads, furiously navigating through virtual Google maps as they tried to locate where in the world they were, based only on the clues visible to them. Every so often someone would rise from his seat, arms raised, and yell out, as if he'd gotten bingo. Employees, now banned from playing any daily fantasy games, restricted from the biggest office pastime, had found a new way to entertain themselves.

They'd all become numb to the headlines, because none of them these days were good. One afternoon the news was that the two companies would no longer provide games in college sports — a chunk of their revenue wiped out, just like that. One day brought news that another state was shutting them down; this was happening so frequently that Justine Sacco, the head of PR, decided that she didn't need to bother sending out press releases when they received another cease-and-desist from the latest attorney general. It was impossible to know where the next hit was coming from, only that another one was coming. As Genetski, who had joined FanDuel in 2015 only months before the storm hit, said, "We were getting punched from one side just as we got our hand up to defend ourselves on the other side."

But there was a football season coming up, the first season since they had become a nation's punching bag. It was time to reboot. One afternoon, in one of the glass-enclosed rooms, the company's new vice president of brand, wearing a gray hoodie and jeans, grappled with a question: *What, exactly, is the story of FanDuel now?* Dan Spiegel had joined FanDuel in 2014, during the company's big expansion. Coming from big advertising — his clients included Coke — he discovered something entirely different and unknown when Nigel Eccles hired him away to join FanDuel's marketing team.

That fall, his first football season, Spiegel was a bystander to what he, like many of the employees in New York, sensed was a campaign gone horribly wrong. "I felt like I was on drugs," he said, describing the experience of watching the ad barrage and feeling no control over the messaging. Now, he said, "people have such a low opinion of us — a really, really, *really* low opinion." An internal focus group reported that 10 percent of the people liked the ads from 2015; 90 percent hated them. "There was no middle ground," said Spiegel. Additionally, the hundreds and maybe even now thousands of promo codes that they'd created had become their own punching bag in the public eye, but had also, Spiegel thought, lost their original function, since the daily fantasy companies no longer lacked name recognition; therefore, giving a promo code credit for people coming to the site was akin to saying that the guy who nudged the vending machine before the candy bar came out was the reason why the candy bar fell, after dozens and dozens of others had been pummeling the machine for weeks on end.

Now they were intent on reintroducing the company to America, and Spiegel was charge of coming up with the concept for its marketing. Spiegel was directing the company's shift from direct-response ads to brand advertising, which was focused on creating awareness and shaping perception; in his head, he had three concepts he was playing around with. The first was a cinematic approach — a "brand" ad that was a radical departure from the direct marketing ads they'd become known for. "Think Ryan Gosling in *Drive*," he suggested. Spiegel knew for sure that the new ads could not have anything to do with winning money. They had to be about the love of following sports and connecting with other fans. The second concept tapped into that childlike ebullience inside every fan. Spiegel cited a recent video that had gone viral, one of Stephen Curry sinking a shot at half-court during a Golden State Warriors practice and a fan coming out and hugging him; watching that, he felt the raw emotion that was the essence of sports. He wanted to tap into that feeling, but given the negative public image of the company, he hesitated. "I just don't know if we have that *right*," Spiegel said.

There was a third option, he said, one that would essentially turn the mirror on themselves. One that showed some self-awareness: "Yup, we were the guys — and we're back," Spiegel said. The ad would have to tell the story of this startup. But what, exactly, *was* the story of FanDuel?

"Right now we have to ask ourselves a question," he said. "At our core, *who are we?*"

FanDuel and DraftKings had been ridiculed, humiliated, shamed — but they were still here. The rocket was still in flight, wobbling through the air now, if not exactly screaming toward the heavens. They'd all made mistakes along the way, and as existential threats still loomed — if they remained shut down in New York State for the rest of 2016, through the NFL season, they were dead. There was plenty of blame and finger-pointing to go around. For the leaders of the companies: How could they have been so blind as to let their own employees play their own games? "We looked at the employee play issue before," said Genetski, "and it struck me as odd that people played. Shame on me, for not realizing the extent of how much people played. I thought that people were playing one contest a week on DK, and who cares? I didn't have the full sense of it." For the investors: how could they have been so short-sighted, flooding an unregulated industry, one with an utterly unproven product, with hundreds of millions of dollars, and then allowing the company to burn through it all? "Shame on us," Mike LaSalle said that winter, "for letting it happen. Nigel and Lesley were right in 2014 — they earned it. But then the 2015 race accelerated what should have been two or three years of growth into just a few months, and neither company was ready for it."

Both companies had made plenty of mistakes. The industry as a whole should have begun the regulatory fight earlier; developed relationships with lawmakers in key states; done everything it could to get bills in motion. In hindsight, LaSalle thought, as a board they should have simply been more vocal. More vocal about the way the brand of daily fantasy sports was being presented in a $500 million carpet-bombing. More vocal about having a brand agency helping with what that brand *was*. More vocal about having different creative approaches on the commercials. More vocal about what they were seeing: that every company has a DNA, and the DNA of the two companies, as much as they were unwilling to admit it, made them direct marketing businesses. Yes, the companies, at the start, had gotten from A to B as shrewd direct marketing businesses, but the next step — becoming a transformative sports media company — well, that was a different thing entirely.

Now the board could be more vocal — and they would be. They would take more control because how, they thought, could they let the company make the same mistakes again? Now, in the aftermath of the near-collapse of their business, it was happening: a power shift from the founders, who were there from the start, to the outsiders, who'd joined and turned the company into a billion-dollar unicorn.

Up until this point, no one — not the CEOs, who led their companies into the middle of the storm; not the investors, who simply kept throwing money at an unproven operation; not anyone at the FSTA, who were too slow in the regulatory process and somehow did not see that a tsunami was coming; not any employees, who played on the sites and may have preyed on their own unsuspecting customers; not the professional players, who targeted inexperienced and unwitting minnows; not Ethan Haskell, who started this mess with his post — had been held responsible. All of them, even the ones who'd been there since the beginning, were still aboard the rocket — a rocket that was about to explode and shatter into pieces. There were still open FBI investigations. There were open lawsuits — casual players who'd lost thousands of dollars and contended that they'd been preyed upon by the sharks were still going after the companies for false advertising. There were attorneys general who had yet to come out with decisions on the fate of the operators in their states. There would have to be changes at the companies. New regulations and new safeguards, for starters. Limits on the number of entries for players. Any sniff of employees playing the games, and they were out. And of course, there would have to be assessments of leadership.

The reality was that the founders at both companies had been ceding control and power for months and even years; with each round of massive funding, they were further diluted financially, and with each expansion, further layers upon layers of people were brought in under them. At the time of the Super Bowl in California, the founders of FanDuel knew that big changes were going to have to be made — all the way to the top of the company. What those changes were going to be, they couldn't say. The founders already sensed a shift in power taking place, with the board being more vocal and the growing number of executives around the founders taking more control of decisions. They'd always known, in a sense, that things were headed this way. From the moment they'd taken money from Shamrock Capital in 2014 and then KKR in 2015, they'd known that the private equity infusion of cash would allow them to reach a fantasy of being a billion-dollar company, even if they were running the risk of losing total control of their business — their baby.

The morning of the big game, Nigel and Lesley had boarded a bus in downtown San Francisco for the one-hour drive to the stadium in Santa Clara. Nigel spent the drive chatting up team executives on the bus. Next to him, Lesley was fast asleep. It had been an exhausting weekend — an exhausting twelve months, really. Lesley awoke as they rolled up to a gleaming monolith. Lines snaked around Levi's Stadium; security was everywhere. As they walked toward the entrance and passed an agent with the letters FBI emblazoned on his chest, Nigel took Lesley over, and together they posed with the agent. Their friends received a text with the line: "They finally got us!"

They were in no rush to go inside. They walked around the grounds, just the two of them, and found a patch of grass removed from the stadium, where they sat down. Nigel's phone bleated.

"Put that away," Lesley said.

They both stared at the sky, cloudless and endless. It was, if they allowed it to be, a perfect afternoon.

"How did we end up *here?*" Nigel said, exhaling for the first time all weekend.

During Nigel's presentation in front of the NFL stakeholders, Lesley had looked at him and seen his face hollowed out as she'd never seen it before. He'd always been the most optimistic person in every room, always quick with a quip to lighten the mood, but these last few days and months had made him miserable. For the first time in the years that she'd known him, she looked at him and saw someone broken.

"You know, when this is all over, after we've sold or walked away, you'll be back to being a nightmare again," she said.

"No, no. I'll be chill . . . for like three hours," Nigel said. "Then I'll be fucking miserable."

They'd been together now for more than twenty years — a duration that stunned even them. Not long after they'd started dating, they worked together running the front desk at Lesley's parents' inn, just outside of Forfar. The inn was in the Scottish countryside, hidden beneath a canopy of trees, a place that felt worlds away at this moment. When Lesley was young, her parents struggled to make ends meet, and opening up an inn, of all things, hadn't seemed like the wisest venture. But the business, while grueling, saved her family. Lesley would say that from that moment a work ethic had been instilled in her. A belief that if you put your head down and put in your work, you'd be rewarded. Nigel and Lesley worked the weekends and filled in when Lesley's parents couldn't be there. So much, and yet nothing, had changed from those years. They were still together, still partners, best friends, all in, together.

"I do try to remind myself," Nigel said, "well, this is what I always wanted to do. I worked so long, and this is what I wanted."

"If we went back to the beginning of this and someone told us we'd be here," Lesley said, "we'd be blown away." It was one of the rare moments when the two took a moment to reflect on what they'd built. It could have been easy to dwell on the missteps at various points over the last year and to conclude, after all the public scrutiny, that they'd been a failure.

A loud roar came from the stadium. Kickoff was nearing, and pre-game festivities were under way. All eyes — 100 billion viewers worldwide — were on their screens. The big game was about to begin.

"We should go," Nigel said.

"No — let's take a moment," Lesley said, holding him back, just this once. "Let's have this moment."

PART III
THE NEW WORLD
2016-2019

It is a matter of integrity. It is a matter of the character of our games, of the character of our fans and a matter of values — especially the values that we in professional sports and our athletes represent and transmit to the youth of this country . . . **WHY SHOULD VEGAS HAVE ALL THE FUN?** *. . . Gambling on a sport is I think the deadliest of all things that can happen. It's evil, it creates doubt and destroys your sport . . .* **LEGAL SPORTS BETTING IN JERSEY? YOU BET** *. . . I believe that sports betting should be brought out of the underground and into the sunlight where it can be appropriately monitored and regulated . . .* **FANDUEL: SPORTS BETTING REIMAGINED** . . . And if you download now, DK will match your first bet up to $200! . . . **THE DRAFTKINGS SPORTS BETTING NATIONAL CHAMPIONSHIP: $2,500,000. GUARANTEED** . . . I'm Pretty Sure These New Sports Gambling Laws Should Make Me Rich Beyond My Wildest Dreams but I Can't Figure Out How Yet . . . **HERE COMES THE SPORTS GAMBLING APOCALYPSE.**

12

A LINE IN THE SAND

Las Vegas, Spring–Summer 2016

Leroy's Horse & Sports Place was a yellow-and-blue-rinsed storefront that squatted in a derelict downtown strip mall, under a Chinese men's club of Las Vegas. At night in the parking lot in front, under the yellow glow of the lamps, as young men in nylon athletic gear who spoke not a lick of English shuffled by, the fleas and wiseguys who'd spilled out from Leroy's, bleary-eyed and blitzed from a full day of listening to games, stood wobbly while they quietly cursed their bad beats.

Through Leroy's front doors was a parlor that smelled of cigarette smoke, gin, 50-cent pickled eggs, and desperation. Strewn with discarded tickets and beer bottles, the carpet on the floor was an indistinguishable color — if there was one sliver of advice from the Leroy's regulars to abide by, it was that if you drop something, leave it there. In one corner of the room, if you could see through the smoke, was a whiteboard hand-scribbled with the daily lines. In another was a TV that weighed as much as a tank and hung from the wall; it had to be replaced the night Crazy Kenny lived up to his name when he reacted to a bad beat by taking out a gun and blasting a hole through it. The long oak bar, starting at seven in the morning, seven days a week, began serving the medley of sharps, wiseguys, and fleas: Crazy Kenny, Dick the Pick, Jerry the Hat, One-Eyed Scotty, Bobby the Midget, and the Hunchback, a group of degenerates who had seen it all. A man ramming his head through the wall after Pisarcik's fumble in the Meadowlands; two men, settling a debt, crashing through Leroy's front doors, one wielding a pickax and the other running for his life; a longtime regular dropping dead of a heart attack at the bar, his dear friends around him not skipping a beat when they carted him out the front door.

The casinos on the Las Vegas Strip catered to the wealthy out-of-towners who'd come chasing luck all the way; Leroy's, the biggest independent sports book in town, was home to the transplant bettors from New York, Boston, Philly, and Chicago who arrived at the only place in the world where they belonged, the place where the search for destiny first came to life, a place that had a way like no other of separating the winners from the losers. And Vic Salerno, the man behind the bar, the man who scribbled the daily lines on the board, who took home the tickets every night from Leroy's and sorted the winning ones from the losing ones, was always more than willing to help them find out which one they were.

By the time he was thirty years old, Vic had made it. He was a dentist serving wealthy patients in an office overlooking the sparkling Marina del Rey, pulling in $200,000 a year working four days a week. On Fridays he spent his afternoons at the old Hollywood Park racetrack, then headed across town to Los Alamitos for the evening races, then — if he and his pals won — drove to the airport to catch the 11 p.m. to Vegas. He found himself spending more and more time in the desert, at the craps tables, in the poker rooms, and, more than anywhere else, the dark and smoky sports books, until finally he decided that, like many before him, he was going to move to Vegas to reinvent himself. Vic decided to walk away from his career in dentistry, sensing an opportunity after Congress lowered the betting tax rate in 1974.

For bookmakers as much as gamblers, sports betting was an unpredictable business. Casino executives, mob-controlled and otherwise, knew for sure that the house won at blackjack or poker. Leroy's was one of the independent sports books in the city, still decades before practically all the casinos in town were run by public companies, their fortunes tied to Wall Street, long before gambling was gaming and the mob was replaced by faceless corporations that were just as cold-blooded. Vic began working at Leroy's as a bookmaker in 1978. Within two years he owned it, and by the early 1980s it was the largest independent sports book in the state of Nevada. Vic first began revolutionizing the industry by taking bets over the phone, which no bookmaker had done before. Then he created an electronic system to take bets, so that he no longer had to lug home trash bags filled with tickets to go through one by one at his kitchen table every night. By the late 1980s, there were Leroy's affiliates all over the state.

When, in 1991, his old friend at the Stardust, Art Manteris, told him about his plan to install sports books at racetracks across the country, linked through Vic's computer line and connected to a hub in Nevada, Vic thought it was brilliant. He was aware of the stigma associated with gambling outside of Nevada; he knew the enormous uphill climb they faced, primarily because of the professional sports leagues playing the public charade in their stance against legalized gambling, going back all the way to the most powerful man in sports, NFL commissioner Pete Rozelle. During his tenure, the commissioner would declare that legalized gambling was "destructive of the sports themselves and in the long run injurious to the public," while at the same time never cracking down on the publication of point spreads in media publications or on TV analysts' habit of mentioning betting lines more and more often as interest in betting rose nationwide. Vic also knew the realities of the business; the vast majority of interested parties had no sense of how bad a moneymaking enterprise sports betting could be for the bookmaker. "People don't understand the exposure" — the amount that a bookmaker could stand to lose — "that we have on an NFL Sunday," he would say, in his low rasp. "It's in the *hundreds of millions of dollars.* Nevada's a tiny, tiny state, and if you extrapolate that with PASPA, the exposure would be in the billions of dollars. And then you're talking about these low margins, 3 to 6 percent, to begin with. *And* if it's legalized, every state will want a cut of that. We give 6.5 percent of our revenue to Nevada. Not every state would be that reasonable. New York Lottery came to me and said they want to get into parlay cards, and they said that a 50 percent hold" — the amount kept by the house — "wasn't high enough. *Fifty percent!* People don't understand, and people are greedy. And greed kills."

Of course, Vic also believed in everyone's right — in everyone's fundamental drive — to gamble. He saw the ridiculousness of the tired debate between what was gambling and what was a game of skill and the necessity to draw a line between them. Poker, blackjack: sure, people gambled with their money, but hadn't Hollywood, in countless, albeit clunky, portrayals, sufficiently established that those were games of skill? "What, exactly, is gambling?" Vic would say. "You and I can play horseshoes and compete against each other, and it's an innocent game of skill. I bet you $5, and that game of skill just became gambling, didn't it? It did just because there's money on the line? The essence of the game is still the same."

He saw the passage of PASPA in 1992 as the best thing that ever happened to the illegal bookmakers and the underground gambling world. He watched as betting in the Caribbean and Asia boomed, watched as others cashed in, like a bookmaker he knew in Singapore who controlled a handle that was in the billions. He watched as online gaming boomed too, not in a legal, regulated environment in the United States but only in quasi-legal enterprises that made gambling available to anyone who wanted to partake in it, their US dollars drained by internet rogues through twisted virtual wires buried deep underground, well beyond the reach of the authorities.

As the years passed, Vic became sure of something else: he would not see legalized gambling nationwide in his lifetime.

Then, in the spring of 2012, someone sent Vic a link to a page on the *Philadelphia Inquirer* website. Vic didn't need to scroll all the way through the page to know what his friend wanted him to see: the banner at the top that read "FanDuel: The Leader in One Week Fantasy Football Leagues. Win a Million Dollars Today." After calling his friend to say "What is *this*?" Vic immediately clicked on the banner and signed up. His reaction was the same as Art Manteris's reaction to the sign he saw at McCarran Airport, touting a company called DraftKings. Like Art, Vic was stunned that this company FanDuel was permitted to operate, as well as shocked by its audacity in flaunting its business. Clearly a sports gambling business, it had nevertheless somehow stayed out of the legal and regulatory grasp of the government.

He knew that in Vegas the Mirage and other casinos had looked into similar games, called daily games, and that their lawyers had concluded that it wasn't worth the risk: occupying a gray area that would be considered gambling, they were games that simply wouldn't stand up under legal scrutiny. And yet these companies were hawking these games in plain sight — flashing a big middle finger to any regulated, legal sports gambling enterprise playing by the rules.

"Obviously, I'm in favor of *legal* sports betting in America," said the man at the table. "I'm opposed to *illegal and unregulated* gambling."

His voice echoed across a cavernous chamber at the Las Vegas city hall, a room that was grand. Joe Asher, the CEO of William Hill US, the leading sports betting company in Nevada, continued: "When we talk about daily fantasy sports betting, we need to be clear and call it what it is. It is gambling and needs to be regulated as such . . . The classic definition of gambling is that you put down something of value to win something of value, based on an uncertain result. Clearly daily fantasy sports is betting."

In the front row behind Asher, listening to him speak, were Jason Robins and Nigel Eccles and if the two CEOs didn't know what kind of day they were in for, they were quickly beginning to sense it.

The piles of money that FanDuel and DraftKings had raised and spent had compelled every venture capitalist and investor to ask, *How are we missing the boat on that?* The vast sums were compelling lawmakers across the country to ask, *Where's our piece of the pie?* But just as significantly, the most powerful casinos and sports books in Las Vegas had been compelled to ask, *Are they taking our customers? Are they coming for us?*

The two CEOs faced a podium that was as long as an aircraft carrier, and gazing down on them were twelve of the most powerful men in the state — among them, the head of MGM; the chairman of the state gaming commission; and the governor of Nevada. Anyone who'd never been in this room and suddenly found themselves facing those men couldn't possibly have a thought other than: *These are men I don't want to mess with.* It was early March 2016, six months since the companies had been shut down in Nevada because they'd been deemed, in October 2015, illegal gaming organizations. The CEOS had flown across the country to convince the men in front of them to allow them to open up shop again. It wouldn't be easy.

Daily fantasy games had arrived in Nevada at an uneasy time in the industry, a time when the city at the center of sports betting in America had serious questions about its place in the world. In an age when everyone was on their phones, where did Las Vegas, the ultimate tourist destination, fit in? For big casinos, investing heavily in mobile didn't necessarily seem like a winning proposition considering that casinos wanted people physically inside their sports books, not in their hotel rooms or away from the Strip. Casinos had begun developing smartphone apps tied to their sports books, but early attempts at a product were clunkily engineered and full of bugs — the state wasn't exactly a hotbed of tech — and of course they were accessible for browsing only from inside the state of Nevada. Even if daily fantasy games weren't a perfect product, if people across the country were getting their gambling fix from those games, that was a direct attack on the sports book business.

As the daily fantasy companies' profiles rose, Nevada gaming regulators began to see every move by their CEOs as a threat to their state's livelihood. The word among the Nevada regulators was that these were two disrupters — two "kids," as more than one of those regulators would put it — from the East Coast who didn't have any interest in complying. "The word we were getting from Washington D.C., was that there were two companies starting to meet with people but they were either clueless or not serious," said one Nevada regulator. "That, for me, was the moment I realized, *Okay, we got some disrupters here, and let's not anticipate them coming in and playing by the rules — certainly not our rules."*

The operators' sudden hiring of an army of lawyers and lobbyists beginning in the summer of 2015 sent up red flags. A. G. Burnett, then chairman of the Nevada gaming commission, said: "The lobbyists and lawyers they were hiring were the über-lobbyists and lawyers. The minute I saw that, I knew that either we were going to get run over by them or we had to do something to speak to the law and keep the regulatory scheme intact. You can have those celebrity lawyers, but you have to dig deep into the law, and *just comply.*"

To "just comply" meant that the CEOs would admit, on record, officially, and once and for all, that they were gambling operations. The problem was that they couldn't exactly admit that while they were in Nevada — and then declare themselves not the instant they stepped foot outside the state. Their situation wasn't necessarily the result of a failed strategy, but it did shed light on just how preposterous it was to try to fit into the fifty different legal frameworks set by the different set of rules of each state.

Then there was the little problem of Jason Robins having already alluded to DraftKings as a gambling operation. Burnett had commissioned a research memo into the legal designation of daily fantasy sports and circulated its findings among lawmakers and gaming officials. The memo included a Reddit online thread in which Jason had said:

"The concept is almost identical to a casino . . . specifically poker. We make money when people win pots."

"This determination is consistent with how certain daily fantasy sports operators describe themselves," the Nevada gaming commission's memo read. "The DraftKings CEO also states that DraftKings' 'concept is a mashup between poker and fantasy sports. Basically, you pick a team, deposit your wager, and if your team wins, you get the pot.' Additionally, the DraftKings CEO repeatedly refers to the payments on his sites as 'wagers' and 'bets,' and the activity as 'betting.'"

The report was damning. And yet here they were, front and center, still refusing to acknowledge that they were gambling operations — a designation that would allow them to operate in Nevada while being taxed and regulated, just like any other gaming operation in the state.

"We're up for any discussion that does that in a way that doesn't significantly damage the business," Jason said into the microphone, his voice echoing across the room. "I do acknowledge the need for regulation is there — I believe everyone in the industry acknowledges this. We've joined hands with FanDuel. We're all for regulation."

One of the men at the podium leaned forward. His nameplate said TONY ALAMO. CHAIRMAN OF THE NEVADA GAMING COMMISSION. Alamo had a desert-tinted face and wore a purple tie as wide as the Hoover Dam. He gazed down and said: "I think you see a theme here today: we *know* how to regulate gaming, and I think we do a very good job at it." Then he asked a simple question of Jason Robins: had DraftKings tried to start the licensing process in Nevada? Jason's response was that he wasn't aware of whether they had or hadn't.

Alamo asked the CEO of FanDuel:

"Have you looked into the details of what it would take to try to fit in as is and the licensure process — calling our local expertise and trying to get that advice?"

Dressed much too well for a public flogging, Nigel shifted in his seat. "I personally have not — but we will do so."

Staring at Nigel, Alamo huffed, "If I could just be a little critical, I think *that needs to be done.*"

In the audience, a few rows back, a large man sat by himself, amused. "They made fools of themselves," Vic Salerno would say of the CEOs who were getting called out for not doing their homework. How could they have flown across the country not knowing whether their people had even glanced at the guidelines spelling out the state's process? Clearly, these two companies were run by two CEOs who simply didn't have time for details.

Still, Vic also had another thought as he watched the two CEOs get undressed: as much as the guys rubbed him and the others the wrong way for their lack of interest in conforming to Nevada regulations, their companies were turning the tide of the national conversation outside of Nevada. What the companies had done was to put the topic of sports betting at the forefront.

Vic got up and walked to a lectern, faced the twelve men, and began to speak. "I think Nevada is the greatest state, we are the gold standard, and everyone should go through the regulations," he said. "Frankly what I hear today is that the people in the business somehow want to avoid going through our rigid process . . . That being said, I believe this is the way to go. I think it's fast, it's fun, it's easy. It could benefit the state tremendously. We would pay taxes. If other states legalize sports wagering and have pools, we can merge pools here in Nevada, into megapools that really benefit the state. We could extend our position in sports books . . . It *is* a game of skill. And it *is* gambling."

Given how all the Nevada men had spent the morning piling onto the daily fantasy operators and their CEOs, perhaps not everyone in the room saw the unexpected turn taking place. Suddenly, the old bookmaker wasn't just making an argument for daily fantasy games. No, Vic Salerno, in a roundabout way, was explaining why *he* was getting into the business of daily fantasy sports.

He still put his left shoe on first. He still did not carry $50 bills. He still drove the same route to work until a winning streak ended, when he changed his route entirely. Vic Salerno was still as superstitious as ever, still the old bookmaker at heart, even if the world around him was changing. In 2012, he had sold Leroy's to William Hill, the bookmaking giant based in the United Kingdom, for $18 million. They razed old Leroy's within a year and put in its place yet another glimmering hotel and casino, some fifty stories high, in a city full of glimmering hotels and casinos. He'd lost track of Leroy's fleas, the high-stakes bettors in town who'd been displaced by quants armed with Wall Street algorithms. Vegas, with its colored fountains and magic shows and roller coasters and $60 buffets and Cirque du Soleil shows, had long since become a playground for wealthy out-of-towners. Where longtime bookmakers like him now fit in this Vegas, Vic didn't exactly know. He didn't know how they fit into the world outside Vegas either. The world was changing. Now commissioners of sports leagues were softening their stances against gambling. The tipping point was when NBA commissioner Adam Silver came out with his op-ed in the *New York Times* in 2014, saying that he believed that gambling should be brought out into the open and regulated. Then other commissioners followed suit, albeit slowly: "All of us have evolved a bit on gambling," said Roger Goodell in 2016 — this comment from the same NFL commissioner who had been as adept as any of his predecessors at playing the public charade. And then, at the NHL owners' meeting in June 2016, Las Vegas's expansion bid for a hockey team was approved by a unanimous vote; signing on on the approval was Commissioner Gary Bettman — the man who had been at the forefront of successful lobbying to Congress to pass PASPA twenty-four years earlier.

In the following months, there would be louder murmurs that the US Supreme Court was considering hearing arguments in a case that could challenge PASPA, some twenty-five years after the law went into effect. Anyone paying close attention had already noticed that suddenly, everywhere, there were companies positioning themselves to flip the switch when laws started going their way, from conglomerates like William Hill — which had gotten a license in West Virginia and opened an off-track betting site in Iowa, getting a foot in the door of those states — to startups offering new kinds of games that would have raised red flags for authorities before FanDuel and DraftKings came along.

In fact, FanDuel and DraftKings themselves were offering new, simpler variations of games: single lineup, pick 'em, contests that would have attracted the wrath of state attorneys general everywhere. "They're moving closer to our model, and we're moving closer to theirs," Vic said. "They accelerated the conversation. And it's driving us to ask, 'What else is in sports wagering, and what is the natural takeoff from that?'"

Months after the Nevada hearing in which his friends on the podium stared down those hotshot innovators from the East Coast, Vic was sitting in a sterile office in a business complex a few miles away from the Strip. Just above his head was a plaque that read: "1991 FANTASY

FOOTBALL. THE WINNER: *SONNY'S SUPPERS*." Below that was "THE REST: . . ." followed by a list of names. In the 1990s, Vic was part of a fantasy football league that got together once a year for a draft. This wasn't exactly twelve old friends meeting up over wings in a sports bar. This was the type of league where a personality like Roy Firestone emceed the draft, held in a grand hotel ballroom. And it included some of the most powerful players in Vegas: bookmakers, regulators, high-stakes gamblers. Salerno's partner on Sonny's Suppers, proud champs of the 1991 season, was famed Nike executive Sonny Vaccaro. He won't divulge how big the stakes were, only that local law enforcement caught wind of the league and quietly asked them to shut it down.

Perhaps the models on opposite sides — Old Vegas's and the daily fantasy operators' — had never been that far apart. Perhaps now the world was finally going to see fantasy games and wagering as one and the same.

Vic could have been enjoying retirement, but just as he had thirty years earlier, he sensed an opportunity to position himself for a world that twenty-five years ago, after their plan was crushed, they never thought was possible. A day that he and others had dreamed of but given up hope on was about to arrive: the day he would be able to take every bet, not just from Nevada but from anywhere in the country. Vic suddenly felt the same energy he had felt many decades earlier when sports betting was about to explode in his state.

As the future began to come into focus, Vic wasn't going to be left behind. On this day in the offices of US Fantasy, Vic was dressed in blue jeans and a red Dri-FIT polo emblazoned with the logo of a new venture. A few weeks earlier, Vic and a few business associates had traveled to Cupertino, California, the home of Apple. Interested in launching an app, they were formally applying for inclusion in the Apple iTunes Store. "It was a real clash of cultures," Vic said. "We were in suits. And we walk in, and there's this girl who looks like she's fourteen. She has holes in her jeans. And she explains that she's the attorney. Then she asked why we were legit, and we had to explain that we're regulated, an SEC traded company. We might as well have had a target on our backs."

Within weeks was the launch of US Fantasy, a fantasy sports site that offered variations of the game. Vic Salerno was the founder of Vegas's new tech startup.

These new fantasy games were doing something miraculous: they were actually moving the needle. Everything was changing. The lines that had been drawn and then remained untouched for decades, lines that had seemed permanent, were suddenly, miraculously, disappearing, like lines in the sand.

13

JASON'S DELUSION

Boston, Summer 2016

What was Jason Robins thinking when he considered the chessboard in front of him, saw the lines that had been drawn for decades, and wondered what one move could blow up the board entirely? Some called what he did in changing the rules of the game "a scorched-earth approach," "crazy," and "reckless." "Ruthless," was the word one early DraftKings employee used. "He knew what he was doing from the beginning." And of course, they called Jason Robins and his cofounders "lucky." Lucky because of their impeccable timing. Lucky because other startups that had come before them had essentially handed them the playbook on how to run a successful fantasy sports business. Lucky because the financial markets were opening up, because the professional sports leagues were becoming desperate for renewed fan engagement, because Americans finally were ready to embrace sports betting, or something that smelled very much like it.

The cofounders at DraftKings were lucky because a perfect storm of technological and social change had cleared the way for wild innovation as venture capitalists, emerging from the wreckage of the financial crisis, set out on a mad hunt to find the next unicorn. The environment created a group of disruptive startups that reshaped industries and were led by entrepreneurs uniquely suited for the moment. Jason would be the first to acknowledge that he was indeed fortunate that a series of events lined up as they did in his early years as CEO. He knew that even a tiny change in one of those events along the way could have made things turn out very differently. Robins cited his favorite movie to explain: "It's the time travel paradox in *Back to the Future:* you change one thing and you don't know how else everything would have changed. Perhaps things would have changed dramatically. I do think back to how lucky we were."

Success in running a startup was no different from success elsewhere in life: skill went a long way in setting the winners apart from the losers, but there was always a good deal of chance involved. Like the CEO of any other disruptive company, Jason possessed a set of traits that carried him in that particular moment: an understanding of technology and the consumer, a high tolerance for risk, an urge to create a little chaos, and delusion. The delusion was essential for any entrepreneur. It gave Jason the belief that he had what it took to change the landscape around him. *Thank God for the delusion,* Jason thought, because when he looked back at himself at the start of DraftKings, he saw someone who was utterly unprepared for what he was getting into.

All three founders were. They worked out of Paul Liberman's spare room nights and weekends, making cold calls around town to ask for help in launching a company. One man named John Hession had returned their message. "If you're willing to get up at seven o'clock in the morning and pick up a $30 check for breakfast — I'll meet with you," he told Jason. Hession was well respected and connected in the Boston entrepreneurial community, and so the three cofounders met with Hession, in corner booths at half-empty diners all around Boston on Saturdays for a month. At their first meeting, the three explained that they wanted to change the world with their new idea . . . but first it would be helpful to know what exactly an incorporation document was. Hession began to dispense the advice, telling them how to save every cent of their war chest *(write your own incorporation documents and option plans, for starters; don't waste your money on lawyers)* and warning that any minute arguing with each other on the finer points and not meeting with an investor was time wasted. He tore apart their pitch decks, told them they weren't going to raise a cent until they walked away from their jobs, and gave them the names of investors and venture capitalists he knew. He gave them what they needed: a map to navigate Boston's cutthroat startup world. After a series of introductions that led them to Atlas Ventures, Jason and his cofounders had the money to get their game off the ground. Finally, as they were all leaving the diner one day, Hession put his arms around the founders he called the Three Amigos. "This is not going to be easy," he said. "But it isn't going to be easy for reasons you don't expect. A year from now, one of you won't be here. And the other two of you will be miserable."

They *were*, according to Jason, miserable in the early months, arguing with each other over the product. Matt, for instance, recalls a particularly heated shouting match with Jason over the CEO's idea that the games should be virtual-currency based. Jason pushed the team to build a more social product. Jason and Paul argued about . . . everything.

Over time, however, the three settled into their roles, and were important to the company in different ways. Jason was the clear face of the company. Matt, in time, could concede that he was never meant for the CEO role; he was, behind-the-scenes, leading the operations and, as a gaming nerd, brought a certain authenticity to the company. Paul was not a sports fan but was the founder who got shit done — he was the one who threw a fit if a new product was launched a few hours later than planned.

Four years later, in 2016, the Three Amigos were all still there, defying the odds. Through the years Jason had begun to appreciate just how fortunate they were. There had been countless moments when the story of DraftKings could have taken a wildly different turn — inflection points where the outcome was decided almost by chance, or by a calculated bet that they ended up on the right side of. Really, what did any startup do other than make a series of bets? They bet big, in 2013, that TV would put them on the map; it did. They bet big, in 2014, that the acquisition of DraftStreet would help close the gap between them and FanDuel; it did. They bet big, in 2015, that their $500 million of advertising would allow them to catch FanDuel and in the process make their name one of the most recognized in America; it did, though with unintended consequences.

In March, not long after his appearance at the Nevada statehouse, Jason Robins was given little choice but to make another big bet. Christian Genetski, working in tandem with Jeremy Kudon, had devised a plan to drop the litigation against New York State, come to a settlement with the attorney general, Eric Schneiderman, and fold up shop in New York, taking the resulting massive hit in revenues and liquidity. With investors becoming increasingly concerned about the long-term viability of the daily fantasy industry because of legal uncertainty in the state with the largest user base in the country, the only way to survive was to face the issue head on and fight for a resolution before the start of the upcoming NFL season. The only way to achieve legal clarity was to have the lawmakers in Albany pass a bill to legalize daily fantasy statewide. Genetski had brokered a deal between FanDuel and Schneiderman's office. But he still had to convince DraftKings that it was the right deal, and DraftKings' high-powered lawyers — which hailed from renowned firm Boies Schiller — weren't convinced.

One day during this moment, Genetski, oddly enough, found himself in the backseat of a limo with Jason, on the way to a meeting with a payment processor; the FanDuel chief legal officer pitched the idea up to the DraftKings CEO. It was the start of a bizarre day. The facilitator for Genetski and Jason's meeting with the bank was Bo Deitl, the former New York police detective turned media personality. A full day's worth of meetings ended with a dinner at a Manhattan steak house in which Pete Rose strolled in and sat down for a drink with them.

Genetski sensed that Jason understood they had to end the war with Schneiderman. Genetski got the late-night call on a train ride somewhere between New York and D.C., where he lived. *Ok, let's do it,* Jason said, holding firm against his own lawyer's wishes.

Eric Schneiderman was still frothing at the mouth — when the cameras rolled at least. "Some of the content of the ads we're looking into because we believe there were misrepresentations made," he said in an interview on PBS. "So beyond the issue of whether or not this is gambling, our investigation is looking at whether fraud has been committed. You're not allowed to lure people into spending their money or betting their money based on false representations." The Schneiderman probe had mystified observers: what was the AG's endgame? "It had just expanded so far beyond from what it initially looked like," said Genetski. "It started with insider trading allegations, then all of the sudden it was about companies not *geo blocking* in states where players are restricted, and then they were pivoting to other theories and asking, Well I also read this story about how many employees win: tell me about that." Schneiderman's agreement to now settle was viewed within the companies as confirmation that he was merely a politician who wanted to create some splashy headlines. When it became clear to him that the issue of daily fantasy sports wasn't going to be big enough to, say, propel him the New York governor's office, then, well he could move on to his next cause.

Every state in which daily fantasy bills were introduced, debated, and voted on offered its own unique drama, but New York, where the stakes were highest, would provide an instructive glimpse into the powerful and hidden forces at work on the state level when an issue becomes a turf war involving gambling interests. One longtime Albany lawmaker would rank the clash in his top three or four most heated issues. "We had a few when I first came into office, like the gay marriage issue, where that was late night, very contentious," he said. "But this one, when it came to last-minute lobbying and how hard-core the lobbying was, I would have to say it ranks number one. I can't remember one where it was just this intense right down to the very last minute, right before the vote was taken. It was that intense."

Through the spring and summer and until the very moment of the vote, a popular exercise was sizing up the odds of a New York bill passing, and the odds would fluctuate wildly by the day. With all the unknowns in play — including the eccentricities of local politics — an element of chance was undoubtedly involved. In those final few days of June leading up to the final days of the New York legislative session, company executives, if they were being honest, would say that a daily fantasy bill passing through the gauntlet of Albany was, at best, a fifty-fifty proposition.

The fate of DraftKings, FanDuel, and the entire daily fantasy industry was coming down to a coin flip.

On a June night, inside a booth in the corner of an Italian restaurant in Albany, New York, Jason sat wondering if the biggest bet they'd ever made was a terrible one. Just blocks away, the New York State Capitol sat in the hazy glow of a sweltering summer night. Only a handful of days remained in the legislature's session, and the daily fantasy companies were no closer to seeing a bill pass than they had been in the spring. If they did lose this bet, Jason was going down with the man sitting in front of him. After another long day spent sweating through their shirts in the musty halls of the statehouse, Jason and Nigel were having dinner and drinks, and for the first time perhaps, they were getting together with no agenda. Nigel summed up where they stood: "Everyone talks about dealing with uncertainty with startups, but I'd never appreciated just how binary the outcomes could be. You go to bed every night thinking, when I wake up tomorrow, will it be the day that we die? Here's another one of those moments where there was no in between: you lived or you died."

At this point, with the NFL season three months away, the two companies were on life support, hemorrhaging money into legal fees. For the last four years the daily fantasy battle had been a tug-of-war between the two CEOS, but after the the fall of 2015, Jason found himself on one side working with the very CEO with whom he'd been engaged in this bitter war, and with the lawmakers who backed them. On Jason's and Nigel's side of the rope were lawmakers like New York state senator John Bonacic, who had been invited a year earlier, with a referendum on casino gaming coming up, to a talk at a Saratoga racetrack. Bonacic's first remarks were: "I don't know why I'm up on this panel, I don't know a damn thing about fantasy sports." Now, as chairman of the state gaming committee, he was the fantasy industry's great hope, the legislator in charge of rounding up support for the bill introduced by Democrat Gary Pretlow.

On the other side of the rope were a group of legislators who opposed anything that smelled of gambling, as well as lobbyists on the casino side, who had a proud tradition of wanting to tie any online or mobile business to brick-and-mortar establishments. The casinos, in short, wanted New York daily fantasy players to get in a car and drive to their New York casino in order to play daily fantasy in person, which was an odd thought since the appeal of these games was that you could play anywhere, anytime. The racinos (the racetracks and casino establishments) "didn't want anybody to spend their sports dollar on some other game of skill that might take away from racinos," explains Bonacic. "They wanted to kill the industry in New York because they felt that there were only so many recreation dollars to be spent, and they wanted people thinking of racinos and not fantasy sports. They lobbied for this every day. But they were playing it a bit over the top." At the end of the day, Bonacic knew, daily fantasy sports was small peanuts in comparison. He noted that the New York racinos in a recent month had brought in well over $3 billion. Bonacic could see from a quick glance at the reports that his staff had rounded up for him that fantasy sports was lucky to bring in $3 billion a *year*, across the entire United States. There was always a big misconception about the size of the daily fantasy sports industry — for that, the industry had the massive ad campaign of 2015 to thank — and lawmakers in Albany, like lawmakers across the country, had a vague notion that daily fantasy sports was bigger than it actually was. Perhaps it just didn't matter; anything that could take a dime from a New York racino's business was a threat that needed to be crushed. Anything that could take a gambler's attention away from the roulette table was a problem.

For the two CEOs, the week had been a series of conversations with lawmakers and various special interest groups and presentations in which they gave impassioned defenses of the daily fantasy sports industry to people who commonly thought that DFS stood for Department of Financial Services. In offices in the New York State Capitol, Jason explained why three hundred employees in Boston were counting on them. "I know this is just another bill for you, but for all these people, you can be a godsend for them, and the entire industry," he said to them. One weekend afternoon Nigel was at a barbecue and had downed a few drinks when his phone lit up. On the line was a racino in upstate New York, an entity that was one of the biggest opponents of the bill percolating in Albany. When Nigel opened FanDuel's New York office, he'd had an outsider's view of the US political system; now he could describe to you each state's cumbersome legislative process and even had a way with charming lawmakers. He composed himself, and went on for half an hour, explaining why a racino should not be opposing daily fantasy sports and, to the surprise of those listening in, just how much he loved the beautiful city of Buffalo. Behind the scenes, FanDuel chief financial officer Matt King had been working feverishly on a deal with the upstate casino. That weekend FanDuel struck a $300,000 marketing agreement; in return, these track owners would flip their support to back the bill.

Still, it was an uphill climb: as other tech companies fighting the regulatory battle in New York had found out, the shrouded process in Albany was unlike any other: the poorly ventilated, unbearably hot halls of the New York state assembly had witnessed swaggering tech companies strutting into town and then leaving battered and weakened. That very month Albany had in fact been the scene of a bloodbath for two prominent startups in their own regulatory fight: Uber, which essentially had to kill its own bill because of backroom machinations, and Airbnb, which was effectively being shut down in New York City, were both being slaughtered in the New York State Legislature. And yet neither of those two startup behemoths attracted the kind of attention focused on the fight involving the daily fantasy industry.

Lawmakers on the sidelines of the fight began to comprehend the stakes when two tall men walked into the statehouse surrounded by cameras and began to speak at a podium. "The main reason I'm here is because I see what fantasy sports has done to my friends — how crazy they get, how excited they get," said former star NFL quarterback Jim Kelly, flanked by fellow former QB Vinny Testaverde. "I'd say probably 80, 85 percent of my friends play fantasy sports."

It didn't matter to the lawmakers that the quarterback was just the latest to conflate season-long fantasy sports with daily fantasy. It certainly didn't matter to the companies that the cameos cost them $100,000. In Nigel's latest lesson in politics in America, he saw that lawmakers love press for a bill they're sponsoring — and feared negative press more than anything. The media attention made opposition to the bill just a bit harder, especially for anyone representing a district where Kelly, who led the Buffalo Bills to four Super Bowls, and Testaverde, who starred for the New York Jets in the early 2000s, were heroes.

And yet local New York special interest groups would not let even these two leave town unruffled. Lobbyists against daily fantasy pushed ethics violations on Jim Kelly as he stood in the capitol signing autographs because he was signing his name to gifts worth more than $15, which was above the value that state officers were allowed to accept. Not even a beloved sports figure — a Hall of Famer, now diminished as he underwent cancer treatment — could step into the cutthroat world of daily fantasy sports and leave unscathed.

Just down the road from where Jason and Nigel dined, Jeremy Kudon sat in his Albany hotel room suffering a crisis of confidence, convinced that he'd just lead the industry off a cliff. The bright side: he could just go back to litigation. Now he could finally take his wife to see *Hamilton*. Kudon knew as well as anyone what defeat in Albany meant. "Neither company was going to be able to operate in New York, because no investor was going to be a believer if there was no clarity in New York," he says. With one day remaining in the New York state assembly session, Kudon was becoming increasingly convinced that he and Genetski might be leading the entire daily fantasy industry off a cliff. That Thursday night he had received an email from someone inside. *We're going to have to pull a rabbit out of the hat in the senate*, it read. He began to draft an email to the two companies. *I don't know what to tell you ... We've done everything we can, left everything on the table ... I'm not optimistic.* They were all bracing for the worst. "You had a good run," Christian Genetski's wife told him that night.

The billion-dollar fantasy sports war was now in the hands of a group of New York State lawmakers, like Bonacic and assemblyman Dean

Murray, the rare Albany politician who had actually been on the Draft-Kings and FanDuel sites. Murray had emerged as a leading voice for the industry after Eric Schneiderman announced that November that he was going to shut down the companies. In that moment, Murray turned to his wife and said: "Oh no he's not — not in the middle of football season." That night he began writing a press release, introducing a bill that would legalize daily fantasy games in his state. On June 17, 2016, he stood on the floor of the New York State assembly, addressing the grand room, arguing that these games were "nothing but day trading for sports fans." The bill now being considered, introduced by assemblyman Gary Pretlow, used other states' templates: Players had to be at least eighteen. No college contests could be offered. Fund segregation was mandatory. Operators were to register with the state gaming commission. Notably, operators would pay a 15 percent gross revenue tax, not a onetime licensing fee, the proceeds going to state education funding. The bill passed that assembly easily, by a 91–22 vote, but the biggest question was always whether it was going to make it through the senate. Not long after his victory, Dean Murray got a text from a senator: *We're in trouble.*

They were in *big* trouble, because now standing on the side of the rope opposing the bill and the daily fantasy sports industry was a man whose mere name sent shudders through the halls of the statehouse: *Feathers.* James Featherstonhaugh was one of the best-known, best-connected, and most feared lobbyists in Albany: a successful plaintiff's attorney, he had gone toe-to-toe as a lobbyist with seven different governors. He was also a minority owner of Saratoga Casino and Raceway, where two million people annually gambled tens of millions of dollars on video slot machines; for decades he had been fighting for a full-scale casino, with live poker dealers and, perhaps one day, a sports book. Feathers was in his sixties and always dressed in pin-striped suits; if you were a Hollywood casting agent looking to fill the role of a powerful lobbyist, you could send along a portrait of Feathers. Votes on the senate bill were vanishing like smoke, Murray had been told. Murray didn't need to know more than that Feathers had stepped into a room of Democrats. By the time he stepped out, a bloc of senators had joined him on his side of the tug-of-war. "Someone was saying, 'I can't believe it, Feathers is here,'" recalls Kudon. "'I've never seen him here that much.' And that was . . . upsetting."

The eleventh-hour turn of events had Kudon now thinking that his next case would most certainly be as a litigator. Kudon received a text with a GIF from Genetski — a play from the Titans Rams game in Super Bowl XXXIV. All they could do was watch from the sidelines as their bill fell one yard short.

The grandfather clock that stood tall in the back of the assembly chamber inched toward 1:30 a.m. A group of senators left the chamber and disappeared into a room. Inside were four senators who had the power to swing entire blocs of their party. One was John Bonacic, whose Republican conference didn't have enough votes to pass it on their own. "It was a poker game they were playing," says Bonacic of the Democrats in the room. "And that's the heart of how we were going to play this. 'Go ahead, you want to vote it down? We'll make sure every voter in the state of New York will know every "no" vote.' This is part of how the game is played, you know."

In his final argument, Bonacic pointed out to his colleagues the two sides of the tug-of-war. He cut through all the lobbyists and special interests to bring their attention to one entity that had in some sense been absent from the process: the voters. Because, as the votes were being taken and politicians held closed-door meetings, something miraculous was happening: the fans were making their voices heard. By late that night, in fact, 250,000 emails had arrived in the inboxes of various representatives. Bonacic in fact had had ammunition for his argument all along: unlike Airbnb and Uber, DraftKings and FanDuel had a community with deep personal connections to the industry, a community that could be mobilized at a moment's notice, thanks to the infrastructure put in place through the lobbying group assembled by Jeremy Kudon, Fantasy Sports For All, whose database with millions of names and emails of DraftKings and FanDuel users was now used to inundate inboxes in Albany at a rate that astounded many longtime lawmakers. It was estimated that "7,500 to 15,000 people were playing for *every* senate

district," says Bonacic. His ammunition was, "You know, this is very popular in your district." All legislators had to do was ask a staffer precisely
how many emails they'd received. In some cases, the number was in the
tens of thousands.

No one had seen it coming: that the final pull in a tug-of-war would
come from an unseen force, outside of Albany, that was as strong as,
and in the end maybe even stronger than, the casinos, the heavyweight
lobbyists behind the casinos, and all the other forces opposing the fantasy sports industry on the other side of the rope. The final pull would
come from the fans. Bonacic added, "Now, look, I've never played fantasy
sports, so to me this wasn't life-or-death. This issue was in my lap because I was chairman of that committee. But because of its popularity, I
just thought it was the right thing to do to carry the ball on this and not
see this new and flourishing industry terminated."

The final vote of the 2016 legislative session came at quarter past two
in the morning. If you woke up later that morning and read the cursory
accounts of the final day in Albany, one that stretched into the wee hours
of Saturday morning, and its flurry of activity before lawmakers headed
home to prepare for their November reelections, you'd read about the
passage of a bill that allowed restaurants to serve alcohol at 10 a.m. on
Sundays; an agreement to allow lead testing in New York schools; the
defeat of legislation that would authorize ride-sharing companies Uber
and Lyft outside of Manhattan; and the passage of a bill legalizing online daily fantasy sports games. Anyone who'd seen the final vote in the
senate — 45–17 — wouldn't have known just how close the bill had been
to defeat.

Even many of those in the industry with so much at stake would only
know, after staying up late until the vote was cast, that a coin had landed
on the right side.

And, so too would the two CEOs.

Every day in their roles, they and those around them had taken countless risks and made countless bets — gambles that had been both infini-

tesimally small and incalculably big. Once again, a big bet had paid off, and the companies would live to see another day. Two months later, in early August, New York governor Andrew Cuomo signed a bill legalizing daily fantasy sports in his state, in time for the start of the NFL season.

One afternoon a week later Jason was in a car headed back to his offices after attending a bill signing at the Massachusetts statehouse. Dressed in a blue blazer and red shirt, he had spent the last hour uncomfortably standing at the front of the room, behind a lectern, sweating through his shirt. "My feet are killing me," he said, after listening to a succession of state officials and then the governor of Massachusetts speak to commemorate the signing of something called "An Act Relative to Job Creation and Workforce Development." With the signing, Massachusetts became the ninth state to legalize daily fantasy sports in 2016, a particularly key moment because of the ongoing federal investigation in Massachusetts, which was looking into DraftKings as an illegal gambling operation. With a state bill in place legalizing daily fantasy sports, it would have been surprising if the investigation went anywhere. The tide was turning, but heading into the 2016 NFL season, he did not feel as if the moment was one to celebrate. For one thing, the outside world still saw DraftKings and FanDuel, less than a year after the *Times* story, as the two startups behind the implosion of an industry.*

Jason was aware of all the negative stories. Perhaps he'd been humbled, just a bit. He certainly was wiser. The last few months had, at least, given him a certain new clarity. He looked back to that vision that had propelled him forward, that belief that he was the only one who could change the rules of the game because he saw the board differently.

"The vision, from the start, was: we can build something that is a new age company that is one of the all-time greats," he said. "In terms of impact on sports, we're aiming for ESPN, but also something on the level

---

* "The implosion of daily fantasy sports is a bro-classic tale of hubris, recklessness, political naiveté, and a kill-or-be killed culture," read the headline on an *ESPN The Magazine* deep dive on an industry's spectacular fall.

of Google or Apple or Facebook. In terms of changing sports, that was always the vision. It was always that big. We were the ones that we felt always had the biggest vision and had the most expansive view — a view of what the real opportunity was. We were the ones who had this very different vision — an idea of what our destiny was — to set the landscape where it wanted to go.

"We were the ones who were going to write the book on this. That idea gave us a greater sense of mission, in the way that a great vision can serve your company in that it can grow your company and survive in a nascent marketplace. The vision was the core of us at the start.

"But it was also a complete myth."

Over these last few months and weeks, he admitted, he had begun to see that it was a delusion from the start. A delusion to think that the story they were crafting inside those gleaming offices was unique; that *they* knew and understood the world better than anyone else; that just because they had the biggest story meant that they could win a billion-dollar war; that a story alone was good enough to win. Jason had begun to see, during his dinners with Nigel in Albany to discuss their business, that it was possible to sit down and talk. Over the next few weeks, during the fall of 2016, the two companies would, in fact, begin to convene a series of meetings in Boston and New York to discuss a merger.

"As I started talking to him," Jason said, "I would hear Nigel say literally the same thing about his company that I would say about ours. It was just a realization: maybe at our cores we weren't different at all. I thought we had these ideas that were going to propel us to become something new — and I just came to the conclusion that it was 99 percent about the execution. The vision itself? Anyone can come up with that."

Neither company was yet close to profitable, and neither company was going to see any growth during the 2016 NFL season, but there were larger dynamics at play in the world around them signaling that the environment in sports and business might once again be perfect for these two companies at a particular point in time. Jason was now seeing the same changes in the world around him that Vic Salerno was seeing out in the desert: a landscape that was bigger than daily fantasy games.

For the industry, the tide had begun to turn many months before the bill passed in Albany. The turning point was May, in Richmond, Va. Inside an opulent hotel that, with its stained glass ceiling and marble statues and columns and antique furniture and oil paintings in the grand lobby, seemed to evoke another time, they were all here: the founders of the two companies, board members, everyone dressed for the signing of a new bill that would make daily fantasy legal in Virginia, the first state to do so. The tide was beginning to turn not just on the legislative front. Shamrock's Mike LaSalle was walking through the lobby of the Jefferson Hotel when he saw Nigel and Jason talking in a corner of the room. *That's interesting*, he thought. An hour later, he walked through the room again, and saw that the two had not moved from their seats. For the first time, LaSalle thought that a merger was possible; the rivalry, the escalating game between the companies was, finally, perhaps, behind all of them.

This wasn't, of course, Jason's first conversation with Nigel. And Jason had run into and even been friendly with Tom Griffiths at various events. But there was one founder at FanDuel that Jason had never met. She was standing alone in the middle of the room at the bill ceremony, dressed in a black gown. Jason had heard much about FanDuel's CMO, of course, heard that she was the most competitive of all of them, that she had as big a hand as anyone in growing the company in the early years — years before DraftKings even existed.

Jason approached her. "It's great to meet you, finally," he said. Lesley Eccles looked up at Jason Robins, and smiled. There were so many questions she could have asked. *Why, for starters, did he view the daily fantasy war as a winner-take-all game? What was he thinking in raising the stakes to such preposterous levels? Is this the outcome he wanted?* Perhaps the other founders had moved on, and could say that they respected the decisions that Jason had made. At least, they would have been able to carry on a conversation with their once bitter rival — but not Lesley.

There was nothing left to say. Without a word, she simply smiled at Jason, and walked away.

14

NIGEL'S DELUSION

New York, Fall 2016–Summer 2017

Nigel emerged from the subway entrance, squeezed through the morning sidewalk crowd, and walked toward the entrance of the New York Stock Exchange. It was one of those bright, crisp Manhattan mornings in September when anything felt possible, and the CEO of FanDuel, donning a black blazer and a neat, sculpted coif, had a bounce to his step. He was making a stop on a small press tour with the start of the 2016 football season set to begin, preparing to get the word out that despite reports of their demise, the companies were not dead. They had survived by the skin of their teeth after the eleventh-hour passage of a bill in the New York state house and the governor's signing of the bill legalizing daily fantasy sports in the state that fed the ecosystem with more users than any other state in the country.

Nigel arrived at the studio that presided over the frenetic exchange floor, a TV set bathed in an iridescent blue, with shiny surfaces and an array of screens and three hosts perched over a long table, tugging at their earpieces, looking down at their tablets, checking their phones. An army of assistants were waiting to mic him up and apply a layer of powder to his face so that it was as smooth as the icing on a wedding cake, and as the seconds ticked down on the digital clock on the wall before he got in his chair, he mentally reviewed the talking points that his communications manager, Justine Sacco, had helped shape: on regulation *(we're back online, now in forty states, including New York)*, on the new mission of the company *(it's still about making sports more exciting, but making it more social and less about the money)*, and on the prospects of a merger with their longtime rival DraftKings *(the industry is shifting toward cooperation)*.

As he stepped onto the set, Nigel stopped in his tracks. He had forgotten to bring something so vital that he felt as if he were about to wander in front of the cameras naked. Nigel had done enough of these interviews to know that the hosts would always, at the end of the segment, playfully ask him for some fantasy football advice — the name of a player, say, to look out for on Sunday. Surely, a softball question to the head of a fantasy sports company. *A name — just a name!* The request had always caused Nigel great anguish. He wasn't Jason Robins, a fantasy sports nerd who could off the top of his head tell you which RB2 just that morning had inched closer to the top of a depth chart. Being the CEO of FanDuel hadn't exactly converted Nigel into a rabid American sports fan, and any time he attempted to answer the question for an audience of sports fans about actual sports was yet another opportunity to expose himself.

Nigel texted a few people back in the office: *Fantasy pick?*

Dak Prescott, someone texted back. *Cowboys QB.*

Okay, Nigel thought. *Prescott. Dallas Cowboys.*

". . . Plus . . . the future of daily fantasy after a long legal battle across the country. We'll talk to the CEO of FanDuel . . ." the host was saying, and with that Nigel was whisked onto the bright set, where he joined the others at the table, the cameras now directed at them like a firing squad. Before he knew it, the red light on the camera flashed. He was on air. "After some extended scrutiny over its legality, daily fantasy is back just in time for football," said the host. "Joining us as Week 2 of the NFL season kicks off is FanDuel CEO Nigel Eccles. Bring people up to date on where they can find you."

"Absolutely," Nigel said. "We're online in nearly forty states . . . We obviously had to go offline earlier this year, a lot of headlines around that . . ."

Days earlier, FanDuel had reintroduced itself to America, unveiling a new logo — a clean, sleek blue shield — and ad campaign that celebrated the joy of being a sports fan. "SportsRich" was the term that FanDuel head of brand Dan Spiegel and his team had landed on and were now using in new ads that featured everyday people in their living rooms watching an NFL game and flipping over snack bowls, jumping off couches, cheering, high-fiving, taunting, hugging everyone in sight in a shower of popcorn. *THIS IS FANTASY SPORTS BUILT FOR EVERY FAN. Passion. Excitement. Thrill. Fun.* No promo codes, no testimonials, no dollar signs.

"Has there been a noticeable dent in customers?" one talking head on the panel was asking Nigel, "because of the fear that they're doing something illegal even if they're not?"

"There certainly was last year. We had a lot of brand damage last year. What we've done over the last twelve months is try and bring those people back."

"You guys spent a ton on marketing. You probably can't keep spending that much."

"I'd say last year was about awareness." Then Nigel added, "We got *a lot* of awareness last year . . ."

That last line got some big laughs: they were all in on it, the CEO, the host, even the other talking heads, this understanding that the ads, the damn ads, *were* everywhere. Now they felt like the ads were nowhere; a year after appearing every ninety seconds, they appeared on average just once every game.

The interview was off to a loose, easy start; Nigel, always a picture of rectitude, looked relaxed, but in reality he was having difficulty focusing. The Cowboys quarterback. What was his name? Prescott — yes, Prescott. Zak. Jak? *Wasn't it Zak??* None of those options seemed exactly right. He could feel a cold sweat breaking through that impenetrable layer of powder. He was mortified. Then he had a thought to just name the first NFL player that came to mind, but quickly he realized there was a problem. In that moment he had trouble naming *any* NFL player! He kept returning to that name . . . *Zak* Prescott? Something about the sound of it in his head didn't seem right.

"Part of that awareness was to shift some of that away from your main rival, DraftKings," the host said. "When the head of DraftKings says a merger is an interesting idea, do you agree?"

A question about the merger: *that* was something Nigel was fully prepared to answer. "It's a very competitive market," he said. "It was true about all startups last year — it was all about growth. Everyone was like, spend, grow, that's all that people care about. This year, for every startup, it's like, no, things have changed. What you're seeing in the industry is a shift toward cooperation."

What Nigel *didn't* say was that a few nights earlier he and one of his board members had met for dinner at a Manhattan Italian restaurant, just a few miles from the Stock Exchange, with Jason and one of the DraftKings board members. This meal came after the many dinners that Nigel and Jason, alone on the road, had shared in Albany, and the many meetings the two companies had held to iron out the details of a combined company. Naturally, the topic of cooperation came up: it made perfect sense to share costs and expenses so that they would be big enough not only to survive the inevitable moment when a media behemoth entered the space, but also to remain the dominant entity in the industry.

Nigel had shown up that night in Manhattan thinking a deal was more or less in place. But not long into the evening the question that always seemed to be at the crux of every conversation about a merger came up once again: who would be CEO? Before this evening, there had been a tacit agreement between the two sides to kick specific issues sideways until a deal went through, or even until it simply seemed imminent. But Nigel and LaSalle realized quickly after they arrived at the restaurant that what had been agreed upon was no longer the plan. Jason wanted to settle the CEO question in that moment. LaSalle was just as floored as Nigel over what he was hearing. Even before the appetizers arrived, they had both walked out of the restaurant.

Nigel wasn't going to tell the world that a merger that had seemed inevitable days earlier now seemed unlikely. Not to millions of viewers on live TV — and so when the CNBC host asked, "When the head of DraftKings says a merger is an interesting idea, do you agree?" Nigel replied, "I can't make any forecasts. We're trying to do the same thing . . ."

But really, something else was nagging at him. After answering the merger question with that autopiloted answer, Nigel suddenly felt the sweat coming on again. It was as if his body could feel it: the inevitable question, coming. *Nigel! Quick! Give us your fantasy pick of the week!*

The quarterback — the damn quarterback. What was his name? Nigel could feel the blood drain from his face. *Prescott — yes, Prescott. Zak. Jak?*

Wasn't it Zak??

Could it actually be *Pak?*

The word he used, half-jokingly, when he was asked to describe what it was like to be the CEO of a startup was *impostor,* which was a bit extreme of course, but it got somewhere near the truth of how Nigel sometimes felt as the head of an American fantasy sports company, a role that he'd never imagined he'd take on. He had felt the impostor syndrome from time to time during his years at FanDuel — in those VIP suites with the team owners talking sports; at the FSTA conventions pretending he was familiar with the oeuvre of the fantasy sports analyst who was the keynote speaker; at live tournaments trying his best to hold a conversation with the NFL Hall of Famer while frantically retrieving mental talking points — the *name* of that Hall of Famer, for starters — from his Wikipedia phone search just minutes before introducing himself.

Now it felt like the fate of the entire company depended on whether or not he could remember the name of the quarterback of the Dallas Cowboys. He felt his entire body freeze; here was the moment, at last, that the impostor would be exposed! The man who ran the biggest fantasy sports company in the world could not offer one bloody fantasy sports tip.

But then, suddenly, he was hearing the host say, ". . . and when we come back, Donald Trump finally admitting the President was born in the United States!"

Saved by Donald Trump. Nigel exhaled. He felt like a fool. He'd nearly had a panic attack on live TV because he couldn't remember the name of a damn NFL player. Just as quickly as he was ushered onto the set, he was whisked away again. He walked through the doors and out of the Stock Exchange, into the bright morning, thinking:

What am I doing?

Nigel wanted to become CEO of a theoretical merged company, yes — but why? He wanted to run the combined company for the sake of his employees; to become CEO would mean, in a fifty-fifty equity split, that by some measure Nigel had won. Under that calm and measured surface, a deep competitiveness had always burned inside Nigel, and a final victory for FanDuel would mean something. He wanted to do it for the cofounders. He wanted to do it for Lesley. The one person he never thought about, it now occurred to him, was himself.

And when he finally asked himself that question, in that moment, of whether he wanted to be CEO of a fantasy company, Nigel wasn't so sure.

He stepped into the cool morning. The flag above the Stock Exchange fluttered in the wind. It was strange, unfamiliar, this feeling he had as he walked away. Once, years earlier, in describing what it was like to be CEO of this company, Nigel had said that it felt like he was holding on to the tail of a dragon. The dragon that Nigel imagined was a sneering, untamable beast that had been roused and then taken flight after the explosion of competition between two companies; clinging to the tail, he felt the alarm and the fear and the freezing wind around him, all of it, but to let go would be to tumble into a hot lava sea below. As the stakes were raised at every turn, the dragon flew higher and higher, and he held on tighter and tighter.

But now, for the first time, he could feel his grip on the dragon loosening.

Lesley awoke, sensing that something had changed. She was in a house tucked away on a narrow gravel road, a short walk from a man-made lake, miles away from the big city, and across the ocean from the city they loved and had left behind. They had been living in this town in the suburbs of New York City for a few months now. They'd finally made the move to the United States, feeling that it was what was needed to save the company and, perhaps, themselves; the expectation, when they uprooted their family, was that Nigel's full-time presence here was going to be essential as he took over as CEO of the new combined company.

The distance between New York and Edinburgh had also taken its toll, with Nigel and Lesley shuttling back and forth, hopping on transatlantic flights for last-minute meetings. When they were house-hunting they noticed that the house a few doors from theirs had the name SCHNEIDERMAN on the mailbox. They had a good laugh about it, but then Lesley did some digging to make sure there were no attorneys general, their nemeses for the last two years, in the neighborhood. When people in their town, like the delightful Schneidermans down the road, or Lesley's personal trainer at the gym, or the kids' teachers at their school, asked what it was they did, they always answered with a question: *Have you heard of a company called FanDuel?* Often there was a pause, a vague recognition of the name. A hint: *You know, all those commercials during football games?* That's what it would take for the recognition, *Oh, yeah, of course!* and *Oh, so you must be a huge sports fan!*

On this morning, the morning after Nigel's appearance on CNBC, Lesley felt that something had changed even before Nigel turned to her and said, "I think it's time." Nigel didn't tell her about his epiphany outside the Stock Exchange, didn't tell her about that preposterous moment on live TV. He told her only that he had come to a realization: it was time for him to step away.

"If that's what you want to do," she said. "You know I'm with you."

In that moment, they could both see, clearly, how it would all play out: a merger of two companies, a fifty-fifty equity split, a board evenly represented by the two companies, merged staffs, offices in Boston, New York, and Edinburgh. The platform would be FanDuel's, the tech lead by DraftKings, an executive team that was a mix of leaders from both companies. Jason Robins would be CEO, Nigel would be chairman of the board. The name would be some awkward mishmash of the two operators, though the limited options — FanKings for one — did not exactly have the right ring to them.

It would be, on the surface, a win for everyone. But at FanDuel there was no other way to feel it than as anticlimactic for some, as a defeat for others. Nigel stepping down would pave the way not just for Jason to become CEO, but also for DraftKings to muscle its way into becoming the dominant presence in a merged company, and the industry. With Jason in position to call the shots, no one at FanDuel was convinced that the DraftKings culture wouldn't become theirs. In New York, there were rumors of even more layoffs in the FanDuel offices.

The circumstances of the merger would even create tension within the FanDuel founding team. When Tom caught wind of how much money Nigel would be walking away with, even he — someone who'd been there from the beginning, who'd had Nigel at his side as one of the groomsmen in his wedding — was taken aback by the sum. They'd all had a hand in the company's success, and Tom felt a tinge of resentment that he and Rob, two founders who were remaining at the company, reporting to the enemy, would be watching from the other side as Nigel faded into the sunset on his golden parachute. The scenario was always hard to even imagine, and the reality was now difficult to swallow: after all these years of clashing with DraftKings, to suddenly now be working as one?

When Jason Robins looked back at the series of events that had led him to this moment, he would say that he wouldn't have changed anything. Ask the FanDuel founders to look back, though, and it's as if they would have changed *everything*. Because they could see now that they had made mistakes — a countless number of them. Their first venture, each of them could agree, was a case study in how *not* to build a startup: *don't* be so precious about your idea that you hole up in a cave for months on end; *don't* roll out your product with an all-or-nothing big-bang launch; *don't* fear failure, because fear keeps you from seeing that the first iteration of your startup was merely an experiment for your next iteration. All of that was before their pivot to fantasy sports, before they became FanDuel. Then they made even more mistakes, more frequently, and larger in scale: the mistake of not striking a deal to acquire Draft-Street and thereby opening the door to the competition; the mistake of letting the ads in 2015 be all about the money; the mistake of letting their employees play even as the companies became more than just niche sites; the mistake of not building more relationships with attorneys general and lobbyists on the regulatory side; the mistake of underestimating, at every turn, just how far Jason Robins would go to win the war.

. . .

After weeks and then months of interminable and agonizing hearings and interviews and meetings between the two companies to figure out how a combined company would work, the Federal Trade Commission released a statement one morning in July 2017:

> The FTC authorized legal action to block the merger of the two largest daily fantasy sports sites, DraftKings and FanDuel, alleging that the combined firm would control more than 90 percent of the US market for paid daily fantasy sports contests.

And just like that, the merger between DraftKings and FanDuel was nixed. There were always reasons why the FTC would strike down a potential merger and put a stop to a deal: the sticking point was always that the combined company would be a monopoly in the market that was daily fantasy sports. But that could also be a misreading of what the market was to those who saw DraftKings and FanDuel as smaller fish in a larger pool: the overall fantasy sports industry, and the sports betting industry as a whole.

A flurry of statements from the CEOs and other spokesmen at the companies ensued, about how this was not a total setback, about how the future of the companies was still bright. The development was met in the media with surprise and confusion about what was going to happen next. In Boston, promises of promotions and new titles were put on hold.

In Edinburgh, still the heart of FanDuel, there was less of a conflict of emotions. The Edinburgh office remained its own island, worlds away from the New York office. The moment the news broke, employees were still on hand in the Edinburgh office, working feverishly to complete the new features for the upcoming NFL season. Many of them in Edinburgh had convinced themselves that a merger was good for the company and that it was what they wanted — but once the news came out, it was like a dam had broken, releasing a flood of emotions. There were quiet cheers. Bottles of champagne. It felt strange, because there were now some real questions about the company's viability, real questions about whether

FanDuel could survive on its own, real questions about what FanDuel, going forward, would be. And a handful of original employees in the company had been on the verge of becoming filthy rich off a merger, and none of them now were going to be a penny richer.

Still, despite the uncertainty that the latest news had wrought, those in the Edinburgh office that night couldn't contain their giddiness. It was clear, here at least, that the news was cause for celebration.

FanDuel — *their* FanDuel — would live to see another day.

It was always her favorite place in the city: the majestic park that sat just blocks from the FanDuel offices in Edinburgh, under the gaze of the university offices where, many years ago, their story began. When the cherry blossoms were in full bloom, as they were today, the Meadows was the most beautiful place in the world. It was always her refuge, as it was on this day when she walked along the path, found a bench, and sat down to begin dialing numbers.

Since the start of 2016, after the shift had begun, everyone at FanDuel could see that Lesley's role was being reduced. Anticipating an internal announcement explaining that she would be stepping away from her duties, Lesley began calling the people with whom she had worked the closest, and for the longest time. She did her best to explain the move to her longtime colleagues, and they listened to her reasons: budgets were going down; they didn't need her, given the size of the new marketing teams in New York and also now in Los Angeles; she wanted to spend time with the children. But they could hear in the way she talked that there was more to the story; this didn't exactly sound like Lesley, who wasn't someone who'd back down and step away quietly. Some listened quietly as she spoke; others started to cry.

Eventually, the announcement would come out with little fanfare.

> Private equity companies Kohlberg Kravis Roberts (KKR) and Shamrock Capital Advisors have tightened their control of fantasy sports business FanDuel which has seen founder Lesley Eccles leave the board. She is one of five directors to leave after the

company was forced to hand over equity to its backers following the collapse of its merger with rival DraftKings. The merger was intended to ease their financial pressures following a long legal battle to defend their operations.

On her last official day at FanDuel, she was in the office in Edinburgh, tapping out emails, when Nigel came by. "Let's go," he whispered.

They were already there waiting for him, Tom and Rob, the two other cofounders. They were at the little pub across the street, where they'd come to celebrate in 2011, when they got the round of funding that saved them; where they'd come to celebrate in the summer of 2015, after another funding round that had established them, officially, as a billion-dollar company. This wasn't a celebration, not exactly, but it was rare for the four of them to be together, in the same country; when they were, the world always seemed to have an unusual clarity to it — overlaid with the inevitable drunken haze. Lesley could always drink as much as the guys, and she wasn't disappointing on this night, when the group in the corner became a loud and raucous mob. When it was the four of them, memories often flooded back, and through story after story, told through one drink after another, they were reminded of just how far they'd come in these nine years.

Another small group passed by their table. It was a group from a startup called SkyScanner, fellow entrepreneurs who worked in the same building as theirs; in fact, SkyScanner was the only other billion-dollar company, the only other unicorn, in all of Scotland. One of them from the group took one look at the four drunken revelers and asked:

"So, what are you all celebrating?"

Once his grip on the dragon began to loosen, it became impossible for Nigel to tighten his hold again. After more than a year of talks and meetings, the merger had fallen through, and, suddenly, just as Jason Robins was not going to be the CEO of a combined company, Nigel wasn't going to be the chairman of the board. Instead, Nigel was back to his role as CEO — but only temporarily. So much was set in motion during the merger process that it was becoming impossible for things to go back to the way they were before it. Whether Nigel did or didn't want to be CEO of a fantasy sports company for the next ten years of his life would not matter. The official announcement came in November, 2017: Nigel was stepping down as CEO and leaving the company.* Soon, Tom and Rob would follow. All the founders would be gone from the company they'd created, ten years after first launching it as a peculiar news prediction site. The tug-of-war between the founders and late-stage investors that began in a small conference room in Edinburgh that August afternoon back in 2014, intensified into a larger power struggle in 2015, and then took hold in 2016 during the company's fight for survival — and now, with Nigel's departure, FanDuel's transformation from a UK startup to a private-equity controlled entity was complete.

Leading up to that moment, Nigel had had countless thoughts about what he would do next. Among them: he would write a book. Whether he was capable of writing one, he hadn't the slightest clue, but one day he decided to sit in front of his computer in his office, collect some memories, and sketch a story. He tapped out a title:

> The Massive Multi-billion Dollar Scheme Intended to Evade the Law and Fleece Sports Fans†

And then he began writing:

> I definitely don't have the background you'd expect from someone who transformed sports, never mind someone who was alleged to have run a multi billion dollar illegal gambling scheme.

---

* His replacement would be CFO Matt King, who'd been hired by Nigel in 2014 to join FanDuel after ten years at KKR

† Two years had passed since the line didn't seem like quite a joke: "It is clear that DraftKings and FanDuel are the leaders of a massive, multibillion-dollar scheme intended to evade the law and fleece sports fans across the country," Eric Schneiderman had said when he sent the cease-and-desist order to FanDuel in 2015.

Brought up in a farm in Northern Ireland and living in Edinburgh, Scotland, I not only had never played fantasy sports before starting FanDuel, I actually don't think I'd ever watched
a full football game. I certainly didn't understand the rules of
either. I also didn't know how to build a company. And unfortunately, neither did any of my co-founders. It wasn't exactly an
auspicious start.

Nigel suspected that these last ten years would make a business story
unlike any other ever told, but the problem was that he didn't know what
kind of story it was — a handbook for how to build a billion dollar company, or a guide for how *not* to build one? A success story or a cautionary
tale?

It was all of those things, of course. To some, the end of the story for
the founders at FanDuel would be the most pedestrian part of an out-
landish tale: the late-stage investor crushes the founders. The founders
paid a price, a steep one, for turning their billion-dollar fantasy into a
reality. "You're solidly an entrepreneur endeavor, and all of the sudden
you're big enough that you've raised private equity, and now it's a different business," one FanDuel investor remarked. "And this conflict between the later stage guys and founders happens all the time.

"In the story of FanDuel, you can go back to the 2015 board meeting
in September, when we're going head-to-head with DraftKings. At that
point you've raised so much money. This is the lesson to any founder. If
you take that much money and spend it all, you have to get it public or
get it bought, because the guy at the top of the stack will crush you."

The truth is that in 2015 FanDuel was on course for an IPO, possibly
as soon as early 2017 — but the unforeseen events of the fall of 2015 put
the company on a different trajectory. FanDuel, under the cofounders,
would neither go public nor be sold. For whatever exit event was going
to happen, they would be on the outside looking in, and whether they
would, in the end, make a small fortune off the silly little game would be
an open question — fully unresolved, possibly, for years.

That summer, Nigel had flown to Ireland and returned to Cookstown, his hometown with a population of twenty-two thousand. His mother still owned the same farm just outside of town. As he gazed out the windows on the drive home with his mom from the airport, he saw that in a world that was constantly changing, nothing here appeared to have changed at all. Later that week he stood in the tiny, damp Cookstown High School gymnasium, where he once played hockey, and in front of a class of two hundred, as well as some former teachers and his mother, gave a speech to the class of 2018.

He began: "You see, I wasn't the model student here, I wasn't head boy, I didn't make prefect, and if I won a prize I certainly don't remember it. So now, some twenty-five years behind my peers, I'm finally here. So thank you." He continued: "My first piece of advice you should hold regardless of what you want to do, whether it is be an entrepreneur or something completely different," he said, "it is simply marry well. Make sure you choose someone who believes in you and will support your dreams."

To this day he was eternally grateful for that moment when Lesley turned to him in the car and told him to chase his dream. Yes, Lesley was at her wit's end with the malcontent next to her, but the easy thing then would have been to tell her husband that he was delusional — that with a massive mortgage and two kids, the mere thought of walking away and talking such a long-shot game was pure insanity. Of course now, looking back, Nigel could see that his belief that he could actually create something of his own, that it might even change the world, had been a delusion from the start. You could call it a delusion, maybe a fantasy, or perhaps something else.

"Starting a business is a gamble," he said to the students. "When you build something new, there is always a risk of failure. But it is fun and it is an adventure. And only by taking a risk do you find out what you are really capable of."

And then he ended with a story: "When my son was five, he was learning how to swim. As part of that he had to learn to jump into the pool. After a big windup, he finally did it. After he got out, I told him how brave he was for doing it. But he said, 'Daddy, I wasn't brave, I was scared.' So I told him that's what bravery is: being scared, but still doing it anyway."

15

THE LAST SWEAT

San Francisco, Winter 2017

I t was funny, wasn't it, how just about all the gambling narratives in existence always revolved around the triumphant big score: how quickly the gambler squandered his money and then how, just as quickly, he won it all back. Rarely did the story linger on the low point because wait a little longer and there was always another beat: another hand, another lineup, another opportunity for a windfall that would change the story entirely.

When Cory looked at the graph that charted his career bankroll over time — specifically the pink line that tracked aggregate earnings, each win and loss recorded from each of the hundreds and sometimes thousands of entries spread across three and sometimes four or five different daily fantasy sites — the line spiked up and down like a seismograph, or more fittingly, like a jittery cardiac monitor: just looking at the financial oscillations, which mirrored his emotional oscillations, made Cory's heart flutter.

There was a sudden spike, for example, at the very beginning of the graph, November 19, 2012. "It was just a sick sweat," Cory recalled. "Bears and Forty-Niners, a Monday night game. Because guys just behind us in the standings had him, we needed Bears kicker Robbie Gould to score either one point or zero points in order to win eight thousand dollars. One of the best kickers in the NFL, and he can't make a field goal and he can only have one extra point. In other words, we need a perfect set of circumstances to happen. So we're sitting there, watching truly one of the worst games you'll ever see, because the Bears cannot move the ball. They're scoreless through one quarter. Scoreless through two quarters. In the third quarter, he kicks one extra point, and it's looking not great. But then it's punt, punt, punt. We're watching him miss field goals, and we're like, Okay, *maybe* we have a chance. And somehow, they're scoreless through the fourth. The game ends, and Robbie Gould has *one* point. First game of the season he has without a single field goal. It was the most miraculous fate ever. Eight thousand dollars. As much as a little blip it is now, that set off our operation. It was off to the races."

Every point on the graph after that was a new day, every high and every low a new twist you could tell in the story of a daily fantasy professional. The only question was whether you wanted to wait around for the next inevitable swing to come around before attempting to tell it.

In other words, as with the story of any gambler, when it came to just about any startup, you could perhaps tell just about whatever story you wanted: a story of perseverance or success, or failure, or survival, or redemption. What was the story, for instance, of the two fantasy sports startups born out of the perfect storm of the US economic landscape of the mid-2010s? It was an unassailable success story — you could hail the two companies' brilliance in acquiring customers and becoming the most successful startups in the sports industry since ESPN. But you could also pick a moment from the downturn that followed, to tell a different story — a story about the shortsighted win-at-all-costs mentality of startup founders barreling toward a billion-dollar valuation, or the madness of the media, or the hypocrisy of lawmakers and politicians, or the greed of the investment world.

And if you wanted, you could even say that the story was emblematic of every problem in society.

Which was the way Cory Albertson saw it in the winter of 2017 as he embarked on a strange journey at a strange time in the world around him — a time when the world seemed to be teetering on the edge. His friends joked that the scraggly beard-and-hair ensemble he'd grown made him look like one of those warriors on that very popular HBO show, and they thought that he was merely taking one of those interesting detours, like the semester he went to Chile to study international economics, or that summer he holed up in a dodgy neighborhood of a Mexican coastal town to play poker.

Then he told them the specifics of his plan: to live out of an RV for an indeterminate period of time, driving east from California, then south, then returning to the coast and driving north — the end point being a particular colony in a redwood forest in Oregon where people lived off the trees, going so far as eating the bark of the trees. They looked at him and thought, *Okay, maybe this is the beginning of the end of Cory Albertson.* He said good-bye to his old life at an RV park on Embarcadero, where he'd picked up a silver RV from a man who'd first given him the idea of this extended road trip. He had met this man — whose Instagram handle was spacetimetimespace — on the beach in Ojai. Cory figured that he was at a place where, if there was anyone to take advice from, it was someone named spacetimetimespace. That decision seemed not so wise one night when the worst rainstorms the area had seen in years hit and he found himself driving his truck up the narrow, twisting roads of the mountains, the silver capsule that he was tugging thrashing around like a rowboat in an angry sea.

Making stops at campsites along the way, he tended to his days in the same highly regimented, methodical way he'd gone about grinding in that other life: after waking to the sunlight filtering through the thin nylon curtains, he meditated to faint Tibetan chants that filtered out of his laptop; practiced an hour of yoga in an open patch outside his RV; took Scout, the eleven-year-old Labrador with the gimpy leg who was his sole companion, for a walk along the river at the foot of the grounds; made himself breakfast, which had become a lot simpler after he went to an exclusively Ayurvedic diet; and finally, turned on his phone to connect with the outside world, beginning with his business partner, Ray, who was already at work in front of his computer thousands of miles away in a bedroom in New Jersey feeding the algorithmic machine that he and Cory had built together.

All the hours of driving and sitting and sleeping in tight, awkward spaces had given him a vicious crick in his back. At Joshua Tree he met two rather attractive twenty-year-olds who were on their own little interesting detour to a Grateful Dead tribute concert in Tucson, and Cory volunteered to give them a lift. This detour took him to another desert pasture, where, under a sky painted strange and intoxicating shades of orange and purple, he danced for eight hours straight, until four in the morning, and in the process miraculously fixed his back.

When he woke up the next morning, feeling as refreshed as a newborn puppy, he went about his routine and then checked his phone, which had a message from Ray telling him that FantasyAces, one of the four daily fantasy sites where they had money deposited, was going bankrupt — just as Ray had predicted. Cory and Ray had essentially been scammed out of $85,000 that they were probably never going to get back.

Cory calmly put his phone away, turned up the volume on the laptop, closed his eyes, and — *ommmmmmmm* — began to chant.

What these last days on the road had given him was a sense of perspective about the games he played. The thing about fantasy sports was that while he loved the money, he loved the games too. He still loved the challenge of them, of trying to stay two steps ahead of everyone else in finding that edge that they could keep pressing. At the moment, he and Ray were obsessing about something that he thought could very well be the final solution to the game. The possible final solution was a model that could accurately predict ownership values of individual players in lineups. Once they could project their competitors' lineups, they could apply return-on-investment prediction for each one and then enter the lineups with the highest ROI. Once that happened, once they understood how they could maximize their portfolio and pick the stocks that were undervalued, daily fantasy games would be solved.

There was a time when he thought that there might be no more games at all — that he could wake up one morning and learn that the feds had raided the offices of the daily fantasy companies and the games had been shut down. But now he saw the bills being passed in states across the country; first in New York — the tipping point — and then in Arkansas,

Connecticut, Delaware, Maine, Mississippi, New Jersey, New Hampshire, Ohio, Pennsylvania, and Vermont, the bills passed in a remarkable regulatory wave. It was becoming clear that daily fantasy games were going to survive after all.

But that didn't mean that the cops weren't onto something when they started looking at the industry in 2015. "I can't tell you with a straight face that I haven't personally been defrauded while playing daily fantasy on one of the sites," he said. "We played on many sites. I don't know. *I'm skeptical.* Probably whatever was happening is no longer happening. With these things probably it's the case that nothing too nefarious was going on beyond maybe some things that have been reported. I'm not expecting some massive bombshell piece of news to come out. It's very possible that people were looking at lineups that Ray and I were submitting to guide their decision-making for lineups that they themselves were making. To me, that's borderline fraud.

"It's a legitimate question at this point: who cares? I mean, compared to what is going on in the world."

After the phone call from the FBI that he received at JFK Airport, Cory never heard from any authorities again.* He'd been shaken enough, however, to wonder if maybe he wasn't cut out for a life with so many extreme swings. He thought back to the pre-2015 days of daily fantasy, back when the prize pools weren't quite as big and there weren't so many ads, before big money flowed into the industry but everyone was having a great time regardless. Who was going to be held accountable for nearly destroying all that?

Cory seemed to be the only one who still cared about how the industry as a whole got to the moment where the feds were knocking on the

---

* Within the daily fantasy community, it was the worst-kept secret in the world that players were testifying. In one odd scene that had already played out, a number of high-volume players who all knew each other but were scattered across the country ran into each other at the downtown Boston courthouse. They were all dressed up, and while they knew what they were all there for, they didn't know *why.* "I've hired lawyers — *lawyerssss,* plural," said one. "I'm not a criminal. I play fantasy football in my underwear! What do they want to talk to me for?"

door. Who was responsible? It was not just the executives behind two main operators, not just the bloodsucking vampire venture capitalists who drained every last cent out of the industry; it was the players, too, including Cory himself, who was along for the ride and did nothing to stop it.

He knew that he, as much as anyone, had benefited and seen his life change as a result of these games; for him to attack the industry was hypocritical. He would allow you to call him out on that, as long as you called out everyone else. "The bummer is that we had a good thing going," he said. "Daily fantasy was chugging along before DraftKings came along. It was primed to be big — it was going to get there, whether or not DraftKings came into existence. They ignited some of the growth, got aggressive with fund-raising, and had overlay and brought a lot of attention to themselves, and it got bigger faster than it was meant to.

"How did this happen? It happened because of casino capitalism and a lack of accountability. If we're trying to assign blame for how the downfall of fantasy sports happened, it was almost like a systemic downfall.

"It was all the heads at the table — no one had enough skin in the game to make themselves responsible enough to make appropriate business decisions for the healthy long-term growth of the industry because everyone was not long-term focused. They were short-term focused. Let's grow quickly, let's dump this company onto a public stock exchange, and we're all going to be filthy rich.

"Venture capitalists are not investing their own money. They're investing the money of university endowments, pension funds, insurance funds, these huge entities, sitting on many billions of dollars, and they dole out some of this capital to venture capitalists who've some kind of compelling story on how they can generate impressive returns. So these venture capitalists, they're not the heart and soul of fantasy sports at all. They're basically ruthless financiers who saw an opportunity to make a bunch of money. And their scheme, they're trying to turn the ten million they invested in DraftKings, they want to double or triple or see it grow ten times as quickly as possible, and then get out of investing and return to their limited partners with this nice impressive check. They get their check and in the process they've nearly ruined fantasy sports for everyone."

Of course, fantasy sports *wasn't* ruined. DraftKings and FanDuel were still plugging away, in the aftermath of the failed merger. The war between the two companies was fading into memory, but the war between the sharks who played the games was continuing. How much longer Cory and Ray were going to be a part of it was an open question — they believed they had another year, at most, before they lost their edge. At their peak in 2015, he and Ray had amassed $4.3 million in less than five years — the last two years being filled with spikes. Their spreadsheets, their research and oddsmaking, the back-and-forth exchange of phone calls and texts — it was all part of a machine they'd built, which had become a million-dollar weapon. But now there were sharks out there with weapons just as formidable as theirs. For the first time, Cory and Ray could see the end for them, and it was near.

From Tucson, Cory had driven north, making stops among the magenta cliffs of Sedona before regretfully parting ways with the two twenty-somethings in Los Angeles. He and Scout were now alone again, navigating through the angriest storms that California had seen in a decade. Finally, days later than he had expected, he arrived at a camping area in Santa Cruz, next to an RV with a pink roof and a Rottweiler tied to its back bumper. He settled in the open portion of a lot strewn with flat needles and seed-bearing cones that looked like chocolate-covered almonds. Cory was also now a week into the Ayurvedic diet, which for him was basically frozen soy nuggets drenched in ginger and turmeric and cardamom. Even though each of his cheeks had been hollowed out like a halved coconut over the last week, he'd never felt closer to that place of balance he was seeking, a balance and sense of permanence that was all around him. He looked up in wonder at the three-thousand-year-old trees, swaying and crackling high above him but never snapping, and he thought that maybe the reason why he loved these creatures as much as he did was because they swayed and crackled and looked as if they

were going to break but had been on this earth for about as long as the
Great Pyramids.

The rains had gone and a cold wind whipped through the air the night
he decided that he would make a fire. Cory stood over the flame, rubbing
his hands, breathing in the air that smelled of burnt wood and the faint
lemony scent of the sequoias and the rosemary oil on his skin that he'd
bought at a reservation in Sedona and the faint whiff from the nearby
outhouse. He was beginning to believe that he was never returning to
his old life — he'd calculated how much he needed to live comfortably in
the silver capsule, driving across the country, going to tribute concerts
and meeting strangers along the way: $3,000 a month would cover the
expenses for this nomadic life, and maybe another few hundred dollars
for storage back in San Francisco. He had already bought the truck, and
now he thought he would buy the silver capsule as well. He would need
just a few days back in San Francisco to pack up his belongings, and
whatever he didn't sell or give away he would put into storage, and then
he would hit the road again, maybe go to that colony in Oregon and live
off the redwoods, if that was what gave him happiness.

On his final night at the campground, Cory sat at the foot of one of
the trees. Yes, he knew that this new life of his was a horrible cliché,
from the beard to the Tibetan chants to the rosemary oil to his belief
that if he could save himself, then maybe he could save the world. And
yes, he knew that anyone could call him hypocritical: despite renouncing
worldly pleasures, he still had skin in the game.

He looked up at the tree in front of him. The crown of the tree was
a perfectly symmetrical spire that looked like a rocket about to take off.
Maybe there was a chance these companies were going to be every bit
as big as they thought they would be in 2015. Maybe there was another
twist to the story coming. Even he could acknowledge that the story of
this industry, and the two companies that had triggered it, was astounding: The unlikely rise, the spectacular fall — and now what? The improb-
able return? Like everyone else in his world, Cory was following with
great interest the movement to legalize gambling nationwide, and he

saw the signs of a changing landscape there as well: the NHL awarding an expansion franchise to Las Vegas, the first professional sports franchise in gambling's holy land; a year later, the NFL owners voting 31–1 in favor of the Oakland Raiders' relocation to Vegas; and in June 2017, the US Supreme Court announcing that it would hear New Jersey's latest attempt to legalize sports betting. The environment was changing into one that would reward only the insanity, hyperaggressiveness, and hubris of the companies and the recklessness of the casino capitalists. The stakes were only getting higher, and as he tried to anticipate what was about to happen next, it was becoming overwhelmingly clear that, out of the rise of this fantasy sports game that he loved, in the end all the wrong people and entities were once again going to come out of this filthy rich, the biggest winners in a crooked game.

16

THE SPEED OF THE GAME

2018–2019

The headline appears one morning in the form of a news alert, the notification popping up on devices with urgency: "The Supreme Court Strikes Down a Federal Ban on Commercial Sports Betting."

Websites everywhere and then cable news outlets pick it up moments later, hailing the news as a landmark ruling in the United States, one poised to upend the $70 billion American sports industry; on a Monday in May, it is the biggest story of the morning. For the last twenty-five years, because of the Professional and Amateur Sports Protection Act, sports gambling has been allowed largely only in Nevada, but soon it can take place anywhere in the country; the ruling has left the states to decide whether or not to allow gambling within their borders. Even to industry insiders who in recent months had predicted this outcome, the resounding 7–2 decision in *Murphy v. NCAA,** which claimed that the state of New Jersey was violating PASPA by passing a referendum allowing sports gambling, is a jolting moment; just a year earlier, it seemed like a long shot that the Supreme Court would even hear arguments on a case challenging the law banning nationwide sports betting, but now the day that many thought they would never see has in fact arrived.

---

* The suit was formerly *Christie v. NCAA;* Chris Christie's name was supplanted when Phil Murphy became the state's new governor.

To some, the news is the latest jarring addition to the unease people across the country are feeling in 2018, which is that the world is going mad. Political unrest, economic turmoil, the dying planet, and now, in the latest signifier of the end of civilization as we know it, anyone, anywhere, so long as there is a device nearby, will soon be permitted to risk one's hard-earned money on the fate of a sports team.

"Now you can bet on high school games. You could bet on AAU games with fourteen-year-olds," says Bill Bradley, the seventy-four-year-old former US senator who decades ago pushed PASPA through, in a statement that feels like a dire warning. "There's no prohibition whatsoever."

A slew of numbers are fire-hosed at the public on TV in the form of graphics, charts, infographics — $2.3 billion, the annual projected revenue from sports betting in just one sports league, the NFL, within two years; fifteen million, the number of Americans at risk of developing a gambling addiction; $1 trillion, the possible overall handle in the United States within ten years — though with little context provided, it's impossible to know what to make of these numbers. The issue is too massive to grasp in the moment.

As they do after a sporting event, pundits quickly assign winners and losers, each compiling their own lists, in some cases contradicting each other. Among the winners, we are told, are the state of New Jersey, every other state in America with a gambling bill percolating in its statehouse, casinos, sports data companies, legal bookmakers, illegal bookmakers, horse tracks, team owners, Twitter, the internet, Chris Christie, Atlantic City, women's sports, e-sports, fantasy sports, the professional bettors, and the betting public. Among the losers are the NCAA, online sports books, Las Vegas bookmakers, illegal bookmakers, the horse racing industry, Bitcoin, Blockchain, Bill Bradley, Sheldon Adelson, gambling addicts, the professional bettors, and the betting public.

Among the biggest winners: the entities whose leaders have forcefully stood up against sports gambling in a decades-long morality play.

In 1993, the commissioner of the NHL, Gary Bettman, was at the forefront of the lobbying effort in Congress in support of Bill Bradley's crusade to pass PASPA and crush the sports betting movement nation-wide. Now, in 2018, Bettman says, "The new sports betting landscape presents a unique opportunity for fan engagement utilizing technology and data that are exclusive to our league."

MLB commissioner Bud Selig said of gambling, in 2012, "It is evil, creates doubt, and destroys your sport." Now the commissioner of base-ball, Rob Manfred, says, "From our perspective, we see revenue oppor-tunities, but most important, we see it as an opportunity for fan engage-ment."

NFL commissioner Roger Goodell, when asked to name the greatest threat to the integrity of football, replied, in 2012, "Gambling would be number one on my list." Now Goodell says, "We have spent considerable time planning for the potential of broadly legalized sports gambling and are prepared to address these changes in a thoughtful and comprehen-sive way."

Like the tens of thousands of settlers in the 1800s in the heartland of America who, in search of riches, lined up along a state border, readying themselves for a land rush, many entrepreneurs who have been lying in wait on the edges are now ready to rush in and file their claims in the land grab. Startups that have been lurking in the shadows, operating in a virtual ghost world while they waited for this moment, are ready to take hold of this opportunity, everyone now creating the products that will be the next step in daily fantasy sports — team owners, Silicon Val-ley entrepreneurs, media companies, racetrack operators in New Jer-sey, even Vegas bookmakers like Vic Salerno, who began building the infrastructure for his company two years ago, in preparation for this mo-ment. As the old bookmaker suspected would happen, his startup, US Fantasy, which is becoming US Bookmaking, focused on the nationwide wagering movement, is just one of many companies rushing in: There's WinView, Boom Fantasy, Proof of Toss, Tappp, Unikrn, US Bets, Sports Handle, Readyfire, the Action Network, all of them tripping over them-selves to proclaim how uniquely positioned they are for this new world, all of them trying to secure partnerships with media companies, some funded by bright-eyed investors and employing talented young tech engineers and product designers. And everyone wants a piece of it. Over the next few weeks and months, senior executives at legacy companies will leave to start their own companies, famous broadcasters will launch their own ventures, doctors and attorneys will drop their day jobs to become full-time betting pundits. A decades-old trade organization started in Madison, Wisconsin, is suddenly making a pivot: the chairman of the Fantasy Sports Trade Association, Peter Schoenke, announces that his organization is now called the Fantasy Sports *and* Gaming Association.

What everyone emphasizes again and again is that they are not simply fantasy sports companies or daily fantasy sports companies or gambling companies — they are *sports entertainment* companies. The term they use is "hybridization"; the hybridization of fantasy sports games and gambling is what this new bright, shiny world is all about.

Over on CNBC, in the days after the ruling, a logo has been made: FROM FANTASY TO REALITY: AFTER THE SCOTUS RULING. On a morning when experts, pundits, businesspeople, and lawmakers have been remotely making media appearances across the country to speculate on the implications of the ruling, the show's host welcomes one of the biggest key figures to consider those implications.

"You guys have long said that what your business is, *is not gambling*, it's a game of skill as opposed to a game of chance," the host says. "But now you are very, very ready to transform — and to fully concede that what you have been providing is, partly at least, a game of chance."

Standing in front of a white screen bearing the logo of his company, the CEO of DraftKings, in a sports coat and a button-down shirt, says: "What we've been providing stays the same . . ." Jason Robins then seems to be directing his company's remarkable pivot almost in real time when he adds, "But we're very excited to offer this new product. The real goal of this is to take something that is an unregulated black market activity and bring it to the light."

This story of the two fantasy sports startups, DraftKings and FanDuel, has been a sprawling, twisting, confusing, complex story, but the news of the Supreme Court ruling crystallizes what their story has been heading toward all along: *this* moment. Because when it's time to declare winners and losers, there is no doubt where the two startups come out: "DraftKings, FanDuel Hit Jackpot" is the headline on one website, and virtually overnight the two leading fantasy sports companies in the world have become sports gambling companies, primed to take every bet in America.

The game — the one playing out not on a screen but on the field in front of him — plods along at an excruciating pace; with all the breaks between pitches, the fits and starts of action, it's no wonder, Mark Nerenberg thinks, why everyone is saying that baseball, as an entertainment product, is doomed. He's sitting among the forty thousand in attendance, in the cheap seats at Yankee Stadium, and the game moves along like an old, broken-down train, jerking along the track; it's an open question whether it will ever reach its destination. That's how it feels on this evening watching the New York Yankees in a regular season game. The stakes are low, and it all feels meaningless — if not the outcome of this single regular-season game, one of 162 of the year, then certainly this particular at bat in the late innings of a blowout game, the fans around him either checking their phones to keep themselves entertained, or already headed to the exits.

The game in Mark's head, though, moves at a different speed, along a different track: that game moves almost incomprehensibly fast. In his game the stakes are constantly changing, sometimes, in an instant, rising almost incalculably high. The game in Mark's head can make every at bat in this ho-hum game feel almost like life or death.

Set it and forget it: that is what he calls the style of fantasy games that people like his father have been playing for decades. It's even what you could call the daily games that Mark's generation began playing years ago — games that are about to feel like a relic of the past. Set a lineup, sit back and watch your fortunes rise and fall. *Live betting:* this is the future, except it's already here. In Nevada and soon New Jersey and other states where wagering has been legalized since the ruling, bettors can bet on games *during* games, the odds changing and renewing after every event in a contest. But the game in Mark's head moves on yet another, even faster track. *Bet building:* stacking up one bet on top of another, as many as a bettor desires in a given moment. "Right now you can only bet on the *outcome* of a game, but let's say you can take an at bat — *this* at bat," Mark says as he watches a hitter stroll to the plate. "You can bet on exactly how many pitches this at bat is going to have, and if it's going to end in an RBI double. You can bet that this next pitch will be a curveball . . . *and* whether the hitter is going to hit a double . . . *and* whether two runs are going to score.

"It's things we weren't even thinking about just a few years ago, but now it just seems . . . inevitable."

So much has changed over the last ten years. It's funny: what now seems inevitable seemed impossible at the time. A decade ago, the world was ready for Mark's game even if it didn't know it. After he and his co-founders sold DraftStreet to DraftKings, Mark took on a senior position at his old rival company, leading the company's New York offices, where he lorded over a team of young, hungry engineers creating new variations of their daily fantasy game. He was grateful for everything that DraftKings had given him, but if you wanted to know the truth, Mark never again felt the thrill he had felt at DraftStreet — the exhilaration of creating something of his own. DraftKings became a large company of hundreds, and Mark was just a small part of the machine.

One morning not long after the Supreme Court ruling, Mark was sitting in the lobby of the DraftKings offices in Boston. He always remembered how his dad told him that he was proud of him for leaving his job and starting his own company, DraftStreet. And since he joined DraftKings, he had been waiting to take his next leap of faith but found it harder and harder to do so as he got older. He was now married, with a young daughter. But then Mark could begin to sense it: just as had happened ten years ago, the opportunities were opening up, everywhere, and he decided it was time.

Mark sat in the lobby, waiting on Jason Robins to give him his two weeks' notice: he was leaving his job as vice president of game operations and development at DraftKings and joining a new startup, based in New

York City and run by a recent Columbia University graduate out of some-one's apartment building, one of those hybrid fantasy-sports-gambling businesses. Mark would serve as its chief product officer, the mind be-hind the odds that they would create and provide. The work he would be doing was in some ways no different from what he'd done as a youngster, when he created games for his friends to make the games they watched a little more interesting, their days a little more dangerous.

"This is the future," he says. "And it's every sport. A football game: It's beyond just that the Patriots will win and Tom Brady throws two TDs. It's this drive will go more than four plays and end with a missed field goal. The key is that you — the fan — you create your own scenario. And we give you the odds, however small or big you want to bet. The possi-bilities are endless. This is combining the instant gratification with that huge lottery payout that everyone wants."

He gazes down at the action on the field. The hitter swings and misses, and even though there is nothing on the line, Mark had, with a mere sug-gestion, made an inconsequential event in a blowout game a bit more interesting. Now if there was actual money on the line — well, maybe the game in front of him isn't doomed after all.

Sitting in the stands, just thinking about this new idea he has, he knows he's onto something, and he has this feeling that he doesn't have any time to waste. The race is on.

Mark feels the impatience that he did on that day in the offices in Bos-ton as he waited on Jason Robins. On that day, Mark waited, and waited, and waited. Finally, he got up, and left.

He couldn't wait any longer.

"AAAAAAAAND, at guard, NUUMMMMMBER EIGHTEEEEEEEEEEN — JAAAAAAASON ROOOOOOBBBINS!"

In the house where Frazier beat Ali, Willis Reed walked out of a tun-nel, Bill Bradley became a hero, Reggie sparred with Spike, and Jordan dropped fifty-five on the Knicks, intruders have taken over the hallowed site.

The voice of the PA announcer echoes across the grand arena, and from the sideline, in a white basketball uniform that says DRAFTKINGS on the front of the jersey, the CEO, lights on him impossibly bright, jogs to the center of the court, where he's met with high-fives, backslaps, and cheers. There's a PA announcer, a ref, two coaches, a working score-board, and a running shot clock; otherwise, it's just Jason and his clan here. His cofounders, executives, and staffers, as well a handful of media members, have the entire place to themselves for a game of five-on-five.

Tip-off, and then what is supposed to be a friendly game among friends and acquaintances quickly becomes intense. Elbows, pushes, hard fouls — a little bit of everything, except for made shots.

The scouting report on number 18: he's a grinder. He's far from the most athletic one on the court, but there's a fearlessness and abandon to his game. He runs from end to end with his slouch, he plays hard — he dives for a ball, slides across the court, scrapes his knee, has to sit out for a few minutes. "It's not that bad," he grumbles when a teammate asks if he's okay, and soon enough, he's back in the game.

When he's on the floor, he wants the ball. And when he has it, he has a quick trigger: he takes a shot along the baseline; it rattles in. Cheers from the sideline and from his teammates.

It is not a game that will go down as one of the finest moments in Madison Square Garden history, and thank heavens no one has kept a box score. Though he has had seats behind home plate for the World Se-ries, box seats at Foxborough, and a perch along the 50-yard line at the Super Bowl, has hobnobbed with Hall of Famers and childhood heroes, he insists that he has not become numbed to these experiences. It has been in many ways a fantasy life for a sports nerd like him — the world has become his playground. And now that he has the most famous bas-ketball arena in the world, thanks to a partnership between DraftKings and the arena, he runs the court as if he owns it.

Afterward, in a meeting room in the bowels of the arena, everyone gathers for a presentation. Jason stands in front of the room and pre-sents his vision. It's many months before PASPA is struck down, and already there are new offerings of games — pick 'em games, social games, season-long games, new variations of the old daily fantasy model that not long ago would have raised the eyebrows and ire of regulators — games for this era of hybridization. But much larger than that is how the Internet of Things will permeate everyone's daily lives and DraftKings is going to be a central part of that — the first thing a sports fan checks when he wakes up each morning, the portal to the online world. Jason talks about how media partners want customers, customers, and more customers, and they have millions of them to offer — paying customers whose habits, tastes, payments, and interests they have tracked for years. Jason explains how they plan to expand, with a new media arm called DK Live, and in foreign markets — not just Europe but into Asia and beyond.

Years earlier, it was impossible to foresee the landscape changing like this — that PASPA was going to be repealed so soon — and yet in the months before the decision, without knowing which way the ruling would go, DraftKings was determined to be ready as soon as the decision came down. They opened a headquarters for a New Jersey operation in Hoboken, hired a new head of sports book, and hired an army of new analysts and coders to get a sports betting app off the ground, all months before the ruling. Jason and his company, once again, were going full throttle.

On a spring morning in 2019, they open the doors to their new offices in Boston's Back Bay neighborhood. The sprawling 105,000-square-foot space is, in fact, the biggest one-floor office space in all of Boston. There are now seven hundred employees, a 65 percent year-over-year increase; over the last year alone they've made more than four hundred new hires. The standing desks, the focus rooms, the podcast rooms, the dining room, the game room, the barbershop, the Vince Lombardi–inspired banner along the wall (WINNING ISN'T EVERYTHING. BUT WANTING IT IS), the names of the meeting rooms paying homage to the gods of fantasy football (BRADY, MOSS, SANDERS) — all of it is part of an impossible vision realized. Still, at its core, DraftKings feels like the same company it was when it started in 2012, and defying the odds, the three nerds who ran it then are still here.

As a scrum of media gathers, visiting lawmakers and local figures stand with the three founders in the office's grand lobby, which glitters with the running ticker of the night's games and the TV screens, flashing overnight highlights, wrapped around the walls. The opening of the office feels like the start of a new chapter. Or perhaps a validation. The founders, after all, were called the suicide bombers once, the ones who almost blew up an industry. The thing is, the three founders at DraftKings had always seen it all as a game, too. "The three of us, what did we have to lose?" Matt Kalish would recall. "When we started, there was no real downside to what we were trying. We were frustrated in our jobs in corporate America. I had nothing in my bank account. We looked at FanDuel's lead, and we just said, Let's catch them. Let's beat them. We knew we could raise the money and find ways to catch them. It was just going to be a matter of time."

Flanked by a group of men in suits, the three founders stand behind a black ribbon, ready to pose for the cameras. Clutching a pair of oversized scissors, the CEO, in a sports coat and slacks, begins to speak. He thanks the employees. He thanks the partners and investors. He thanks the guests who have come today, a contingent that includes the governor of Massachusetts, Charlie Baker. He thanks his cofounders. Those who have been with him since the beginning say that in the early years Jason, then a midlevel analyst with no experience running a business, would be a ball of nerves, stumbling on his words, when he made his pitch in a room full of investors. With each presentation, however, he got better, and now, those first few rocky years for Jason and his founding team feels like a lifetime ago. They pose together for a photo, at the front of their latest, and perhaps, last DraftKings office.

He speaks, and like in every room he's in now, he commands it. Then he leans over, ready to cut the ribbon and begin this new chapter. But first someone murmurs something. "Oh," Jason says. "I think the governor would like to say something."

One late summer afternoon in New York City, months earlier, Jason was having lunch in midtown, sitting in a booth in a restaurant that overlooked Central Park. He talked about the war, one that, by many measures, he and DraftKings were winning, perhaps had already won.

DraftKings, years ago the third-running horse in the race, had held an edge over their longtime rivals since their ad blitz in 2015, and was positioned to be the leader in the industry.

It had begun as a battle between three fledgling startups, then a fight between two. Brian Schwartz had long ago left DraftStreet behind; now Nigel Eccles was gone too. Jason Robins was the last CEO standing.

What was he thinking when he considered the chessboard and wondered how he could blow up the board entirely? "The thing that people don't understand," Jason had said, "it was fear. I have felt that way since the moment we started and to this day. Constantly fearful for our survival, constantly fearful that someone else will come around and do it better, constantly fearful of others. Constantly fearful of this not working, and going back to — what? How I see it now is when you stop feeling that way, it's when your company is too big. What pushed us? It was not greed. It was the opposite. It was fear."

It was fear, he now said over lunch, that compelled him to keep raising the stakes. What, looking back, did he regret?

If you'd asked Brian Schwartz or even Nigel Eccles that question, they would have detailed the endless number of different moves they would have made. *Of course we made mistakes — I don't know where to even start!* they'd have replied.

Asked what he'd have done differently, Jason looked up from his lunch. He wore a dark sports jacket with a pocket square over a button-down shirt. He sat up straight, perhaps aware of that slouch. In this moment he looked the part: the CEO of a billion-dollar company with one of the most recognized names in America.

And then Jason Robins answered a question with another question:

"If you were me, would you have done *anything* differently?"

"It's all so ironic, isn't it?"

The question is posed in another restaurant booth, this one a dimly lit establishment on the main street in a quiet suburb of New York City. It is a Wednesday afternoon, and a husband and wife are trying to have a quiet lunch without the screaming kids or distractions from work, but as always, they've been reminded that there's no escaping the world they've both left behind, no matter how hard they try. The news of the Supreme Court ruling had come some time earlier, but the story is not going away: on the hanging TV set in the corner, the channel is tuned to CNBC, and the anchor behind the desk on this live segment is concluding an interview with the CEO of a gambling company over a chyron that reads SPORTS BETTING BONANZA.

"It's just so ironic," Lesley continues as she stabs at the pieces of pasta in front of her and listens to the meandering thoughts of yet another commentator attempting to say something insightful and interesting about this news story that few, including him, actually have a handle on. "All those years we wouldn't dare utter that we were a sports betting company, and now, just like that, it's, *Look at us, we're a sports betting company!*"

Nigel, sitting across from her, has no reaction. He looks up, and as if on cue, the chyron reads: REPORTS: FANDUEL TO BE ACQUIRED BY UK BOOKMAKER PADDY POWER BETFAIR. The news now is coming at a breakneck speed: on the heels of the repeal of PASPA, one of the biggest gambling companies in the United Kingdom, the conglomerate whose stock shot up 25 percent within two weeks of the Supreme Court ruling, is making a play for the US gambling market, and FanDuel is its way in. In this new world, FanDuel has made an even more jarring transformation than DraftKings: seemingly overnight, it's partnering up with a bookmaking titan that has been around for more than three decades. Now FanDuel is not a daily fantasy operator but a global sports entertainment company; it is led not by a group of Brits but a CEO who, before coming to FanDuel, was a director at the private equity behemoth KKR, and by a board made up of current and former executives at the world's biggest media companies, like Comcast Ventures and the DISH Network, including a member who remains one of the most influential voices in the company: Mike LaSalle from the private equity group Shamrock Capital. To this moment, FanDuel has raised $416 million and is still not profitable, but after years of negative headlines, years of high legal costs, years of making a game that perhaps was never meant to go mainstream, the news is a jolt to the company, giving it new life: here is the path forward, and the path is sports betting.

Within months of the completion of the acquisition, FanDuel's ad campaign begins in earnest: they will be offering risk-free bets and inundating the public with promo codes, ads, billboards, direct marketing ads that seem a bit familiar — all hailing the arrival of the FanDuel Sportsbook, the new online operation ready to service every bet in America.

It is odd, of course, to watch the FanDuel story barreling ahead, without the founders. Later this summer, stories will surface that the four, in the Paddy Power acquisition, are coming away, astonishingly, with *nothing* — the latest story of a late-stage investor crushing the founders. This, of course, is not how they imagined their story to end. But it may be also be just the start of a new saga: three months from now, the founders, led by Nigel, will file a lawsuit, saying they are owed more than $100 million.

"If there's any consolation," Nigel says, "*the name* will live on. That's something to be proud of."

There's this too: in these last months since his final day at FanDuel, he and Lesley have almost become a normal couple again. For starters, they were able to travel, together, and not to some NFL city or fantasy sports conference. They spent a few days in Tennessee, where they watched the sky go dark in the moment of total eclipse. At home they have settled into the simple, easy routines: errands, pickups, even exercise classes. When news of the Supreme court ruling appeared on his phone, he was next to Lesley in cycling class.

Just as they finish lunch and prepare to leave, Nigel looks up at the TV one last time. On the screen is the FanDuel logo, reports of the sale, now imminent, and then the basic facts: "A company founded in 2009. Headquartered in Edinburgh and New York. Originally a company based in the UK called Hubdub."

A group of Brits walk into a room with an idea for an American fantasy sports game — it still sounds like a clunky joke at a bar, Nigel thinks, but it was the start to a story that wasn't half-bad either.

Now the cofounders, all of them, are ready to move on — each of them on their own path. A few weeks earlier, Lesley had been across the country, in Menlo Park, California, on a wide avenue lined with oak trees. Its stretch of office buildings housed the most expensive rental properties in the country, and its famous name, Sand Hill Road, was known as the place where the most powerful venture capitalists in America made their decisions. Lesley was there to pitch them her little idea that just might change the world. The last few months in New York she had been waking up every morning inside a quiet house, and in the moments just before the kids were awake, her head spun with plans and ideas. She'd told only her closest friends that she had a desire to start her own company and held the idea close to her vest until things were really in motion. After months of bouncing among half-baked ideas, she landed on one that would stick, a creation that one might even say couldn't be further removed from the business of fantasy sports games: an app to help couples find happiness in their relationships.

When she began reaching out to potential investors, the name of her old company on her résumé, to her surprise, didn't carry as much baggage as she'd feared. Sure, there were the requisite jokes — "We *may* not need to spend $500 million on marketing" — but more than anything, being the founder of a company that was hailed as a unicorn and was now regarded as one of the rare success stories for a startup in the sports industry got her a meeting with any venture capitalist she wanted. On Sand Hill Road, it got her face time with one of the most influential VCs in the world. For this new venture, Lesley would be the CEO. This was her baby, and she was ready. All she needed was money and time.

For Nigel, these last few months away from FanDuel have also been exhilarating: he wakes up every morning with new ideas spilling out of him. He's planning his next venture, and every day he's been taking the train into the city for meetings with potential partners, possible investors, and old friends.

It's been a decade, really, since it has been like this, just him and Tom and Rob, the three of them kicking around new ideas, and the familiar floods back.

Yes, these last ten years have been full of doubt, regret, and uncertainty. But if they've learned anything during that time, it's that only out of uncertainty can the things truly worth doing emerge.

Because there was a moment nine years ago when it seemed like the end for them. They had been attempting, unsuccessfully, to get their little startup off the ground, but it was clearly over; their silly idea for a news prediction site was dead. They needed to latch onto something new. Nigel and Lesley's savings were nearly wiped out. Tom and Rob had no interest in disappearing back into their cave. What was next for them, if anything, they didn't know. They agreed to meet up during South by Southwest in Austin, at a festival of ideas, in a moment when they felt they had no more ideas in them. They rented a house, and it felt like rock bottom at the time, even as they set up chairs in the backyard, next to a shed and for five days scribbled down the things that came to them on scraps of paper and passed them around.

For some time the side of the shed stared back at them, like a terrifyingly blank canvas. After a few days, though, it was covered in notes with their ideas, notions, plans, and dreams.

On one of those scraps was perhaps the most ridiculous dream of all: FANTASY SPORTS.

Now, looking back as they sit together again, staring at the blank canvas and thinking about what is next for each of them, they can see that what had felt like the ending of one story was really just the beginning of another.

Nigel knows this familiar feeling, one that he can only describe as a delusion — this belief that he's onto an idea that might just change the world. They've been at it these last few days, and now he thinks they may have something. Maybe — something.

"Okay," he says, at last. "Let's get started."

ACKNOWLEDGMENTS

Back in 2016, when first I set out to tell this story, I quickly encountered a problem: the narrative kept changing at every turn, as the fate of the two startups at the heart of story hung in the balance. Writing a book on events occurring in real time was difficult enough, but there was another challenge: the business of gambling and fantasy sports can be impenetrable to anyone who doesn't speak the language of overlays, rakes, stacks, fades, and contrarian plays. I thought of what the great Michael Lewis has said: if his mother can't understand what he's writing, maybe there's no point in writing it. To write a book about gambling and fantasy sports that my mother — a Taiwanese artist trained in brush painting — could understand *and* also want to read might well be impossible, but I tried my best to explain a complex world in a way that might be compelling to anyone. To do that, I had to write a story with rich characters at its center, characters who were also trying to understand this complicated world in which they'd found themselves. The only way would be for those individuals to tell me their stories and, even though they had little to gain from talking to me, they did — much more, in fact, than I expected. I'm blown away, still, at how raw and candid they were about what was, in many cases, a harrowing time in their lives.

This book is the result of more than 100 interviews with those individuals but also many others whose names do not appear in these pages. I'm grateful for the countless hours they spent with me, for all of their insights and their willingness to explain the story underneath the headlines and, yes, the ads.

My agents, Scott Waxman and Jeremy Bell, remained unwavering believers in this project when none of us knew exactly where the story was going to take us. Without Jon Wertheim's encouragement, this project would not have gotten off the ground. Nathaniel Posey and Ashley Lopez offered wonderful support and advice along the way. I have no idea what this book would be without the guidance of the relentless Will Green, who was instrumental in laying the foundation. Craig Williams read early drafts and offered brilliant thoughts on how to shape the narrative. Jeremy Fuchs was there to track down every last query, until the very last hour. Jill Jaroff made the book dramatically better — and saved me from myself — with her keen eye.

Thank you to Susan Canavan, for her exceptional guidance, enthusiasm, and zeal. I couldn't have asked for a better editor for my first book. I am also grateful to everyone at Houghton Mifflin Harcourt: Heather Tamarkin, Megan Wilson, Brooke Borneman, Lisa Glover, and Mary Cait Milliff, without whom I'd never have reached the finish line. Cynthia Buck's perfect touch is on every page.

I had the help of countless others as I grappled with the subject. Scott Gramling and Zach Cohen set me off on the right direction. At various points, Nick Dunham, Charles Chon, Paul Zimmerman, Dan Back, Lee Asher, Stephen Murray, Jonathan Joseph, Art Manteris, Cal Spears, Vic Salerno, Tom Willer, and Robert Walker were invaluable guides through the DFS and gambling jungles. Since October 2015, I relied on the excellent reporting of many terrific writers who have covered the industry, including Michael McCann, Ryan Rodenberg, Dan Barbarisi, Chris Grove, Dustin Gouker, Daniel Roberts, Dan Primack, and David Purdum.

The seeds of this project were planted in the fall of 2014, after I pitched a magazine story on a peculiar little industry to Adam Duerson at *Sports Illustrated,* and I'll always be grateful that he said yes. I'm indebted to Chris Stone and Steve Cannella at *SI,* where I've had the pleasure of having spent my entire career working with them and many of the most talented writers and editors in the business. I am also lucky to call them my friends and would not have gotten here without their support: Richard Demak, Gabe Miller, Hank Hersch, Larry Mondi, Stefanie Kaufman, Ryan Hunt, Mark Bechtel, Sarah Kwak, Stanley Kay, Jack Dickey, Trisha Blackmar, Ben Reiter, Marguerite Schropp, Taylor Ballantyne, Prem Kalliat, Chris Chambers, Larry Burke, Ted Keith, Jim

Gorant, Emma Span, Scott Price, Mike Rosenberg, Greg Bishop, Tom Verducci, Joe Lemire, Eric Single, Stephanie Apstein, and Gary Gramling. I certainly wouldn't have been qualified to write this book without Dave Hogue, Jeff Sussman, Mike Merrill, Noah Monick, and the rest of the degenerates from the League of Ordinary Gentlemen, of which I am a three-time champ (alas, over the span of, well, a few decades).

My wonderful friends and family have been my most important source of support: Irene Chen, Ronald Chen, Fiona Griffiths, Steve Yang, Alex Woo, Whitney Friedlander, Kayleen Schaefer, Alex Chung, Greg Kirschling, Julia Chang, Sara Isani, Ryan Martin, Ryan Mauban, Liz Mauban, Lew Gleason, Sandy Chung, Michelle Umali, Tommy Craggs, Marc Pomplun, and Andrew Gurman.

The biggest thank you to Yud-Ren and Jing-Jy Chen, who with their wisdom, grace, and unconditional support have taught and inspired me from the beginning.

Finally, this book is dedicated to Leo Chen, who makes my heart grow each day, and Andrea Woo, who over these last three years put up with way too much, experiencing every high and every miserable low, every step of the way. I don't know how she makes it all look so easy, only that she makes me the luckiest of all.

NOTES

1. Betting on Brett Favre with Bar Mitzvah Money
(And Other Hidden Origin Stories)

page

6   "*An idea hatched on a cross country flight.*": Chris Ballard, "Fantasy World," *Sports Illustrated*, June 21, 2004.

7   "*The first documented fantasy draft was, fittingly, held in someone's basement*": Patrick Hruby, "The Founding Fathers of Fantasy," *Sports On Earth*, December 2, 2013, http://www.sportsonearth.com/article/64244480/.

20   "*If you're not embarrassed*": Reid Hoffman, "If There Aren't Any Typos in This Essay, We've Launched Too Late," LinkedIn, March 19, 2017, https://www.linkedin.com/pulse/arent-any-typos-essay-we-launched-too-late-reid-hoffman.

24   "*Does Turning 60 Bucks*": Daniel Roberts, "This Man Is Blowing Up Fantasy Sports," *Fortune*, September 24, 2015, http://fortune.com/2015/09/24/draftkings-jason-robins-40-under-40/.

5. The Output Is Insanity

91   *worth $250 million:* Kurt Wagner, "DraftKings Will Pay ESPN $250 Million for Ads over the Next Two Years," *Recode*, July 20, 2015, https://www.recode.net/2015/7/20/11614842/draftkings-will-pay-espn-250-million-for-ads-over-the-next-two-years.

6. Friends and Foes

99   "*Insider Trading Scandal Rocks Fantasy Sports Industry*": Joe Drape and Jacqueline Williams, "Scandal Erupts in Unregulated World of Fantasy Sports" (first published as "Insider Trading Scandal Rocks Fantasy Sports Industry"), *New York Times*, October 5, 2015, https://www.nytimes.

com/2015/10/06/sports/fanduel-draftkings-fantasy-employees-bet-rivals.
html.

111 *"a global hate figure"*: Lucy Waterlow, "'I Lost My Job, My Reputation
and I'm Not Able to Date Anymore': Former PR Worker Reveals How She
Destroyed Her Life One Year after Sending 'Racist' Tweet before Trip to Africa," *Daily Mail*, February 16, 2015, https://www.dailymail.co.uk/femail/ar
ticle-2955322/Justine-Sacco-reveals-destroyed-life-racist-tweet-trip-Africa.
html.

113 *"The most controversial woman in public relations"*: *Post* staff, "PR Guru
Who Posted Racist Tweet Surfaces in Fantasy Sports Scandal," *New York Post*,
October 6, 2015, https://nypost.com/2015/10/06/pr-guru-who-posted-rac
ist-tweet-resurfaces-in-fantasy-sports-scandal/.

"And Now, a Funny Holiday Joke": Sam Biddle, *Valleywag*, December 20,
2013, http://valleywag.gawker.com/and-now-a-funny-holiday-joke-from-
iacs-pr-boss-1487284969.

"Justine Sacco Is Good at Her Job": Sam Biddle, "Justine Sacco Is Good at
Her Job, and How I Came to Peace with Her," *Gawker*, December 20, 2014,
https://gawker.com/justine-sacco-is-good-at-her-job-and-how-i-came-to-
pea-1653022326.

7. Open and Notorious

115 *Times* (London), *November 15, 2015:* Michael Glackin, "Fantasy Turns
into Hard Facts for FanDuel": *Times* (London), November 15, 2015; https://
www.thetimes.co.uk/article/fantasy-turns-into-hard-facts-for-fanduel-f6zx
dtpwj03.

120 *"Unicorn to Unicorpse?"*: Peter Evans and Kiki Loizou, "Unicorn to Unicorpse?," *Times* (London), November 22, 2015, https://www.thetimes.co.uk/
article/unicorn-to-unicorpse-pftpxxwg5p2.

not clearly defined by law in her state: Ryan Kartje, "Daily Fantasy
Sports Industry Waits for California's Next Move," *Orange County Register*, December 26, 2015, https://www.ocregister.com/2015/12/26/
daily-fantasy-sports-industry-waits-for-californias-next-move/; Ryan
Schlager, "Georgia Gambling Regulators Question Legality of Daily Fantasy Sports," *Sporting News*, October 19, 2015, https://www.google.com/
search?q=sporting+news+georgia+daily+fantasy&oq=sporting+news+
georgia+daily+fantasy&aqs=chrome..69i57j69i60.4607j0j4&sourceid=
chrome&ie=UTF-8; Marc Tracy, "NCAA Distances Itself from Daily Fantasy Websites," *New York Times*, October 20, 2015, https://www.nytimes.
com/2015/10/21/sports/ncaa-distances-itself-from-daily-fantasy-websites
.html.

8. Nightmare at 35,000 Feet

136 *"A Fantasy Sports Wizard's Winning Formula"*: Brad Reagan, "A Fantasy Sports Wizard's Winning Formula," *Wall Street Journal,* June 4, 2014, https://www.wsj.com/articles/a-fantasy-sports-wizards-winning-formula-wsj-money-june-2014-1401893587.

9. Crowning the King

141 *"the best was ahead of me"*: Ray Kroc, *Grinding It Out* (New York: Henry Regnery Co., 1977), 13.

147 *leaned into his microphone:* "Here's Where the Federal Investigations into Daily Fantasy Sports Might Be Focused," *Legal Sports Report,* March 18, 2016.

10. The Circus

156 *"Fantasy Sports Convention Gets Cold Welcome"*: Chris Sadeghi, "Fantasy Sports Convention Gets Cold Welcome in Texas," KXAN.com, January 20, 2016, https://www.kxan.com/news/fantasy-sports-convention-gets-cold-welcome-in-texas/1049766349.

162 *Wiegert and the industry won:* Eric Fisher, "Judge Rules for CDM Fantasy Sports in Fantasy Rights Lawsuit," *St. Louis Business Journal,* August 7, 2006, https://www.bizjournals.com/stlouis/stories/2006/08/07/daily30.html.

163 *he ran an $837,000 office pool:* Steve Politi, "How Running an $837,000 Office Pool Destroyed This Man's Life," *NJ.com,* March 16, 2015, https://www.nj.com/sports/index.ssf/2015/03/the_800000_office_pool_how_a_teacher_got_busted_an.html.

11. The Most Miserable Man at the Super Bowl

177 *"Betting on professional sports"*: Adam Silver, "Legalize and Regulate Sports Betting," *New York Times,* November 13, 2014.

12. A Line in the Sand

198 *at playing the public charade:* Justin Rogers, "Goodell on Betting Ruling: He'll 'Protect Integrity' of NFL," *Detroit News,* May 5, 2018; https://www.detroitnews.com/story/sports/nfl/lions/2018/05/21/nfl-commissioner-roger-goodell-weighs-sports-betting/628944002/. "It's a very strongly held

view in the NFL, it has been for decades that the threat that gambling could occur in the NFL or fixing of games or that any outcome could be influenced by the outside could be very damaging to the NFL and very difficult to ever recover from," Goodell said.

13. Jason's Delusion

210 *Saratoga Casino and Raceway:* Michael DeMasi, "10 Minutes with Albany Attorney James Featherstonhaugh," *Albany Business Journal,* March 21, 2014, https://www.bizjournals.com/albany/print-edition/2014/03/21/10-minutes-with-albany-attorney-james.html.

16. The Speed of the Game

239 *"The Supreme Court Strikes Down":* Adam Liptak and Kevin Draper, "Supreme Court Ruling Favors Sports Betting," *New York Times,* May 14, 2018, https://www.nytimes.com/2018/05/14/us/politics/supreme-court-sports-betting-new-jersey.html.

241 *crush the sports betting movement nationwide:* Terry Lefton, "Industry's Elite Talk Gambling at Sports Summit," *New York Business Journal,* November 29, 2018, https://www.bizjournals.com/newyork/news/2018/11/29/industry-s-elite-talk-gambling-at-sports-summit.html.

"The new sports betting landscape": MGM Resorts International, "National Hockey Announces Landmark Sports Betting Partnership with MGM Resorts" (press release), October 29, 2018, https://investors.mgmresorts.com/investors/news-releases/press-release-details/2018/National-Hockey-League-Announces-Landmark-Sports-Betting-Partnership-With-MGM-Resorts/default.aspx.

"It is evil, creates doubt": Ben Fawkes, "Rob Manfred: MLB Reviewing Stance on Gambling; Sees Las Vegas as a Viable Market," *ESPN,* February 21, 2017, http://www.espn.com/chalk/story/_/id/18736620/rob-manfred-says-mlb-reviewing-stance-gambling-sees-las-vegas-viable-market.

"From our perspective, we see revenue opportunities": Dan Waldstein, "Rob Manfred Addresses the Shift, Gambling, and That Viral Terry Collins Video," *New York Times,* June 18, 2018.

"Gambling would be number one on my list": Leigh Steinberg, "Sports Gambling Is Evolving More Rapidly than Expected," *Forbes,* November 28, 2018, https://www.forbes.com/sites/leighsteinberg/2018/11/28/sports-gambling-is-evolving-more-rapidly-than-we-expected/#6798af74eaf3.

241 *"We have spent considerable time planning"*: NFL, "NFL Commissioner Roger Goodell Issues Statement on Gambling" (press release), May 21, 2018.

243 *"DraftKings, FanDuel Hit Jackpot"*: Dana Olsen, "DraftKings, FanDuel Hit Jackpot as Supreme Court Opens Door to Sports Betting," *Pitchbook*, May 14, 2018, https://pitchbook.com/news/articles/draftkings-fanduel-hit-jackpot-as-supreme-court-opens-door-to-sports-betting.

INDEX